CONFESSIONS OF A STOCKBROKER

You, Too, Can Find Tomorrow's Blue Chips Before Wall Street Finds Them

Andrew A. Lanyi

Managing Director,
Lanyi Research
Ladenburg, Thalmann & Co., Inc.

PRENTICE HALL

New York   London   Toronto   Sydney   Tokyo   Singapore

10 9 8 7 6 5 4 3 2 1

This publication is designed to provide accurate and authoritative information in re-
gard to the subject matter covered. It is sold with the understanding that the pub-
lisher is not engaged in rendering legal, accounting, or other professional service. If
legal advice or other expert assistance is required, the services of a competent professional person should be sought.

*—From a Declaration of Principles Jointly Adopted by a Committee of the American
Bar Association and a Committee of Publishers and Associations*

Mine is a true story, told as accurately as memory allows. Although in
some cases to tell the story I have created composite characters,
changed names, and dramatized events, in no instance has anything
been distorted.

A. L.

Library of Congress Cataloging-in-Publication Data

Lanyi, Andrew A.
    Confessions of a stockbroker : you, too, can find tomorrow's blue
chips before Wall Street finds them / Andrew A. Lanyi.
    p. cm.
    Includes index.
    ISBN 0-13-175746-6
    1. Stockbrokers—United States. 2. Stock-exchange—United States.
    I. Title.
HG4928.5.L36 1992
332.63'22—dc20   92-25479
                                                   CIP

ISBN 0-13-175746-6

PRENTICE HALL
Professional Publishing
Englewood Cliffs, NJ 07632
Simon & Schuster, A Paramount Communications Company

PRINTED IN THE UNITED STATES OF AMERICA

To the memory of my son,
George Robert Lanyi

Contents

Preface

First of all, let me confess that I don't believe in Wall Street's number one sacred cow: the *price/earnings ratio*. *It doesn't count—except if you do very superficial research!* No one will convince me that the key to major profits is the ability to divide two numbers; most 10-year-olds are good at that. Often you don't even have to figure out price/earning ratios—you can *read* them in your newspaper!

Most other ratios also mean substantially less than the public believes. What counts is *understanding the essence of the company.* Understanding it not only the way its top managers see it but, even more importantly: the way its main customers, suppliers, and printers see it.

❊

The biggest profits aren't made in the *efficient market*, where a company is already followed by 10 or 25 or 50 analysts. The largest gains take place in the *inefficient market*, when the analyst, the broker, and you, the investor, *do your homework way ahead of the crowd.*

And *the tools you have to use are incomparably more complicated and time consuming* that the ones you employ *in the efficient market.*

❊

You've probably met very few people in your life who come from a poorer background than I.

During World War II, I was a slave—forced to build military installations for the German Army.

When, more than a decade later, I arrived in the United States from my native Hungary, I had two professions, neither one marketable. I had a pregnant wife, and I had no job. I spoke very little English—and I certainly didn't know the first thing about the stock market.

Today, in spite of a tragedy two years ago that nearly shattered my life, I made peace. I am content. I have a son I love. I have a wife I love passionately. And—so everyone tells me—I have become one of the most successful and best know individual brokers in Wall Street's history.

❉

I do my own research. I do not sell a brokerage firm's, its management's, or research department's products. It's a major difference! I decide what I will recommend—but I have *to find common stocks for my clients that make them money, or I will be out of business.* No side products, no "lifesavers," no substitutes!

It took me a long time and endless numbers of mistakes to develop *the "Indicator" Approach.* But now customers like and enjoy what I am doing! And so do I.

❉

During my 34 years on Wall Street, most analysts and money managers I met called themselves "value investors." The term means "recognizing undervalued assets," that is, businesses that with better management could increase the dollar value of the investment by 25, 50, or even 100%. With the proper use of leverage, they could increase their worth even more.

This approach, though it has become almost a religion on Wall Street, never played any music to my soul. I have much admiration for its geniuses, but it just isn't my way.

I believe in *earnings*, more than assets. I believe in *growth*. I believe in the creative genius of man, in his brilliance producing ever-increasing earnings.

Investing takes *knowledge, discipline,* and *patience.* A hardworking and thorough growth stock investor may end up with a several hundred percent, and occasionally with a several thousand percent, gain. Naturally, when an investor accepts this challenge—the projection of earnings—he is climbing up a much more slippery pole than if he concentrated on assets.

What is the key?

He has to find those exceptionally rare companies that, for one reason or another, have a high likelihood of continued growth.

❋

In this book you will read extensively about my six criteria:

1. Fast growth
2. Industry, niche, or area domination
3. The ability to increase earnings even during recessions
4. Wall Street's lack of familiarity with the company
5. Ever-growing repeat orders
6. The "cookie cutter" factor

❋

Occasionally, my associates or I have found a company that satisfied these criteria and experienced phenomenal growth. Since going public in 1961, *Automatic Data Processing* shares have appreciated *185,900%* to their early 1992 high, and since *its* first offering on Wall Street in 1962, *H&R Block* shares have appreciated *101,150%.*

I will give some more recent examples. For instance, during the last four years, the price of *HealthCare COMPARE* grew 1,118% and *Surgical Care Affiliates* 1,821%.

❊

Don't consider my approach to investing the only method: there are many other ways to make money in the market. It is simply the approach that fits me, that I have been using for quite a while, and that seems to produce considerable profits for both my customers and me.

At the beginning, I made a great number of mistakes; my associates and I kept discussing them, again and again. Eventually, our ratio of winners to losers kept improving, and today my customers, my team, and I are quite comfortable with the results. We now seem to discuss more frequently why some investments work out better than we expected, rather than the reverse.

❊

This book is a loose web of three related subjects:

1. How to find tomorrow's "blue chips" before Wall Street finds them.

2. How to find a good stockbroker—or how to become one yourself.

3. The experiences that drove me to get involved with— and intrigued by—these questions.

When I began to write this book, an old friend warned me: stick to one subject; write either about finding tomorrow's biggest winners or about finding a good stockbroker. And don't mix into either stories about your life, however important they may have been in initiating later ideas. And, for heaven's sake, he said, do not mix any humor into it. No one will take you seriously.

I didn't take his advice. I teach my team: "Don't talk to the customer's *logic* only. His *emotions* are important. His sense of *humor*. He has to get involved in what he hears on several levels."

If you are interested in only one of the three subjects, you will probably have no difficulty recognizing it in the coming chapters—and skipping the rest.

❄

Before I continue, let me give you one piece of advice:

Don't expect, don't even hope, to buy only big winners. You will have many many false starts. This is not a game of vanity and pride; this is a journey of nonstop research, of admitted errors, and of modified direction.

And, I hope, some very happy results.

The amateur panics, the pro investigates.

1

Where It All Began

I share with you this early part of my story, because I hope it may help to explain how some of the ideas of this book developed. My eventual success as a broker has as much to do with wartime and postwar experiences as it has to do with my learning to sell mutual funds door to door, stocks on the phone—or analyzing companies late into the night.

The Carpathian Mountains, 1944

I was 19 years old. Since September, we had been in a labor camp: about 250 frightened young Hungarian men building a military airport for the Luftwaffe in the northeastern part of Hungary. It was backbreaking work but vastly better than being locked into a concentration camp. Here at least we were fed.

In October, the Russian army pushed very close to our camp. We could hear the guns day and night. The Germans decided to abandon the airport and move us toward the center of the country. The idea was to march us to complete exhaustion and death.

We had been marching, with little food, for several days when we arrived at a relatively large city. A number of us were gathered at the main square, trying to recover from the day's march. Supervision was very lax. It never crossed the minds of the soldiers that anyone would try to escape. It would have been suicide.

Tom Roboz nudged me and pointed: "Andy, look at that."

"What?"

"That building," said Tom. "I think the Germans are using it as some kind of a barracks."

We watched them for a while.

"I'm hungry."

"So am I," said Tom.

"How's your German?"

"Pretty good. My grandmother was German."

"Let's try it."

We took off our jackets with the yellow star and walked over to the sentry at the front door.

"Wir kommen von Bustyaháza; wir bauten einen Flughafen. Ist hier eine Stelle wo wir etwas zu essen bekommen?" (We came from Bustyaháza; we were building an airport. Any place we can get some food?)

The sentry pointed to the far right corner. *"Geh zurück!"* (Go in back.)

We walked through the courtyard and found a door marked *VORRATE* (SUPPLIES), guarded by a soldier.

"Wir bauten einen Flughafen in Bustyaháza und wir müssen zurückgehen nach Budapest. Wir haben keine Vorrate." (We have been building an airport in Bustyaháza and are supposed to get back to Budapest. We ran out of supplies.)

The soldier just pointed to a book. *"Unterschriebe hier."* (Sign here.)

We signed our real names.

"Vorrate für zwei tage." (Two-day rations.) He handed us two medium-sized packages.

When we got back to the square and opened the boxes, it was unbelievable! Meat in aspic and other delicacies we hadn't even dreamed about. (This was more than 40 years ago, and meat in aspic still does something

2

special to me.) Tom and I shared one of the boxes. Our friends took the other one.

Two others who were fluent in German got up, took off their yellow-starred jackets and walked into the warehouse. Then one more. All three came back with boxes. The rest of the group did not dare to go; the process would become too obvious.

This experience made a very strong impression. Whenever you do something *new*, whenever you do something *unusual*, whenever you do something *contrary to the accepted wisdom*—you have to be *the first to do it*. The second one may succeed, the third one may succeed, but there is a major advantage to being the first.

❄

We had been marching with aching feet, with our eyes practically shut, just putting one foot in front of the other. We learned to march while nearly asleep, just keeping up with the rhythm of the people around us.

Tom had been one of my best friends for the last ten years. He was an exceptionally nice guy—with a lot of street smarts. But no amount of street smarts prepares you for a forced march!

One evening, the guards dispersed us to several dozen peasant homes. Tom and I spent the night in a hayloft. Next morning, I just couldn't continue any more. I told Tom I had a plan.

He stared at me: "They will catch us and shoot us on the spot!"

"Maybe not, maybe we'll get lucky. And if they shoot us, it's better than marching us to death."

"We can't just run off. This is enemy territory, even if we were born in this country. There's no place to hide."

"Maybe we should *not* hide. Maybe we should just walk right in the open."

"Are you crazy?! With these yellow stars?"

3

"At least they'll know we are not hiding. We could be legitimate."

"Without papers?"

"I will make us some papers. At the lithography shop where I used to work, they showed me how to forge rubber stamps, both seals and signatures. All it takes is a simple compass, some transparent paper, and a purple or red pencil that bleeds on wet paper and looks like a rubber stamp."

"But where will you get that stuff?"

"I brought it along when we were drafted. It takes up absolutely no space."

"And if they searched your luggage?"

"The stuff looks innocent—no one would care."

We took a postcard—the only paper we had—and wrote out a longhand marching order for Tom and me, stating that we were under orders to go to a military hospital in Budapest. I copied the rubber stamp of our unit and the commanding colonel's signature from my troop pass.

We guessed that getting away from the approaching Russians would be more important for our guards than trying to find us.

An hour later we climbed down from the hayloft.

❋

Tom and I passed through two villages. People stared, but no one stopped us. Finally the sign on the roadside said the next village was the one we were looking for: Dombó.

At the crossroad stood two Hungarian MPs. This was it! Within the next few minutes we could be dead.

Trying to appear calm, we approached the soldiers. Tom simply said: "Good morning!"

Both MPs had mustaches. Nice Hungarian peasant boys, trained to be animals: "Where are *you* going?"

"To Dombó."

"Why? Whom are you going to see there?"

"The Judge." (The chief of the village aldermen was called "The Judge.") "We want to ask his permission to stay for a few days," said Tom.

"Your papers?"

I handed him the postcard with the fake seal and fake signature. The front was collapsing and military orders could have been written on any kind of paper, even on a postcard. This was nowhere as absurd as it sounds.

"Where do we find the Judge's office?" asked Tom.

"Just continue on this road. It will take you straight to the village square." He handed me back the postcard.

We started to walk. Not a sound behind us. Who knows, we just might make it!

❋

The Judge: "What do you want here?"

"We want to stay for a few days."

"So?"

"We need your permission."

"You have it."

"Would you write it on our document?" He scribbled something on the postcard. "Could you put a rubber stamp on it, and sign it?" He did.

"Do you have a place to stay?"

We didn't.

"Try Peter Csorba's. The third house on the right." Mr. Csorba put us up for the night.

❋

During the following 10 days, we stayed in three other villages, working our way toward the nearest railway station. In each village we obtained another rubber stamp, another signature. By now, in addition to our two fakes, we had four real stamps and four real signatures on our postcard.

The last village was only about 10 kilometers from the railroad. In the morning, our host said, "If you want to go home, you'd better get to the station soon. I doubt there will be many more trains leaving for Budapest."

✤

Four days later the train approached Budapest. "There is a curfew," the conductor told us. "After 9:00 no one is allowed out on the streets."

"What time is it?"

"Seven. We will arrive before the curfew."

I was eager to see my mother. Tom planned to join his family; they were hiding in a gentile friend's apartment.

About 5 kilometers outside of the Budapest Eastern Railroad Station, the train stopped. It sat there until 10:00. The conductor warned us: "You better stay in the railroad station. If you are on the street during curfew, you might get shot."

By the time the train stopped in Budapest, it was a quarter past 11. We took our backpacks and—curfew or no curfew—walked straight out of the railroad station. No one stopped us.

Budapest, November 1944

"Irene! Irene! Your son is downstairs!" The cry reverberated throughout the old stove factory. We were in the ghetto. The ghetto of World War II Budapest. My mother came, running.

Family and friends began attacking me with questions—and then with anxious warnings. "You can't stay here. They check every few hours to see if we are hiding anyone. They are looking for people who escaped from forced labor camps, other ghettos or . . . "

"Where can I go?"

"Downstairs, in the basement of the factory, we have a small cubicle hidden behind the stacks of bricks."

Someone took me downstairs. My beautiful 17-year-old second cousin, Sylvia, and another, unusually bright, young relative, George, were hiding there. The little room had a weak light that was turned off most of the time.

"Are we safe here?"

"When they come to check, they generally don't climb down to the basement."

"They" meant the Arrow Crossers, the Hungarian version of the German Nazis.

Mother appeared with a big pot of 80 dumplings. They would have normally lasted me about a week. Two hours later, 60 were gone.

❊

"We hear reports that there are people hiding in this basement."

It was a rough, uneducated voice. We froze. It had to be one of the Arrow Crossers. He was tapping on the walls. "The reports say there is a cave somewhere behind the bricks." He got tired of tapping, right before getting to the wall of our little room. The hollow sound would have given us away.

"I will be back." His footsteps grew fainter.

An hour later I was on the street again.

❊

When the Nazis or the Arrow Crossers pick up someone, my relatives had said, they take him to the Danube and simply machine gun him into the river. The body floats down to Yugoslavia or maybe all the way out to the Black Sea.

"Where am I going to find a place to hide?" I asked myself in panic. It was an hour and a half to curfew.

Someone stopped me: "Andy!"

I didn't recognize him.

"Joe, from the gymnasium."

A half hour later, I was with his friends, in an abandoned dental laboratory. There was nothing to eat except some dried-out bread—and not much of that.

*

The day after the last piece of bread disappeared, the Germans began withdrawing from Budapest. In a few days, they were gone.

I walked about ten blocks to our former home. My mother was already there.

We had nothing to eat. One of our neighbors discovered a dead horse two corners away. We borrowed an axe, went out, and cut off a hind leg. Everyone had a feast.

From time to time, my mother would get on a train with some of our towels or whatever else of value she could find. In the countryside she swapped our belongings for corn meal. Cornbread was our only food for weeks.

Mother's apartment had two rooms. There were too many homeless. The city assigned our second room to a family of three strangers.

Budapest, 1945

The war was over. Some degree of normalcy returned. I decided to go after my dream of becoming a stage director. I studied, passed a special exam, and was hired as an assistant director of the leading privately owned Hungarian theater. I was a stage director for almost ten years.

*

On a hot Sunday afternoon in 1955, I went to the beach and ran into an actor from the theater. He was with a stunning young woman. I asked him if she was an actress. No, she was a medical student.

Several weeks later, a distant relative asked me if I'd like to meet her roommate, Vali. It was the girl from the beach.

We had a whirlwind romance. By the time I took her home in the evening, the buses had stopped running. I had to walk home. It took me about an hour and a half. Within 11 days—after six dates—we decided to get engaged. Vali—we call her Valery now—still claims the only reason I proposed was that I wanted to avoid the hour-and-a-half trek home.

❈

In 1956 Hungary revolted. The country was fed up with its puppet government. At first, the revolution seemed to be winning. Then the Russians sent in their tanks. They drove them through the Kórút—the main artery that formed a semicircle around the heart of the city. The Soviets systematically blasted with cannon fire every twelfth or fifteenth building—just to let the Hungarians know they meant business.

Hungary was always a country receptive to "black humor." The day after the attack, on the front of what used to be one of the city's most beautiful buildings, a sign declared: "Stunning fifth floor apartment available. You can inspect it on the ground floor."

❈

Many thousands of Hungarians died or were wounded. Other thousands, including several of our friends, had been rounded up and jailed. My wife—who was now pregnant—and I, along with a few of our friends, fled for our lives.

We took a train to a village near the Austrian border. Then we started to walk. It would be hard to exaggerate the danger. There were children with us. Their mothers gave them sleeping pills to make sure they didn't cry out in the night and betray our presence. Our little group was captured anyway. Fortunately, our captors were Hungarian soldiers, not Russian troops, and they were ambivalent about turning us over to the political police. They put us up overnight in a barracks attached to the railroad yard.

It was relatively easy to escape. This time, with the help of a railroad man, we made it to the border. An Austrian customs officer lent me some coins and I called Christl, a distant relative in Vienna.

9

She took us in, of course, but we were eager to be out of Europe. Our first choice was to go to the United States. We gave ourselves a time limit of one month: if no American visa came within that time, we would try for Australia. The United States relaxed its immigration rules and allotted an extra quota to Hungarians. On the thirtieth day, our visa arrived.

New York, December 1956

I had an uncle who lived in New York. He represented the dream of every European: Uncle Sigmund started penniless, got a job in a company rebuilding machine tools, and became the chairman of the second largest corporation in the country specializing in buying closed-down factories, selling off the real estate, rebuilding the machinery, then selling that, too. At age 75, he was a multimillionaire.

The morning after the U.S. Army delivered us to Camp Kilmer, Uncle Sigmund, accompanied by his younger son, Bob, came to pick us up. Watching Bob, I received my first lesson in what it is like to be a citizen of a free country. With none of the subservience I expected, he approached an officer and said, "I've come to take my cousin and his wife home."

The officer was courteous: "I am very sorry, sir, but that can't be arranged yet, certainly not today."

Bob simply walked into the adjoining room and talked to another officer. The answer was the same. He went into the third room, and a fourth, reaching officers of successively higher rank. In the fifth room, he repeated his request to a colonel. The colonel pushed a piece of paper in front of Bob: "This is where you sign."

I learned a lesson that morning. *Don't give up!* Push a little more. Keep asking until you get a "Yes." It didn't cross my mind then, of course, but this is one of the basic tenets of what later became my American profession—salesmanship.

Uncle Sigmund owned a Cadillac limousine. We had never seen a car that size. I turned to Valery, dumbfounded: "I wonder how many families have to share this?"

❊

Uncle Sigmund and Aunt Sadie lived in one of Manhattan's poshest areas, Sutton Place. We walked into the foyer with the mud of Camp Kilmer still on our shoes. Uncle turned to us and said: "There are two bedrooms, a pink one and a blue one. Which one would you prefer?"

I couldn't describe our feelings. That morning we had awakened in our Army barracks, with more than a dozen people sharing the room. A month earlier, we had been fleeing for our lives—over land from which the mines had only recently been removed. And now this nice elderly relative asks us *what color* bedroom we prefer?

❊

I had to find a job.

The demand for Hungarian stage directors was surprisingly low. Through an agency that specialized in helping immigrants, The International Rescue Committee, I got a job at *The New York Times*—as a filing clerk. I worked in what was called "the morgue," filing clips of yesterday's stories.

On May 29, 1957, our first child, George, was born. Beautiful, bright-looking—and an American citizen!

My wife, Valery (for some reason we misspelled her name with a "y," rather than an "ie" and it stuck), had learned that there is no reciprocity between New York State and Hungary. After being a full-fledged doctor in Hungary, here she would not be allowed to practice medicine for approximately four years. She became an intern and then a resident at several large New York hospitals.

We were totally broke.

❊

After three months with my uncle and aunt, we were desperate to find a place of our own. I asked one of the real estate editors of the *Times* for suggestions.

"I'll try to get you an apartment in one of the low-income city projects."

The next day he handed me a very long questionnaire. I filled it out and gave it back to him. He read half of the long document, then laughed out loud. "Andy, this will be the first application in the history of New York City low-income housing where the applicant gives his present address as Sutton Place South."

❋

After a while we got notice from the housing authority: our turn had come. They offered us two bedrooms and two baths in a brand-new low-cost project, for only $60 a month, gas and electricity included. We moved into a building at 125th Street and Amsterdam Avenue.

In the housing authority office, I asked one of the managers: "Could you please tell me something about this project?"

"Sure. It's an integrated project."

"What does 'integrated' mean?"

"There are black families living here and there are white families living here.

"How many apartments?"

"1,440."

"How many black and how many white?"

"We have 1,439 black families and"—he pointed his finger at me—"you!"

❋

Since my wife and I were both working, we asked a neighbor, a young black woman, to take care of our child during the day. She also had a son, only a week or so older than George. We bought a double stroller, so she could take both babies to the park. People would smile at the very attractive young mother and the two gorgeous chil-

dren—and then do a double take: how could this woman
have one beautiful blond, blue-eyed boy and one beautiful
black-haired darkskinned one?

❄

We were broke. Vali suggested we might earn a few
extra dollars by getting on a TV game show. Producers
might think refugees from Hungary would make interesting contestants. I wrote to several networks.

A show called "Do You Trust Your Wife?" invited us.
Johnny Carson, then the host of the show, introduced us:
"This couple has a very convenient career arrangement.
Val is a doctor and Andy works in *a morgue.*"

We won $1,500! The next day we bought a used car.

2

So You Want to Be a Stockbroker?

September 1958

I was still at the *Times*, working at a miserable job, making $64 a week, before taxes. When everyone sent out for a cup of coffee, I didn't. I couldn't afford it.

One morning I decided to splurge; it was the day of *the big interview*. I walked into a coffee shop—the first American coffee shop I had ever seen from the inside.

Two men were sitting at the counter. I joined them. The waitress stopped in front of the first one. He looked over the top of his newspaper and said: "English."

She stopped in front of the second one. He said: "Danish."

She stopped in front of me. I said: "Hungarian."

❀

"You want to be a stockbroker?"

Pete McKenzie wasn't amused. The young man in front of him barely spoke English.

"What makes you think you could sell securities?"

"I have been selling mutual funds for the last six months."

15

"You *have* been selling or just *trying* to sell?"

"I have made more money selling them part time in the evening than I have made during the day in my full-time job." I was careful not to spell out how little that day job paid.

"How did you get into it?"

"I read every ad in *The New York Times* and they all said 'previous experience necessary.' The only ad that said 'no previous experience necessary' was to sell funds part time. I was starving and decided to try it."

"Any problems?"

"Only three: I never sold anything in my life, I didn't know what a mutual fund was, and I didn't speak any English. At least not any that someone could understand. I was a perfect candidate! But then, they hired everyone who could pass the simple exam."

"Who in the world did you sell to?"

"I looked up Hungarian names in the Manhattan telephone directory and called them."

Pete McKenzie started to show some interest. The firm, like most of the old-time Wall Street firms, had recently embarked on selling mutual funds. He was eager to hire salesmen with some experience in the field. His established sales force had no interest in the new product.

"Do you plan to see any other firms?"

"I've already seen three and plan to see five more." Pete didn't react. "What do you pay your trainees?"

"Four hundred a month."

❋

Two weeks later I was back. "I would like to work for you."

"Did you speak to all the other eight firms?"

"Yes. Seven of them offered me a job."

"What did you tell them?"

"That I plan to be completely self-supporting within six months. If I am not, I expect them to fire me."

16

The custom was that a firm supported its trainees for at least three years, giving them ample opportunity to develop some business. To fire someone after six months was unheard of. If a salesman made only a few really good trades, he more than made up for his modest draw.

"Any reason you'd prefer working for us rather than the others?"

"I checked with several people. Everyone told me that you are a very high-class firm. And you offered four hundred dollars a month. The others offered three."

"All right, start next Monday," said McKenzie.

"Thanks! But I have a problem. My wife is a doctor and she is working as an intern. You know, 36 hours work, 12 off, and then another 36 hours work. She gets paid only $64 a month."

"A month?"

"We have a one-year-old baby and I can't support them on $400."

McKenzie was a good guy: "I know they wouldn't allow me to pay you six hundred, but I can get away with five."

❄

Training? They gave you a set of books and six months to get prepared for the New York Stock Exchange exam. No one spent a minute teaching you or explaining anything. If you had a question, you went to one of the older salesmen for help. Most of them considered me a strange creature from an unknown world.

During those years, and I guess even before, being a broker with a major investment banking firm was a gentleman's profession. You finished some very good school, preferably Ivy League, and started to sell to your parents, relatives, their friends, and your friends. Who was this crazy Hungarian who wanted to make it in this business without any contacts?

The rules of what a new salesman was allowed to do were completely different then. After a month with a Stock Exchange member firm you were allowed to sell mutual

17

funds; after six months you were allowed to take the exam and, if you passed, to sell anything your firm approved.

I knew that even a generous $500 draw would not feed us; I had to start to prospect right away. I went to the New York Public Library, looked up the Budapest telephone directory, made a list of those names that took up more than a page and then added a random few. I ended up with 110 names. Back in my office I opened the Manhattan directory looking for, and then dialing, every single one of those names.

Thirty-two days later, I made my first sale.

✻

At the beginning of the fifth month I walked up to Pete. "Mr. McKenzie, I am flat broke. The last two months I made about four times more in commissions than my draw. Could you give me the extra money?"

"I don't know. Let me check with the lawyers."

An hour later he was at my desk, funds in hand.

"Why did you have to check?"

"To make sure that the firm doesn't lose much money on a new salesman on a draw, he is expected to produce enough to have one month's payout in reserve before he gets paid a penny over the regular amount."

"Well, then I *was* entitled to the extra over the reserve, wasn't I?"

"The rules apply to *salesmen*. I had to see whether they also apply to *trainees*." Pete was grinning. By now he had developed some pride in me, his *discovery*. "And I never had to ask the question before."

✻

When I had been with the firm for two years I asked for a private secretary. Pete thought I was nuts. The rule was that every four men shared a secretary. He thought it over for a day or two and decided to go half way on my request; Jim Peppercorn and I would share a secretary. Jim was the top producer in the office; he was bright, good-looking, and came from a very wealthy family. And I happened to like him a lot.

We hired a young woman named Beverly. She was very smart, extremely hardworking, and had a great sense of humor. She also had a son to support, and for a decent salary she was ready to work her brains out.

One day I had a number of emergencies, but couldn't get any help from Beverly, because Jim had been dictating to her from 9:30 to 4:30, almost nonstop. When she finally became available—I would not dream of interrupting them, as Jim never interrupted me when Bev was working on my projects—she told me that they had spent the whole day making plans for rebuilding his summer home. I wasn't thrilled. I needed help to survive; he needed it to live elegantly.

One day Jim proudly informed one of our colleagues:

"My wife bought a new dog yesterday. It's the most fashionable breed these days, I understand: a lhasa and apso."

Our colleague, with a grin:

"A lhasa *and* apso?"

"Yes."

"I thought the most fashionable breed today is the German *and* shepherd!"

❉

"Everybody to the research meeting! Come on," said Pete, "let's go—all except Andrew. He's only a mutual fund salesman." "*Only?*" Right then and there I decided to switch to stocks.

For the next several years I didn't sell a single share of a fund, only stocks. By the end of the fourth year, in an office of 40 well-connected salesmen, most of them old-timers, I was the top producer.

There were two simple reasons:

1. I put in more time, substantially more time, than anyone else.

19

2. I listened to the advice that everyone gave me and then considered whether *doing exactly the opposite might be more beneficial*. Very often it was!

One of the typical "wisdoms" imparted to all young salesmen was to prospect in the middle-class areas. "Don't prospect on Sutton Place, Beekman Place, Fifth Avenue, or Park Avenue. Everyone there already has three or four brokers."

For a year or two I listened to the advice. Then I decided that if those rich people could afford several brokers, they could probably afford one more. Especially one who works harder for them.

I sent out several thousand double postcards to addresses in Sutton Place, Sutton Place South, and Beekman Place. The cards said something like: "We have a new research report on IBM. If you want to receive it, please return the attached business reply card."

As a result of the returns, the *number* of my trades increased only modestly, but the *size* of my orders tripled and quadrupled! So did my income.

Just in time! On March 29, 1962, we had another son: Paul. He was adorable.

We needed a larger apartment!

❊

By this time I had enough confidence to talk with non-Hungarians; not only had my speech improved a bit—my accent was *still* very bad—but I found that most Americans, and especially New Yorkers, were quite willing to do business with people whose English was far from perfect.

As one of my customers explained: "I thought that anyone who can make a living with that horrible accent must be pretty good."

And another client told me: "Andrew, you have a *perfect* accent—no trace of English!"

✳

One of the postcards I sent to Sutton Place was
returned by a middle-aged lawyer. When I called him, he
bought 200 shares, and from then on, anytime I reached
him—which always happened to be on Mondays—he
bought 200 shares of whatever I suggested. For a beginner,
that was good business.

"Why can I reach you only on Mondays?"

"The rest of the week I am in Washington. Let me give
you my number."

Whenever I called him in Washington, *he* picked up.
No secretary, not even a switchboard. I decided he must
not be a very successful lawyer; he probably inherited the
money.

On the day of the Kennedy inauguration he walked
into my office. It was the first time we had met in person.
He gave a terrific impression—a warm, obviously very
well-educated man with a twinkle in his eye.

"I know that you are a lawyer," I said, "but I am
embarrassed to say I have no idea if you are a tax lawyer,
a corporate lawyer, a divorce lawyer, or what?"

During those years I worked 16 hours a day, 7 days
a week. I never had the time to read newspapers or watch
TV. I had become one of those morons who does nothing
but concentrate on one subject.

My client was grinning. "I guess *from today on* I am a
freelance corporate lawyer."

"Why? What have you been doing up to now?"

"For the last eight years I have been a member of the
Eisenhower administration."

That's why there was no switchboard or secretary! He
had given me his direct number; he didn't want anyone to
know about his personal business.

✳

I come from a country where business was done by
telling a prospect: "My uncle, the president of X Corporation, and your cousin, the chairman of Y Corporation, play

21

bridge every Wednesday." *Then* you could start to talk about business. To pick up one of the top members of the Eisenhower administration on a simple postcard gave me a hint of the possibilities.

Getting Ahead

I spent five years with that firm. I got lucky and started to make a living. A very modest living, but far better than a filing clerk makes.

You can call people at work, you can call people at home, so my day stretched very long. (Even today—I am past my 66th birthday—I still put in 85- to 95-hour weeks.)

I love the work. Selling stocks is not like selling vacuum cleaners; not that I have anything but admiration for vacuum cleaner salesmen. Door-to-door selling may be the best preparation for becoming a successful stockbroker. But we brokers are not asking someone to buy a product: we are selling *an intangible*—an idea, one that, we hope, will make money. We're selling our knowledge, selling our research.

Good brokers spend most of their time on the phone, talking to clients, and trying to get new ones. The investment ideas they propose come from the firm's analysts. If they read or hear about a company that intrigues them, they generally ask the research department for an opinion. At many firms, brokers are forbidden to invest clients' money in any stock that hasn't been approved by the research department. It cuts down on lawsuits.

Unfortunately, after a while I began to suspect that the quality of my firm's research wasn't as good as I had thought. My clients weren't making money. When clients lose money, they don't blame the firm's analysts; they blame the broker. They close their accounts, and the broker has to start from scratch, working even harder and even longer hours and making even more calls in an attempt to stay ahead.

I asked the firm to transfer me from the branch office in midtown Manhattan to the main office on Wall Street. That was where the top players were, the brokers whose brains I wanted to pick. Maybe I could find better investment ideas that way. That was also the office where the wealthiest clients tended to go. My requests for transfer were always turned down. The firm didn't think I fit its image. I was more Iron Curtain than Ivy League.

❈

I decided to look for another employer.

By that time I had built up a pretty good book of clients. Most firms I contacted said they would love to have me.

The big brokers and investment bankers generally had two sales departments: one, the *institutional*, serviced mainly "house accounts"—big banks, insurance companies, investment managers, and so on. Most of these accounts were assigned to the brokers, who were expected to recommend to their clients as many of the firm's products as possible.

The *retail* sales department was generally staffed with more entrepreneurial types: people out to prove themselves—and doing pretty much whatever it took to achieve success. The best ones were working 16 hours a day; the worst were overtrading their clients.

Much of the institutional sales was face to face; it included a lot of entertaining, such as taking clients to sports and similar events. The retail business was heavy on telephone work and lighter on personal contact.

These distinctions weren't rigid; there were aspects of each that mixed with the other. And a few salesmen, generally the most successful ones, were allowed to cover both retail and institutional accounts.

I generally contacted the retail sales managers. After meeting them, I took home stacks and stacks of research reports from some eight firms and pored over them. It seemed to me that the best research originated from an old-line firm—good sized, but not one of the giants.

I told its retail sales manager that I would be willing to join his firm, with one stipulation: I wanted to bring my secretary, Beverly, along. Bev had been working with me for three years by then, and she was very good.

Today a broker who is a "big producer"—who generates an exceptionally high level of commissions for his firm—has the power to make requests like that, and much more. In those days my demand was unheard of.

The sales manager laughed. He asked whether I was romantically involved with my secretary.

"No. But she has the same insane work habits I do."

They hired both of us.

October 1963

At first everything went along just the way I'd hoped. The analysts at my new firm were sharp, digging hard to find stocks that could move up. My clients were doing much better, they sent other clients to me, and my commissions kept growing. What's more, by this time I had some savings and my investments were making money for me, too.

The firm had about 600 salesmen nationwide when I joined. During my stay there, as the market continued strong, they added people; at one point there were about 900 of us. Within a few years I became the number one "retail" broker. I brought in more commissions that anyone else.

❊

My English pronunciation was still terrible. One day I tried to convince one of my best clients to buy 5,000 shares of a stock.

"Andy, what's the name of that company again?"

I told him.

"Sorry, I didn't catch it."

I repeated the name.

A pause, then: "Okay, Andy, let's buy it."

Two minutes later Beverly started laughing.

"What's so funny?"

"Your customer—the one who just bought the 5,000 shares—called back. He didn't want to insult you by asking for the name of the company again, so he called *me* to find out what he had just spent $75,000 on."

❄

I wanted to reach more potential customers.

By this time the firm had assigned three people to help me. We developed a new system for phoning prospects. My assistant, my secretary, and our bookkeeper would all chip in. We used 3″ × 5″ index cards with names assembled from various lists: people who lived in affluent neighborhoods, owned fancy cars, yachts—you can buy all sorts of lists. The firm checked the cards against a master list, to make sure the same prospect didn't get calls from two brokers within a short period.

As soon as I finished talking to someone, my three associates stopped whatever they were doing and all of us started dialing the next four people on our 3″ × 5″ cards. Whoever among my little group reached a possible client first signaled to me, I picked up the phone and started to talk.

It was something of an assembly line operation, but it worked. As far as I know, it was the first step on the way to a brand-new—and since then very much abused—prospecting technique on Wall Street.

By the way, assistants, secretaries, bookkeepers, and others helping a producer are getting a fixed pay, and sometimes a bonus, from the company—no commissions. Generally, the salesman gives them an incentive from his own pocket. More often than not, this incentive is tied to *his* production—so if the different associates do a good job, their own income grows with his. The dollar amounts are smaller, but expressed in percentage terms, the additional income can be meaningful.

❊

I lost Beverly: she became a saleswoman—a very good one! I needed a new assistant—and hired one of my wife's friends, Veronica.

She was superb! Not only in doing her own job, but also in teaching others how to do theirs. Her principle was: "Don't just tell them what to do, but figure out what they will misunderstand, and *prevent the mistakes before they happen.*"

Once I overheard her explaining the principle to one of the administrative managers: "If you teach someone how to walk, it is not enough to tell him: 'Pick up your right foot, put it forward and put your weight on it, then pick up your left foot, put it forward and put your weight on it.' You also have to tell them: ' . . . and don't pick up both feet at the same time, because you will fall on your behind.'"

❊

My clients were making money and so was I—for awhile. Then the research began to slip. The top-notch analysts left, one by one. They were offered more money by other firms, or they wanted to manage money themselves.

Up until then I had totally depended on the investment ideas of my firm or on the advice of analyst friends at other brokerage houses (which later had to be *approved* by my firm). But lately the recommendations did not seem to be working. I had to find a way to stop depending on others.

I had no idea how to go about it.

❊

Brokerage offices used to look very much like the newsrooms of the big metropolitan papers. Dozens of, sometimes more than a hundred, salesmen—women brokers were a rarity—worked in these "bull pens." We each had a desk with a phone and several card files—there were no desktop computers back then. Some of the brokers made a good living, but the very big producer, one with such a volume of business he could more or less write his own ticket under threat of leaving the firm and taking his clients with him, was rare.

After I had been at the firm about four years, the executive vice president in charge of national sales called me into his office. He was a relatively young guy, but exceptionally talented.

"Andy, congratulations! We are making you a partner. The first salesman to achieve this great honor in the firm's history!"

I asked why I was being made a partner. He grinned. "Because, Andy, the chairman and the president are upset that you had a higher income this year than they did."

Now we both grinned.

"What does it mean—being a partner?"

"Well, first of all, you have to take a 67% pay cut."

Guess who didn't become a partner.

❈

A stock salesman can practically decide how much money he really wants to make. His income is in line with the time he is willing to devote to the business. His take-home pay is not determined by talent alone. Leverage has a lot to do with it.

Let's assume a salesman works 7 hours a day: he will spend 5 hours with the daily routines—reading the financial papers, reading the reports, doing all his administrative duties—and there will be only 2 hours left to talk to clients. If he spends 10 hours a day, he will sooner or later rate a good secretary or assistant, so his miscellaneous duties stay constant—but he will be able to spend 5 hours a day with the clients. If he spends 13 hours working, he will eventually get additional help and be able to spend 8 hours a day with his clients and prospective clients.

The leverage comes not only from the time invested, but also from the fact that the more time he spends selling, the more his skills will improve. The time invested increases his results arithmetically. The improving skills increase his results geometrically. The combination of the two can help his income explode.

In almost any other business, when a salesman's income becomes very large, management can cut back his territory. Even in the brokerage business, institutional accounts are considered the company's property—and the institutional salesman is somewhat at the mercy of his superiors. If he starts to make too much money, the management can take away part of his accounts and assign them to someone else.

The reverse is true about a *retail salesman*. He *owns his accounts*. He is the person the client likes, is involved with, feels a close relationship with, not the company. When he leaves, most of the accounts will probably go with him.

A brokerage firm wouldn't dream of cutting back a retail salesman's commission rate, just because he grew too big. It costs more or less the same amount to process a $100 order as a $100,000 order, but the commission on the latter one is incomparably larger. The brokerage firm will do everything *to please its star salesmen*—and will try to reduce the number of the smallest producers.

❊

I was being wooed by several firms, and the manager of my office knew it. He was worried: I might be tempted. So, when I said that I'd like to get out of the bull pen, that I would be more productive *in my own office*, he ran to his boss.

"If you don't give Andy a private office, we are going to lose him."

"I can't, there's no room. We can't get any more space in this building for money or the love of God."

"Do you want to lose your top producer?"

Next day the boss came over to me. "Andy, I want you to take my office"—which, by the way, was very, very large—"and I'll take your space and your secretary's. *I'll* move into the bullpen."

❄

In 1973-74 the stock market collapsed. So did our business.

I had two children in private school, a modest weekend house in the country, a small co-op for my mother, and one, not much larger, for myself.

My assets and my income disappeared at the same time.

Sure, there were negatives to explain investors' fear—but there are *always* negatives when stocks are cheap. You could have bought General Electric or Merck and made a 787% and 1,823% profit, respectively, since. A few younger growth companies, if you had the courage—and luck—to invest in them did even better: Loews is up more than 5,000%, Waste Management 14,300%, and Wal-Mart more than 64,000%. You may have bought some lemons, too, but all in all, it was a great time to buy.

You have to be a contrarian whether you invest in stocks, bonds, commodities, art, or real estate. There is a medieval saying: "When the enemy surrounds the fortress, buy real estate. When the liberating troops arrive: sell it!"

❄

After a number of years I slipped to number 2 in the ranking of producers—behind my good friend Steve, another Hungarian. In my business, almost everyone has an occasional disastrous year—and there were a few years when I didn't even make the top 25.

Steve is the nicest guy anyone could ever meet—and he has an accent that, if possible, is even thicker than mine. We both got a kick out of the fact that two salesmen, who had to start from scratch after they had passed 30, made it.

One day the firm decided to find out what creates a top producer. It hired an industrial psychologist to develop a detailed questionnaire. We were asked about our background, education, habits, interests, and so on. Eventually the pros tallied out the results, and all of us were sent the winning profile: Midwestern, Protestant, graduate of a reasonably good American university, 2½ children, member of several social clubs, works about 40 hours a week.

Steve and I looked at each other. He said, "It's sheer luck that we already have our jobs; they'd never hire us now!"

3

The Fundamental
Factor of Success

After 15 years with my second firm in 1978, I decided to join a real Wall Street powerhouse: two of the best established investment banking firms, both substantially more than 100 years old, had recently merged. Joining them seemed to me like a once-in-a-lifetime opportunity.

When a broker switches firms, it is completely unlike any other employee leaving an organization. He doesn't give a two-week notice. A broker, or trader, announces that he is leaving—and walks right out the door the next minute. The same happens if he is fired.

The departing broker's manager jumps into action. He immediately distributes the abandoned accounts among the other brokers. The most successful producers get the biggest accounts, the mediocre brokers share the moderate-sized accounts. In most cases, before the departing broker arrives at his new firm, even if it's next door, most of his customers have already been called.

The callers, in most instances, are careful not to say anything illegal. They will not say that the broker has been stealing his customers' money; they may only insinuate it. They will not say that the broker has been fired for improper conduct; they may only insinuate it. In essence, they will try to make the customer feel that following the broker to the new firm would be a horrible mistake.

Naturally, the switching broker employs the reverse tactic. When he arrives at his new firm, he calls all his clients—the largest ones have probably already been contacted by his former colleagues—and tells them that he made the move because *the research at his previous firm was extremely bad.*

He probably switched firms because many of his clients had such large losses that they were ready to dump him. Now he can tell them that they lost money, not because he was doing a sloppy job, but because the research department was hopeless. He will also try to convince them that the new firm has the best research on Wall Street.

As soon as possible he will get out a letter that ballyhoos everything positive that can be said about his new firm. He will enclose a transfer sheet for the client to sign, a sheet instructing the old firm to send all his securities over to the new one. A high percentage of clients usually sign.

April 1978

The firm I was leaving planned to move uptown; I chose that moving date to make my switch. I guessed that in the turmoil of the move, there would be many problems more urgent than reaching my freshly reassigned customers.

The plan worked better than expected. When the members of my old firm arrived at its uptown quarters the telephones weren't working. Hysterical brokers were desperately trying to get in touch with their regular clients; no one even thought of trying to reach mine.

❋

By this time, I had a new assistant—Maureen. She was an athlete with boundless energy—and spectacularly bright. I concentrated on investment ideas and selling. She took everything else off my shoulders. We hired a telephone clerk, someone to handle the duties of dialing and spending time with telephone operators and protective secretaries.

We went to work.

❊

My new shop was a great place. At least for *an education in selling securities*, there was no better shop in the country. The man who ran our division was brilliant—and totally results oriented. In plain language, all he focused on was making commissions for the firm. And commissions for the firm meant commissions for the brokers.

I had been doing well before, but now I learned how to really make money. After about two years my "gross" quadrupled, which meant that I was taking home as much as—or more than—the president of a large corporation.

You'd think that I was deliriously happy. In slightly over 20 years I had moved my living quarters from Harlem public housing to the 47th floor of a stunning new midtown building.

But something was wrong. It was soon clear that the research at my new superfirm was about the same as at the first two. When it came to fast-growing young companies, it was strictly average, which means useless. If that was the best that I could do for my clients, why did they need me?

The firm understood—though would not admit—that its research was not going to make its retail customers rich. The partner in charge of our division, a brilliant marketer, urged us to open more and more accounts. Anyone who had $10,000 was welcome. He had to assume that many of our clients would lose money and be gone—but he also assumed that casting a net every day would bring in plenty of new clients. And he showed us salesmen *how* to do it.

It would be unfair to say that he was the best sales manager I have ever met. He was the *only* real sales manager I have ever met on Wall Street. Most of the others were simply administrators, trying to convince everyone to sell the firm's products. Larger, quality firms never try to *force* their salesmen to sell certain products, but there is a steady effort to brainwash.

This brilliant manager decided that educating young salesmen is a waste of time. For quicker, better results he would pirate the most successful young producers from other firms. He had much to offer: the impressive name of the firm, a good education—in *salesmanship*, not in stocks, bonds, options, and other products of a securities firm—and *good commissions*.

Compensation was the main attraction. The regular commission structure was similar to that at other firms, but there were "specials," providing unusually high commissions, available to those who were willing to go for them. The firm's trading department, led by a very able, very experienced man, would accumulate large blocks of stock, sometimes from institutions getting out of big positions. If the salesmen could distribute this stock among the retail customers, their rewards were high.

❄

I considered again changing firms—but I wondered if it made any sense. Most had the same policies, and few had a name to compare with my present company—and names are door-openers in this business. But more than that, I now knew that research at other houses, with a very rare exception here and there, was not much better. By now I was convinced that *most of Wall Street research shoots for mediocrity and never quite makes it.*

❄

A new, interesting company was offered to the public: the shares of an athletic shoe company whose sales and earnings had skyrocketed during the great running fad.

34

Unfortunately, many at the firm believed that "the running boom was over." All they had to do was attend a "road show" or sales meeting for the stock or read the prospectus carefully to find out that *the company's backlog of orders was at an all-time high.*

I bought a great deal of the stock and held it for over a year. Its price moved up about 50%—at which point my firm finally woke up and began to recommend the company aggressively. The recommendation gave the stock a sharp boost upward—and I started selling.

※

There was something to learn from this experience.

It brought back memories of 10 or 15 years earlier. At my second job I met a brilliant young analyst, Merrill Berman, who discovered a few companies in which no one else had taken an interest yet. At first I didn't believe him, but several of his recommendations became major winners. When I went along with his ideas, the experience became highly profitable.

He discovered a company in New Jersey that offered a new service: it prepared, by computer, payroll checks and all the forms that go with them. The beauty of the service was that it translated a *fixed overhead* for a company into a *variable expense.*

Let me explain. In a cyclical business, in which a company may have substantially fewer employees one year than another, maintaining a fully staffed payroll department is a burdensome *fixed expense.* This organization offered its customers a deal that was hard to refuse: its fee was based on the number of paychecks prepared. When business is weak, at least one expense will drop; when business is strong, the payroll expense will go up, but the company can afford it. *Automatic Data Processing* had created a very appealing service. It also created *a brand-new industry.*

I purchased a lot of the stock before most analysts and salesmen on Wall Street had ever heard of the company. It developed into a *very large* winner for my clients.

This experience with ADP taught me some other important lessons. One was that meeting management is very important. Through Berman, I met Henry Taub and Frank Lautenberg, the chairman and the president: knowledgeable, hardworking, impressive people. I had an easier time convincing my clients to buy the stock, because I knew the quality of the principals.

Another lesson gained was recognition of the importance of an *ever-growing repeat-order factor* for a service company. If you teach your client how to do a job—for instance, how to prepare a payroll—you get one single fee for one single sale. However, *if you prepare his payroll yourself, then that order will probably keep coming back biweekly or weekly.* Your original customer keeps returning regularly—and you proceed to sign up new customers, most of whom will also come back and give you more business regularly. *You created a company that will keep growing, probably for quite a while.*

Merrill Berman also recommended that I look into H&R Block, the company that prepares tax returns. Just like ADP, it also had an ever-growing repeat order factor. And its business was literally exploding.

When I first offered H&R Block to my clients, especially my accountant and lawyer clients, they told me I was nuts. "Andy, how can you suggest that we invest in a company that disappears on April 16th? For the following nine months we won't even know whether or not it still exists!"

I told what I had learned. "Of every 100 clients, 72 come back the following year and bring some of their friends and relatives. Of each 100 friends and relatives, 72 come back the following year and bring *their* friends and relatives. This company may have a tremendous future."

H&R Block proved to be another huge winner for my clients.

❉

I kept asking myself: "How do I find stocks like that? How do I spot opportunities consistently, *relying on discipline and not on luck?*" I wanted desperately to get away from calling clients with the latest recommendation from our lackluster analysts. I wanted to sell ideas *with a conviction* that they had a better than average chance of turning into winners.

I decided that *the only solution was to do my own research*, find stocks I could wholeheartedly recommend because I had done the homework myself, because I had examined the facts and trusted the management!

I had no idea where to begin.

❋

I knew about four major schools of research:

1. The value school
2. The low price-to-earnings ratio school
3. The growth stock school
4. The technical analysis school

The Value School

The value school's bible is a book written by Benjamin Graham and David L. Dodd, *Security Analysis*. The value school theory states that when you buy a stock, you are buying a piece of the company, and how much you should pay depends on how much the company is worth. If you sold it all off and divided up the proceeds among the stockholders, would each person's share of the proceeds be more or less than the current price of a share?

You should look for stocks whose actual value is higher than their market price and hold them until the market price goes up to near book value;* then sell.

---

* "Book value" measures the net worth, per share, of a company at a given moment in time. It does this by dividing the shareholders' equity (without preferred equity and without intangibles) by the number of shares outstanding.

A couple of years ago, many undervalued companies were being bought up by "raiders," who often sold off the parts of the company to realize its full value. Soon everyone started looking for the next target—book values are relatively easy to figure out—until there were few "cheap" companies left.

Not only are sharply underpriced values scarce; there is no assurance that the market price will ever rise to meet "intrinsic value." If a company's earnings aren't growing, if it is a mature, fuddy-duddy company, investors who aren't in a position to break it up and sell off its pieces just won't be interested in the stock.

Leading a company to success, like all other human endeavors, takes character, talent, knowledge, drive, and discipline. I want to find a company with creative and dynamic leadership that is taking it to new heights—not a company that is worth more dead than alive. As one old-time Wall Streeter said: "Everyone knows how to read a balance sheet. I have to know how to read a person."

And as I later realized, success also depends on industry and market *domination*, which increases a company's chances of maintaining good profit margins.

The Low Price-to-Earnings Ratio School

I am not against the use of price/earnings ratios as *one of many tools* in evaluating stocks. Of course I prefer to buy stocks whose price is a low multiple of earnings per share rather than those selling at a high multiple. But, again, *numbers are not the total answer.*

As with book values, *there may be a reason* for the low valuation the market has put on these stocks. The P/E ratio reflects the last 12 months' earnings; earnings during the *following* 12 months could go even lower. Or maybe investors aren't putting much value on a company whose earnings are growing at a ho-hum pace.

Some of the companies I buy are young and their earnings are still slight. After careful research, I sometimes become convinced that earnings will not only grow, but may explode. The *current* P/E of these stocks means relatively little.

Generally speaking, price/earnings ratios and price/sales ratios are much more important in the efficient market (that is, for stocks that are followed by many analysts) than in the *inefficient market* (for stocks that have a zero or near-zero following). And, as you know, it is in the inefficient market where the most money can be made.

❅

Let me insert a little story here that illustrates how I think you can make your biggest profits.

Someone mentions a totally unknown company that for some reason appeals to you: usually it's because you like the service or the product it provides. You write the company and ask to be put on its mailing list.

The first communication informs you that the company is only a few years old and still in the research and development stage. It has yet to record its first sales, and it has never earned a penny, but, for the first time in its history, it has a $1 million backlog in orders.

Three months later the company informs you that the backlog is now $5 million and that it produced its first profit, 1 cent per share. It is in the black! Because you are intrigued, and like what the company is doing, you buy a modest number of shares at $3 each. You feel terribly guilty—you paid 300 times one quarter's earnings per share.

Three months later the backlog is up to $10 million and the company earned 10 cents per share. You buy a few more shares at $5 each.

A year later the company is earning $5 per share and it is selling at $50. The backlog of orders is sky high. Other investors now are offering you $50 for your shares—and because you are a nice person you sell them some of your stock.

You made a big profit! Why? *You used more than just your calculator: you also used your head!* You may keep holding the rest of your shares, monitoring the company, in anticipation of a very substantial additional profit.

Be careful. I have presented an ideal situation. Very few investments ever work out this neatly.

❄

Any approach based on book values or price/earnings ratios or other formulas is going to have thousands and thousands of followers. These days everyone has tons of data on companies and computer software to massage them every way imaginable. For any individual investor to have an advantage in information on big companies, well followed by Wall Street, is almost impossible, and it's just about as impossible for any mechanistic evaluation system to create outstanding results based on that information.

Any approach that a horde of investors uses in a more or less identical way is self-defeating. If your computer screen flashes "bargain," thousands of other investors are reading some similar output and are placing orders when you do. To make substantial money in the market, you must have a meaningful advantage over other investors. *You have to do a thorough and detailed investigation, not just juggle statistics.*

In all fairness to my many friends who use computers, some have refined their technique so that their basically modest advantage applied month after month, year after year, provides reasonable returns.

Many years ago I developed a manual screening process for identifying high-yielding stocks. Mechanically selecting, according to certain criteria, from among high dividend payers did work, but it was a soulless, boring job. It required total devotion to the numbers, all human factors excluded. No personal contact, only statistics. My system was manual. Since then, my friends have created far more sophisticated screening processes using computers. Their approach appeals to me even less. I want to find—and meet—human creativity, human brilliance.

Looking only at statistics and never talking to the management just does not intrigue me.

The Growth Stock School

This school preaches that you should invest in companies that already have had 8 or 12 up quarters in a row. Wait until management has proven its ability, then leap in. In my experience if you wait that long to buy the stock, you are often setting yourself up for trouble.

First, when a company has had that kind of record, many people will have already become aware of it and bought the stock. By the time *you* get it, the price is scary. The theory says that such a company deserves a premium in the marketplace. Fine. Let someone else pay the premium.

Second, the more straight growth quarters a company has had, the closer it may be to its first really bad quarter.

In the early 1970s the biggest banks promoted the idea that a company which had shown above-average growth in earnings year after year was a jewel to be locked away and treasured. These were the "one decision" stocks—IBM, Xerox, Polaroid, Avon Products, Eastman Kodak. The list was long, and so the whole bunch went by the nickname of "the Nifty Fifty." And their prices rose and rose!

"Why are you paying 40 times earnings for a mature, well-known stock?"

"Because five years from now, with the way earnings are growing, the price I paid will be only 6 times earnings. And by that time everyone else will see what a goldmine I have and they will offer me 50 times *that* year's earnings for it."

Along came a recession, and wham! As earnings collapsed, so did the Nifty Fifty.

Look for growth, all right, *but look much, much earlier*—way before everyone else knows the story and has pushed the stock to dangerous heights. Often the best time is when a company, after steadily diminishing losses, reports the first penny of profit. The company's youth and adolescence, the period of its most dynamic growth, lie just ahead: that's when you want to own it! And you want to get out when what remains is middle aged with slowly hardening arteries.

The Technical Analysis School

I look at monthly, weekly, daily, and intraday charts—with moving averages overlaid—on every stock in which I have, or consider taking, a major position. Graphs provide a good quick account of a stock's *past performance*, a kind of picture that shows you how the stock has been progressing. But I would never claim that charts can tell me anything reliable *about the future*.

At one time I thought they could. I read many, many books on charting; I watched channels, tunnels, pennants, flags, W's, M's, and triple bottoms until my head was swimming. Sometimes they worked, and the stocks did what the charts said they should, but most of the time they didn't cooperate.

Consider the chart of an oil stock that shows it is "poised to advance." Fine. Then one of the big oil producing countries starts a war, or the whole market takes a nosedive because of some action of the Federal Reserve, or the price of oil falls because of a major find, or it rises because OPEC had a meeting in Geneva where no one openly quarreled, or the government decides to lower the budget deficit by taxing gasoline at the pumps or the oil companies' "excess profits," or . . . ; well, you get the idea.

If a stock hasn't been going in one direction, but backing and filling between two points, the chartists say, "Keep a close watch on it." The stock has been fluctuating between 5 and 10 for months—and then finally it goes to 10⅛. Aha! An *upside breakout*. The typical chartist will shout, "Buy!" and, if the stock happens to go in the other direction and reaches 4⅞, "Clearly we have experienced a *downside collapse*." The chartist would say, "Sell."

I have never seen a more perfect system for buying high and selling low.

This approach does work twice in each market cycle: at the beginning of a bull market, when the charts show that stocks which have been going down, or "forming a bottom," are starting to turn up again—and at the beginning of a bear market, when the opposite is happening. On every other occasion, when the market or individual stocks are neither bottoming nor plateauing, when they are fluctuating up and down, if you try to leap on the backs of one after another, you are going to be whipsawed.

❊

A more sophisticated form of the technical approach to the market considers *relative strengths*: ranking all stocks on the basis of market action, that is, by what percentage they have moved up (or down) over a given time frame. Then buy those on the top of the lists; they have momentum going for them. Again, ride with the winners. Follow that system and you will always buy the stocks that are already expensive—in the hope that they will become more expensive.

As strange as this method sounds, there are many studies that support it. And, through their individual talent, some investors use the relative strength approach very skillfully and produce remarkable results. Confusing? It sure is.

Many chartists claim that they can predict the future, and as a proof quote their past record. Many of them claim that following their approach, you can make enormous profits. I believe in them, just as I believe in Santa Claus, the Tooth Fairy, and cheap and effective lawyers!

During the past 33 years, I have been subscribing to many market letters. I guess I, too, wish someone could read me the stock prices from tomorrow's newspaper.

Some of the technical letters are written by very bright people, and their opinions and predictions raise considerations you may not have thought about—points that might be useful. And sure, for several months or even years these gurus may be "hot," but I've never seen any of them, over the span of several years, who was right more often than wrong.

A *market indicator* is a tool that helps the trader or investor to predict if and when the market will turn up or down; a *market timer* is an expert who has the rare talent that enables him to use these tools successfully.

From my extensive experience, I have developed another definition of a market indicator: "Something that always worked throughout history—until the day I started to apply it." And my definition of a market timer: "Someone who walked on water—until I started to listen to him."

Maybe I just lack the talent, the ability to read these letters correctly and am not smart enough to understand the charts.

❋

The truth is that the vast majority of individual investors don't follow the gurus; they switch direction on their own, reacting to what they read in today's paper. Ah, but the trick in this business is to trade *against* what you read in today's paper. Very often it is better to buy on bad news and to sell on good news. (Yes, I know, this is a gross oversimplification. But in this pursuit there are few rules that apply in every situation.)

Timing is a very tempting idea. Yes, I've been seduced by the concept, too. Stocks go up and down, and with the wisdom of hindsight, it seems so easy to have called the turns. And the writers of the market letters sound so smart and sure of themselves. It would be nice to have a sure thing, wouldn't it?

I'm totally convinced by academic studies that most stocks *do* move with the market, or are at least heavily influenced by the market. It is very hard for a good stock to climb in a bear market. And yes, I believe that I could make incomparably more money if I knew what the market will do next. Unfortunately, I don't. You don't either. And unfortunately neither does he, the guru. Don't let him kid both of us.

❊

The fundamental factor of success is to find an exceptionally good company, and, we hope, to find it exceptionally early. There are no shortcuts, no answers that apply to every case. You should sell some stocks relatively soon, and in some other cases you should let your grandchildren do the selling.

You have to *stay on top* of every situation you own. Don't get too confident or too nervous. Most important, *don't sell a company that is strategically attractive because of short-term tactical considerations.*

❊

Forty years ago, two brothers inherited 1,000 shares of IBM each. The stock went up for a couple of years, and then it started to retreat. The "smart" brother sold it right away.

The "stupid" brother still owns his IBM.

❊

Unfortunately, you have to be *sure* that that what you're buying is an IBM. As sure as a *hardworking, bright human* can be. No magic, no miracles.

Everyone seems to be waiting for the Second Coming, for the Redeemer, for the Messiah. Face it, when He comes, He won't be a broker or a stock market guru!

4

Finding Blue Chips Before Wall Street Does

What is the way to identify winning stocks?

I had no notion of the specifics of a method, but at least I had a firm idea about what I did *not* want to do. I did not want to follow any of the four accepted paths to investment wisdom. After I examined them all, I came away believing that there must be a fifth, and maybe more satisfying way.

I started with the daily newspapers and concentrated on reports of sales and earnings. I looked for companies reporting exceptionally good quarterly figures—up substantially from the same quarter of the year before.

I wrote to several of these companies asking them to put me on their mailing list. They sent me annual and interim reports, 10Ks and 10Qs (reports the companies have to file with the Securities and Exchange Commission), proxy material, and public relations releases. I started reading without having the faintest idea of what I was looking for. Some nights I would be up until three or four in the morning, poring over endless stacks of papers.

After several months, I began to develop some very preliminary notions of where my search was leading.

47

I won't bore you with a play-by-play account of my explorations; I'll ignore the dead ends and false leads—and just describe what my group and I do now.

Let me state emphatically: what you are going to read about is not a final product. It is simply *the present stage in an ongoing search.* In investing you are always learning, fine-tuning, discovering, adding on, improving. And yes, discarding. And sometimes reexamining and reaccepting the discards.

❁

Over time, with lots of trial and error, I developed an approach to investing that my team and I now call the *Indicator Approach.* It has three key elements:

1. Our method of selecting stocks
2. The way we do research
3. Our effort to sell early, before the bad news hits

How Do We Select Stocks?

Over the years we have focused in on six criteria that we evaluate when we look at companies:

First, is fast growth. We check every single company that publishes a sales and earnings report in *The Wall Street Journal* or in *Investor's Business Daily* (that's way over *27,000 reports* a year) to find *companies whose sales increased by more than 15% and earnings by more than 30%* over last year's identical quarter.

Second, we prefer companies that, because of their patents and know-how, *totally dominate their industry, niche, or geographic area.* In plain English, *they are monopolies or near-monopolies.* If you and I own a piece of a company that has zero or near-zero competition, we will sleep well.

Third, we try to find companies that even during recessions can increase their sales and their earnings every year, like clockwork. If this sounds as though I am looking for companies *that are growing almost totally independently of the economy*, that's exactly what I am looking for. And you know very well *how rare* they are!

We eliminate cyclical companies, those whose earnings fluctuate with the state of the general economy. That means no big industrials, financials, mass retailers, commodities-based, or real estate-related companies. We want enterprises that have at least a fighting chance to keep growing even if the economy goes to hell in a handbasket. Many of them are service companies in certain niches of health care (for instance, physical medicine or home infusion therapy) or in special niches of the computer software business (mainly companies which offer computer software that reduces the need for labor or for additional equipment).

We try to concentrate on those companies that have *exceptionally high order backlogs* and *exceptionally high incoming order rates*, indications that the growth will probably continue. If a company has a very high backlog and a very high incoming order rate, competent management should be able to deliver more than just all-time high sales. It should also deliver all-time-high profit margins, all-time-high net income, all-time-high per share earnings, and, God willing, all-time-high stock prices.

Our fourth criterion is the most important one: *the stocks should not yet be very well known on Wall Street.* We try to buy them before they become the favorites of the major wire houses.

Why?

A famous American journalist, Walter Lippman, used to say: "What everybody knows, isn't worth knowing." We would like to invest in those companies that—in addition to meeting our other criteria—have not yet been discovered.

By our definition, "discovered" means that several major brokerage firms published reports about the company and that their hundreds of salesmen are calling clients repeatedly, suggesting that they invest in the company.

How about a favorable newspaper article? Since it is not followed-up by hordes of salesmen, an article generally does not create a lasting up move. And an up move that was caused by some good news and by the participation of a limited number of alert investors does not mean that the stock has been discovered either.

Our fifth criterion is the *ever-growing repeat order factor.* The present customers come back for more, and the company acquires additional customers, who probably will also come back for more. The level of orders, and repeat orders, keeps increasing.

When we mention the repeat-order factor, everyone first thinks of Gillette. If you own a razor, you have to buy more and more blades. Nobody seems to mention Eastman Kodak, which is also a very good example: it makes more money on people buying *film,* and more film, than by making the cameras.

The biggest winners in the last 30 to 50 years seem to have been companies that had an ever-growing repeat-order factor.

When you apply this factor to service companies, you really start to have fun.

A kid went to buy a hamburger and then went back and brought his friend, and then both of them brought their fathers: an ever-growing repeat-order rate. Then the management of McDonald's took *a cookie cutter* and copied the original three hamburger stands and replicated them at 30, 300, and 3,000 locations. The stock went up several hundredfold.

Dick and Henry Bloch also took *a cookie cutter* and copied the original three offices (where they prepared tax returns) into 30, 300, and 3,000 locations—and the stock went through the roof.

That is our sixth criterion: Does the company have, or lend itself to, a cookie cutter approach?

❄

The most important question is: Where can we expect to find similar combinations of the *ever-growing repeat-order rate* and the *cookie cutter factor* in the future?

❄

There is one final consideration in applying these six criteria; we want to *stay flexible.* We do not want our criteria to turn into a straitjacket. If a company had one bad year for some very understandable reason, we don't necessarily exclude it. And, when we find brilliance—an exceptionally talented manager or a management team that has created something brand new—we may sacrifice some of our criteria. We may make an exception and simply *buy their talent.*

This kind of an exception should be very rare. Maybe one of several hundred companies examined, rather than one out of each dozen. *Too many* exceptions would demolish the discipline of the approach.

Our past experience is that an overwhelming percentage of the exceptions did not work out well; it seems the closer we stick to our criteria, the safer we are and the more money we make.

Out of the over 27,000 quarterly sales and earnings statements that we look at annually, we call maybe 400 companies, and we consider it a good year if we end up with 7 or 8 we can buy.

Obviously, with the growth requirements we have, these are modest-sized companies. Most that we buy have revenues of under $250 million a year, some as low as $20 million! A small company that brings a great new service or product to the market can experience *tremendous percentage growth.* A giant can't.

How Do We Do Research?

When we read a good earnings statement, we pick up the phone and call the president of this totally unknown company: "Your figures are terrific, but we can't find anything about you in any manual."

Most of them will say: "We're not doing anything *that* special."

We say: "Thank you"—and hang up.

Maybe one of several dozen will say: "We're doing something here that's never been done before!"

You can hear the excitement in his voice. He will explain his company, and if it is really something quite exceptional, we will *invite him to visit.*

Let's assume the president tells us that his computer software company last year increased both its sales and its earnings by 50 percent. We tell him that *we are much more interested in his backlog and his incoming order rate.* If he answers that: "Our backlog and our incoming orders are double what we had last year at this time!"—then we will want to meet not only his chairman and financial vice president, but his marketing manager as well. Why the marketing manager? Because he knows more about backlogs and incoming orders—our main indicators—than anyone else at the company.

We talk to the companies that supply his raw materials, his computers, and so on. If they say that he has been ordering substantially more supplies than last year, we will start to call a long list of the company's customers to find out if the orders they are placing are indeed up, and why, and by how much? We will make an effort to contact at least ten of his most meaningful customers. If the customers tell us that his company has new software that is a major breakthrough and that they are ordering twice as much of the product or service as they did the previous year, then we do something that very few analysts on Wall Street ever do: we call the company's *printers.*

What does a customer receive when he orders computer software? He gets the product in a *box* with a *brochure.* We talk to the people who print the boxes and the brochures, and if *they* say that the company's orders doubled since last year, then we pick up the phone and call our customers, or prospective customers, and say:

"Charlie, we've found something exciting. I am sending you a report that I think you will love."

✸

Let me give you an example. It happened many years ago.

We read a company's earnings report in Standard & Poor's *Current News Edition*; the company was too small for the daily financial papers to bother with.

The numbers were exciting. We called the president.

He explained: "We have a chain of clinics treating alcoholics."

That was, sure enough, a new one for me.

"Is that a good business?"

"Alcoholism is the number four killer disease in the country—you know, Andy, car accidents and so on. There are today 900 times more alcoholics than beds available to treat them."

I asked him to come visit us. Both the president and his second in command were very impressive.

Until then, I rarely bought more than 15% of any company's float. (The "float" means the shares *in public hands*, not the total shares outstanding.) I don't want to be "larger than my market." In other words, I want to have a reasonable chance to sell—when the time comes—without driving the price down.

The difference between a cat burglar who is free and a cat burglar who is in jail is that the first one made sure that there is an open window behind him.

I made an exception with Comprehensive Care. I bought for my clients and myself what amounted to 19% of the float: most of it between 6¼ and 9¼. When I'd finished buying, I put together a few sets of literature and mailed them, with my business card, to several security analyst friends. I didn't even bother to write on the card "Please read!" I knew they would.

It took only about two months for a giant brokerage firm to recommend the stock. One of the largest circulation

53

investment advisory letters followed. That did it. The stock picked up in a big way.

Within two years it reached 26 and we sold our holdings.

By the way, most analysts are not fools. They wouldn't have picked up our recommendation if it hadn't been a good company and if we hadn't done a thorough research job to make sure that it was. Never try to tout second- or third-rate companies to your friends; you'll lose your reputation, your ability to do business, and eventually you will lose your friends!

❀

I prefer to invest in first-generation management, people who work 16 hours a day, 7 days a week, nonstop for years in a row.

They can't just be workhorses, of course. We look for creativity and vision—and, above all, for character. Young companies sooner or later run up against make-or-break problems. I want to be confident that when they do, management will have the knowledge and the backbone to handle the crisis.

Other than the underwriter who brought it public, often we are among the very first people from the investment community to call a company. The man we are talking to is its founder and is proud of his accomplishment—he is almost invariably eager to answer questions, delighted to find investors interested in his baby.

When we invite him to visit our offices, he doesn't necessarily come right away—but most of the time he will come see us on his next trip to New York.

We compile a long list of questions. We grill him on many areas, but, as I mentioned, particularly on our indicators: *backlogs, incoming orders,* and *inquiries.* And we ask him, over and over: "What can go wrong?" and then, "What else can go wrong?" and then again, "What else can go wrong in addition to that?"

❀

As I mentioned, we try to talk with several people in the management group and also to several outsiders. We try, but we don't always succeed. I don't know anyone on Wall Street who can do it all in an ideal way. We try to do as much as possible, and that is often less than we would like to do.

Today we are able to do more of this *all-around research* than ever. There was a time when we were often frustrated. We simply didn't have the resources, didn't have the personnel, to be as thorough as we wanted to, and we had some unpleasant surprises as a result. Some managements were honest but overly optimistic, and since we couldn't check their stories as thoroughly as we would have liked, our investments didn't pay off.

And some managements were probably less than honest.

The kind of digging that we try to do is very expensive. We need big winners. Successful ideas generate the money to do good research on the next potentially successful ones.

❄

The companies that we buy are almost always traded over the counter; most have been publicly held for fewer than four years. The entrepreneurs who started and still run them own plenty of the stock—with all the incentive in the world to see that the stock goes higher.

If the *Fortune* 500 companies are first-tier stocks, and the other stocks listed on the New York Stock Exchange and American Stock Exchange and some of the bigger stocks traded over the counter represent a second tier, you'd have to say that ours are third-tier stocks. They are, I believe, the ones with the most potential. (And the most risk; *you have to do incomparably better research.*)

Study after study has shown that over the long term, the stocks of little companies, taken as a whole, outperform those of big companies. The reason is simple: the companies have *far more potential* to grow.

Stocks followed by few analysts, which, of course, tend to be those of small companies, generally outperform well-followed stocks in the long term. And we prefer to buy stocks followed by *no* analyst!

And something else: *most of the top performers in every new market cycle are companies that were still privately held during the previous cycle.*

❄

Investment advisers often tell you to "start by identifying the most attractive industries, and then decide which are the best companies in those industries." Fine. But before McDonald's, there *was no* "fast food industry" to speak of, and before H&R Block, there *was no* "tax preparation industry," and before ADP, *no* "payroll servicing industry."

We look for companies opening up whole new industries, or serving established industries in a way never seen before. We look *for companies, not industries*—period.

And if a company is creating a new industry, all the better for us, because *there are no analysts covering it yet*!

❄

How risky is this approach?

Our total approach is devoted to *minimizing the risk* by concentrating on market domination and recession resistance—and at the same time trying to *maximize the profits* by looking for fast-growing, still undiscovered companies.

The greatest risk is not taking any risk. If you are totally in fixed income securities, chances are that in the long-run inflation will more than eat up all of your income. And if you buy nothing but the largest blue chip companies—"yesterday's blue chips" rather than the ones that may become "tomorrow's blue chips"—you are like the guest who arrives too late at the party.

❄

To summarize, we try to find companies that have some protection against competition and some protection against the fluctuations of the economy, companies that grow very fast and are still relatively unknown. We talk to several of their officers, and also to their suppliers, customers, and printers. And finally, most important, we will put our very best effort into getting *out* of the stock *before* the sales' and earnings' slowdown becomes obvious.

Are we going to take our client out at the very top? I wish we could, but, as Bernard Baruch said: "No one buys at the bottom and sells at the top—except the liars."

❋

We buy healthy, fast-growing companies, not distressed ones. In our experience, the biggest problem with the quality of *Wall Street research* is that it is *often geared to cheap companies, not to good ones.* We want nothing but the best, and, if it looks to us that there is a high likelihood that it will be the best, we are willing to pay for that. We are not proud of the fact that we know how to divide a price by the earnings: everyone is able to do that. We are proud of the fact that we do an incredibly wide-based research which gives us some hint about the company's future: Will it be able to deliver, we hope for an extended period, superb results?

I spent my first 25 years on Wall Street going to research meetings where the biggest part of the session was devoted to analysts *explaining why their last idea did not work out.* More often than not, they bought companies that looked cheap. And the reason they looked cheap, the reason they had low price/earnings ratios, was that either the analyst used the *last 12 months'* earnings or that his *expectation of the next 12 months' earnings,* his estimate, *was* totally *incorrect.* Generally, the stock was so cheap because better analysts—and people who had information in and from the company, the kissing cousins, and the golf playing buddies—were already selling.

Nine times out of ten, if something is cheap, it is cheap for good reason. It is cheap because it isn't worth more. We want to buy paintings by Rembrandt, and we are willing to pay for the quality. Naturally, we have to make it as sure as humanly possible that what we're buying is a *real* Rembrandt painting and not a fake. This means more work, more research, and even more work and even more research. So be it!

When Do We Sell?

Buying is relatively easy. The hard part is figuring out when to add to a position, or when to reduce it—and the hardest, but most important decision is *when to get out.*

In my experience, most individual investors and most retail brokers are very poor sellers.

The great majority sells on "gut feel," obviously, not an ideal way to make decisions. Some sell using charts. That is black magic: sometimes it works, most times it doesn't. Many look at sales and earnings, buying on good news and selling on bad news. That means they are doing what the majority is doing; they are running with the lemmings.

Indicator Analysis means trying to gear decisions to backlogs, incoming orders, and inquiries. They are often very hard to find out, but they much more than justify the effort.

When the orders slow and turn flat, *sell!* Waiting around, hoping, can be extremely costly.

Let's assume that you bought shares in a computer software company at 10 and that you got very lucky. It is now selling at 20. Then it goes down to 19½, then it goes to 19.

We call the company and they claim that business is better than ever. We call the suppliers, and if the suppliers say: "Andy, you remember, last year their orders doubled, and today they are still on that incredibly high level," I start to worry. "Still on the *same* level?"

We call several of the company's clients, and the clients also say: "Andy, you recall, last year we doubled the level of our orders. Well, our orders are still on the *same* very high level!" When I hear this, I panic, get on the phone and start to call everyone who, according to our computer cross-reference, owns the stock: "Incoming orders turned flat, let's get out! Six months from now sales will probably be flat and earnings will start to turn down—and everyone else will panic!"

Napoleon said that "Ninety percent of each battle is *information.*" Wall Street, in a way, is warfare, and you and I have to have the best possible information at the earliest time, and we have to have the discipline to *act on it.*

❈

Hard as you try, this is still a world of surprises, and not all of them pleasant. Negative situations have a tendency to feed on themselves and go from bad to disaster. Many analysts believe "there is no such thing as just one down quarter." When earnings stumble, they tend to keep falling. We naturally *try* to catch the decline before it shows up in sales and earnings. We would like to know when the *incoming orders* start to flatten out.

The belief that one piece of bad news will be followed by further pieces of bad news is known on Wall Street as *the cockroach theory.* If you find one cockroach in your kitchen, chances are there will be a number of additional pests. If you have one piece of bad news, odds are that more is on the way.

❈

We believe in *admitting mistakes*, accepting our imperfections *as fast as possible.*

Many investors live in a world of hope. They hope the mistakes will go away. They hope that the stock that produced some negative surprise will stop dropping, will find its base, and will go up again.

It happens. But counting on it is a mistake. Redo your research, and, if you were wrong, run for the hills—run immediately.

For brokers this is, if possible, even more important than for investors. Don't be afraid that admitting the mistake will alienate your customers. They won't like it, but they will sooner or later appreciate the fact that you consider it more important to cut their losses than to try to save face.

The question is: If we lost part of the profit and the stock is down from its peak, or if, God forbid, we have an actual loss, *how can we make up for the decline* fastest? It's very rare that we will succeed by just holding. Mostly, we have to decide where we will make up for the decline fastest and shift the money into that security.

The key question is: When? And the answer is right now, this minute. Nine times out of ten, empty hope, unsupported by additional research, will create a bigger loss.

If the fundamentals change, your attitude has to change too, your portfolio has to change too. If the basics of the stock are different from what they were, or you thought they were, you might as well divorce it. If you think the change is temporary, look at the stock occasionally. If you have any reason to suspect that the bad news is over, start your research from scratch. Unfortunately, this latter situation happens very infrequently.

❀

We should never take a profit just because we have it. You should never sell a stock just because it feels good to lock in the profit, and certainly not just to brag to your friends!

Hold on to your winners! At the very beginning, when the stock makes its first violent up move, it may make sense to sell a small part of your position, as insurance and as seed money for buying other new stocks. But after this one move, your hope should be that the other two-thirds you can hold forever. Your hope, not your conviction! As the saying goes, *plan as if you will live forever, but live as if this is your only day.*

It is somewhat similar in investing: try to find stocks that you will still own at the age of 95 and that will be sold by your grandchildren and your favorite charity. But if anything happens that, after careful investigation, convinces you that the company might have a slowdown ahead, *sell*, get out, *right away.*

Of course there are tax considerations. I do not suggest that you ignore them. You simply have to change your attitude. If you bought a stock at 10 and it is now 20 or 200 or 2,000, in your mind the profit should never be 10 or 190 or 1,990; in your mind the profit should always be the above-mentioned amount *minus taxes.* This attitude will make it easier for you to take your profits when the company's future changes. If you don't, you will end up with a stale portfolio of has-beens. You will end up with a list of companies which used to be very good to you, but which, you know in your heart of hearts, are not going to be as good to you in the future.

❊

We believe in *diversifying.* There is no easier way to lose a big percentage of your assets than by risking too many of your marbles in a single game. We always suggest that new investors should start with at least 4 companies. We show them 8 or 16 and ask them to decide which ones they like most. More often than not they turn the table on us and ask that we should suggest which 4 they should start with.

In our experience, if the research is good and the client is successful, he will come back for more, and more. He will buy some of the other stocks, too. There will be a few securities that we may suggest he should sell, and whenever we do finish our research on an additional security, we will show it to him. And very often, he will decide to add it to his portfolio.

Depending on funds available during the next few years, he probably will build up a portfolio that includes many, or most, or all the stocks that we consider the best in the country—or at least the best when measured by our criteria.

＊

We are *not market timers*. That is our *conscious decision*.

Warren Buffett, the greatest of all value investors, who took the approach to formerly unknown heights, says: "We do not have, never have had, and never will have an opinion about where the stock market, interest rates, or business activities will be a year from now." I couldn't agree more. (By the way, executed with the kind of brilliance that Buffett delivers to "value investing," it creates superlative results. But then, he is the Michelangelo of the approach, which in less talented hands unfortunately often becomes childish "painting by the numbers.")

Many consider *Peter Lynch* to be the all-time greatest mutual fund manager. In his book he advises investors: "Don't try to predict the economy. Forget the overall stock market. Concentrate on the company!"

And the third in the triumvirate of the greatest modern-day money managers, *John Templeton,* is also more a long-term investor than a timer. Just as the former two, *he concentrates more on the what*—on the process of finding the best—*than on the when.* If you asked Templeton what he thinks of the immediate future course of the market, chances are he would explain to you that in the next 20 years the standard of living will probably double and you should keep your eyes on that horizon.

＊

As I mentioned before, a few years after joining the powerhouse combination of two giant old-line firms, I became disillusioned. I had three choices: two that were obvious and one that, at this point, I wasn't even aware of. I could have gone to work for another top Wall Street investment banking and brokerage house, or I could have started my own firm. I assumed that I could raise the money to start my own show, but friends with whom I discussed my plans warned: "Andy, this is not for you. You like two things: to do research and to explain the results to your clients. If you have your own company, you will spend 90% or more of your time with managing and with doing administrative chores."

The surprising solution came from a totally unexpected source.

The president of Ladenburg, Thalmann, a prestigious, medium-sized, old-line investment banking and brokerage firm—it has been in business for way over a century—somewhere picked up the word that I might be "on the market."

"Andy, why don't you join us? We will start a division for you, and will make sure that you have time to research and sell; we will take off your shoulders as many of the management duties as possible."

We made a deal. To ensure that they have an income to pay for the firm's contributions, they will take an "override on the ticket charges"; in plain English, they will make a profit *on the top line*, a profit if I produce *any* gross commissions. At the year's end, *we will split the net profits, if any*: they'll take half, I'll take half.

❄

April 1, 1983—the date brought me good luck—I walked in with several bottles of Dom Perignon and started to make the rounds. I put a bottle of champagne on the desk of seven or eight people who were exceptionally nice to me while I worked at my third firm.

When I walked into the chairman's office and put the champagne on his desk, he flashed a friendly smile. "I guess you're leaving. Sorry. I know you will be successful wherever you go."

I wondered if that was his standard goodbye sentence. But, then, no one likes to lose a big producer; he handled it with grace.

❄

At 7:30 in the morning two limousines picked up my crew and our books (we left the originals behind, legally they belonged to our former company—these were copies) and 20 minutes later we were at our new firm calling customers to tell them about our move.

"We are at a new company, and *we are starting our own division.*"

5

Principles of Successful Investing

When the market has been going up and up, and most "experts" are predicting that the Dow will be many hundreds of points higher within the next year or two; when everyone is telling you how they made a killing in this or that stock; and most of all, when you look in the paper and see that the stock you were thinking of buying two weeks ago has already moved up 30%—it is hard to resist the euphoria. Everybody's making money! Most investors don't want to be left behind. They empty their pockets and place their bets.

And, conversely, when the market's been down and out for months and pessimism reigns, they don't want to even hear about stocks.

There are some important things in life that we can't control: where and when we were born, to what kind of family, what kind of schooling we had in our early years, and so on.

But then come the major decisions of our own: our higher education, our career, what kind of person we marry, how we bring up our children.

These decisions are our big, strategic decisions. Our future, our family's future depend on them. Almost all other decisions are tactical, secondary.

In investing, there are only two basic, major, *strategic decisions*:

1. Buy nothing but the highest quality
2. Start buying soon after you finished your research and became convinced of the stock's potential.

If the market is bad and the stock is cheaper than a while ago, so much the better. You may want to wait for a few upticks, but *start to nibble.* And hold on. And buy more.

Your selling generally should be independent of market timing. After you've bought a stock, try to redo your research frequently, and as long as the company's incoming orders keep growing, hold onto the stock, disregarding market considerations. Your hope is that a very few of the companies you own will keep increasing their incoming orders almost forever; your hope is that some of these stocks will be sold by your great-grandchildren or favorite charity.

❄

It is human nature to want to buy when you feel happy and to sell when you are depressed and discouraged. Most people invest with the consensus and by their gut feelings. That's not what they say; that's what they do. Everyone will tell you that he wants to buy low and sell high. But, and I'm saying this as a broker who has been talking to many tens of thousands of customers and prospects, in real life *too many people feel irresistibly compelled to go with the crowd and end up buying at the top and selling at the bottom.*

❄

Both rules are correct:

1. Never sell a stock just because it went down.

2. Never double-up or triple-up just because it's down and looks cheap.

In either case, *do your research again* and act on the new, additional information.

Never trade on the basis of the stock's *action* alone; do your best to find out the facts *behind* the action. Unfortunately, many investors are too influenced by a stock's price, and the influence is the reverse of what it should be. The stock drops: "There must be something wrong with it." The stock goes up: "It is probably a terrific buy."

As Charles H. Dow, one of the founders of Dow Jones, said: "The problem with most investors is that they know prices, not values."

You have to trade against those "price watchers," against the people who think price fluctuations always tell you the facts. You want to know the *real news*, and you want to know it *thoroughly*. Trade against the uninformed, the lazy, and the trigger-happy!

You can count on it: most investors are too lazy to do the homework—and many of their brokers are the same.

❈

It has happened many times: a company in which my customers owned stock kept reporting terrific sales, terrific earnings, and terrific backlogs—and, because the general market was good, it went from 10 to 20; then the atmosphere changed, and, while reporting several additional stunning quarters, the stock fell back from 20 to 10. It became ridiculously cheap, totally oversold, without ever having one disappointing quarter. Yes, it was probably the best possible time to buy.

I called hundreds of clients and prospects and found that for some mysterious reason *no one* had any money to invest. Everyone's children had just been enrolled in expensive private schools, everyone's wife had just started redecorating, and everyone's brother-in-law was launching a new business for which he needed family capital.

❈

A short summary of a stockbroker's life: "Charlie, I have a terrific idea, it sells at 5."

"Andy, it sounds fantastic, but in my opinion the market is going to drop much lower."

A few months later: "Charlie, the stock is now selling at 10. I think you should own it. Are you still bearish?"

"No, Andy, I am very bullish now—but I would feel crazy to pay 10 for a stock that I missed at 5."

A year later my phone rings: "Andy, this is Charlie. Your darn stock is at 25. I can't stand it any longer. I'm selling my grandmother's home. Buy me the stock."

Next month the stock is down to 23. My phone rings again: "Andy—*why* did you let me buy that stock?!?"

❈

Now don't get the illusion that I am always right. Nonsense. I have been known to be wrong. Many times. But then, occasionally, I have also been known to be right.

All you and I can hope for is to be right a few more times than wrong.

❈

Remember this: *what you buy is incomparably more important than when you buy*. The *what* can be based on facts. The *when*, in spite of all historic precedents and abstract conclusions, will always contain more risks.

Take the *January Principle*, for example: buy some highly volatile stocks that got depressed in December and make money on their rebound in January. Or the so-called *Dead Cat Bounce*, suggesting a last rally in something that has no future. Those principles worked for many, many years. But then, when the press picked them up and sold the idea to just about everyone, they didn't work that well anymore.

Something similar happened to the classic *October Collapse*. When just about everyone became convinced that this effect would return every year, most investors decided to take some profits in September, so they wouldn't get hurt the following month. The sharp October collapse turned into a mild September decline and an October that produced the reverse of expectations.

Recognizing and examining a situation is only 10%, if that much, of making money. The other 90%, or more, is *the ability to act* on our own knowledge and conviction. To do what almost no one else is doing. This is the point where discipline becomes the all-decisive factor. *Investing is not the art of contrary thinking: it is the art of contrary action!*

❅

Customers and prospective customers keep asking me: "What is your opinion of the market?"

My opinion is that anyone who has an opinion about the market will be wrong at least 51% of the time—and probably much more often. I am not in the business of predicting the market. I'm neither an economist nor a stock market technician.

How about the opinions I hear from the general public? Is their input of any use?

Yes, it is of great use. I have learned to do the reverse of what I hear.

Between 1984 and early 1991, the negativism of the general public went from bad to worse. After the October 1987 crash, it became extreme.

I speak to between 30 and 50 investors daily. For the last several years, the overwhelming majority has been telling me, *every day*, that the market is ready to collapse and that tomorrow is the "End of Western Civilization."

I don't know who influenced them to form this opinion: their favorite daily or weekly paper, the local TV or radio station, or their neighbor? But I know that while very substantially more than 90% of the input I got through the phone was negative, the market did exceptionally well. A great number of the individual securities we bought did even better. No, not all, but the trend, especially since the 1987 crash and during the subsequent flood of extreme pessimism, was strongly upward.

Everyone kept talking about "the second shoe" that is going to drop within the next few days. *It never did.* The truth is I am unable to find one single example of this drop-of-the-second-shoe phenomenon anywhere in the history of the American or any other major exchanges.

It brings to mind another one of Walter Lippman's sayings: "When all think alike, no one thinks very much."

❈

There are a very few occasions when I do become influenced by *technical factors.* For example, if I am ready to start buying a stock, but its chart indicates that the stock is under distribution—there is a big seller—I wait until the selling is over, the stock price turns sideways and shows its first upticks. At *that* point, I start to buy.

If one of my traders tells me that there is only one major seller in the market (and after checking around he can't discover anyone else on the heels of the first one), I will probably instruct him to tell the seller that we are interested in buying the last 20,000 or 30,000—or whatever portion—of the block. This is known as "buying on a cleanup." It means that I want to buy the last piece, at the most depressed price, we hope, presuming that when the selling pressure is over, the stock will rebound.

My risk? That in spite of the traders' most careful checking, an unexpected second seller may show up. I have to depend on my traders' expertise to be right more often than wrong.

Occasionally I am convinced that I know more about a company than the sellers. Still, it isn't a good idea to buy into a waterfall collapse. I wait.

It is not enough to buy a good stock; you have to try to buy it when it starts *to act like a good stock*. Damon Runyon, the writer of *Guys and Dolls* and a lot of terrific short stories, used to say: "The race is not always to the swift, nor the battle to the strong—but that's the way to bet."

Colleagues and customers sometimes ask, watching the unusual amount of fundamental research we do—and the special research done by our traders—whether we are not overdoing it. Can't we get so much information that we won't be able to absorb it? Some feel that we might be doing too much of a good thing.

I would rather agree with Mae West: "Too much of a good thing—can be wonderful!"

❄

I believe the approach I have developed over the years offers a relatively high degree of safety.

And still, many things can go wrong.

Some ideas look great, but *they are years too early*. Our hopes for solar energy were ill-timed. The price of oil went down, and, as a result, the government let the tax breaks for solar energy expire. We lost a bundle.

Sometimes our research falls short. We do what I think is incredibly thorough research. We talk to everyone we can reach to uncover all possible "booby traps." But I doubt that anyone can claim he checked every source that has potentially valuable information. He would be forever investigating and never buying anything.

Sometimes it takes a long while for other investors to find the truth that you discovered with painstaking research. Check and recheck, but maintain patience. However, if you ever find that your data or conclusions are incorrect, get out as fast as you can. There is no place in this for vanity!

❄

Checking back with management, you—or your analyst or broker if he is following the stock—can occasionally sense that something's wrong.

If you find that executives once so eager to talk are now ducking you, then do some very fast checking with your outside sources, and if the news is not reassuring, get out. If you have to, take a loss!

The two major crimes a management can commit in its broker and stockholder relations are *dishonesty* and *lack of communication*. If you find that a management, which bragged loudly when things were going well, suddenly becomes incommunicado, check, double-check, and triple-check. You just might have seen your first cockroach!

When you asked around before buying the stock, the most important thing you tried to find out from the people who know the company is *its executives' character*. If the suppliers and customers and printers had the slightest doubt about these people's knowledge, discipline, talent, and backbone, you would have stayed away from the stock—even if everything else looked perfect. If you develop a doubt now, do even more careful research, and if necessary, head for the exit.

❊

When things are going well, everyone is a hero. When things start to go poorly, some "heros" get shaky knees. That's one reason I try to avoid buying on substantial margin. The man whom I could not talk out of using full margin frequently chickens out just before the stock hits its bottom. If he had been less greedy, he would be able to accumulate more of what had become an outstanding bargain.

❊

When you buy and sell major companies listed on the exchanges, you can put a *stop loss order* under your stock. If it declines, it will be automatically sold.

Many experts recommend this, though I have met very few investors—including the experts—who actually do it. Using stop loss orders may be counterproductive in the long run. You can be sold out when you should be *adding* to your position. No easy, automatic solutions! You have to find out, to *know—and act on that knowledge!*

Placing a stop loss order is nothing but an admission of ignorance and laziness. The right thing is to find out if you can use the drop to your advantage.

In the past, when our research was substantially weaker, I wish I had stop loss orders to avoid some of the sharp declines. Today, when our research is, I think, much better, I prefer to *try to turn the sharp fluctuations to our advantage*: *sell* if and when we are convinced that the future prospects have deteriorated, and *buy more* if we find that the future prospects are as good as or better than originally expected.

In over-the-counter issues, stop loss orders are of no use: most brokers don't even accept them. They may be willing to "watch" the price level of your stock, but refuse to put on their books a limit order that is binding in any way.

When you are accumulating stocks that show an unusual degree of volatility (in professional jargon, they have a high *beta* factor), you have to decide whether you have the will and talent to do research so thorough that it actually may help you *benefit from the volatility*.

I have been told that the Chinese character for *panic* is the combination of the characters for danger and for opportunity. For the gambler who didn't do his homework, volatility means *danger;* for you and me, who try our best to do exceptionally careful research, volatility means *opportunity*.

❋

Sometimes it seems the whole world has turned on you, that you need the patience of Job. For instance, if around midsummer of 1986, you invested in a list of small, fast-growing companies, companies that were supposed to outperform the blue chips by a very wide margin, you ended up in bad trouble. These stocks fell asleep and widely underperformed the blue chips.

Then, more than four years later, on October 11 of 1990, they exploded!

To understand this explosion, we should devote a few lines to a relatively new market phenomenon: the fast growth of professional and amateur short selling.

Short selling is the practice of borrowing someone's stock, selling it, trying to buy it back cheaper, and finally returning it to the lender.

Not only did the number of short sellers vastly increase during the years of pessimism, but most "shorts" discovered that they can sell stocks over the counter much easier than on the exchanges. To sell listed shares, they have to wait for an "uptick." There is, at present, no uptick rule over the counter, so you can bomb a stock without interruption, until it gets practically demolished.

In addition, many short sellers "went naked"; they failed to borrow the stock before selling it. If a short seller finds a cooperative broker, he can leverage to the extremes. The law says that the seller has to borrow the stock (has to find someone who owns the certificates or is in control of the certificates and lends them to him). A broker is allowed to sell short the stock for a very short time, as part of his daily trading operations, without actually borrowing it. Some short sellers did their best to create a gray area, a loophole between the two principles.

During 1990, many stocks dropped to totally unjustified levels. When the market turned, these stocks acted like coils. The shorting binges turned into short squeezes and, in the following three months, a substantial number of these undeservedly depressed companies moved up 100% or more.

There is a misconception about short sellers on Wall Street. Supposedly they do much better research than the long-side analyst. In reality, some do, some don't. But investors—and the press—are so inundated with buy recommendations that they are delighted to see someone recommending sales or short sales. Some of the best financial journalists in the country devote long columns to the praise of short sellers. Why? Because the readers want to hear about shorting and about the more successful practitioners of the art.

Our best trader kept telling me how good most of the "short research" is and warning me that I am going to be hurt badly if I keep accumulating the stocks that the short sellers are destroying.

Table 5-1 is a list of some of our major positions and where they sold at the worst part of the short selling orgy. The list also shows their subsequent percentage moves by the end of October 1991.

Table 5.1
Major Positions and Their October 1990–1991
One-Year Price Changes

	October 1990 Low	High for the 12 months Ending October 1991	
BMC Software	17.75	58.75	+231%
Health South Rehabilitation	15.25	41.25	+170%
Novacare	6.5*	25.75	+296%
Occupational Urgent Health	9.5	25.75	+171%
Surgical Care Affiliates	9.5*	43.25	+355%

* Adjusted for subsequent splits.

❊

It takes a lot of nerve to add to a depressed position. You have to sit back and wait and wait; then when you see that the selling has exhausted itself and the stock starts to go up, you buy a little and then you buy more.

One of our stocks—Compression Labs—was beaten up several times by the short sellers. On every occasion when it started to uptick we called clients and suggested that they buy it or add to their positions. Some did, some didn't. In the first week of October 1990 it reached a high at 16⅝. By the first week of January, the short sellers depressed it to 8⅜. By the last week of March the stock was up to 24⅞—almost tripling during a three-month period. Then the short sellers did a job on it again. By July 26 the stock dropped to 14¼, just to recover to 27⅛ by October 23.

Meanwhile the trend of the company's backlogs kept improving.

❊

Most of the time, the two main factors that move stocks are *value* and *demand*. We try to find exceptional value, buy it, and own it until the demand materializes.

The fact that the price of your property is quoted every day in the newspaper should not disturb you.

If you figured out that there is going to be a super-highway built somewhere and that the announcement may come within three years, you would probably buy some land, or an option on some land, in that vicinity—and then wait. You would not walk out to that spot every day and wonder how much you could sell it for at that moment.

You bought your stock hoping that, when it gets discovered, people will pay the value that you see in it now. *You should not confuse tomorrow's value with today's price!*

When discovery does come, your profit may be enormous. What makes you a winner is the quality of your information. It has to be *reliable*, and you have to have it *before* everybody else does.

❊

To summarize, *you should buy* whenever you have finished your research; checked several members of management, several suppliers, and a vast number of the company's customers and talked to their printers; and come to the conclusion that you have an exceptional stock.

Never buy into a waterfall collapse! If, in spite of all the positive facts you have found the stock is dropping, try to find out: Why? If there is a major seller, wait until he is finished and *then* start to nibble.

If the whole market is in a waterfall collapse, give it a little time and wait until it starts to uptick. You will never be quite accurate on your timing. As Bernard Baruch said: "They don't put out flags at the lows or highs."

Don't get swept away by the general pessimism: this might be your best buying opportunity. Be comfortable with the knowledge that the stock may go somewhat lower after you've started buying. That is OK. Give yourself time. Nibble. Accumulate. There are no solid rules; this is not mathematics or engineering.

Never get swept away by the consensus. You have to turn the consensus to your own benefit—by using it, going against it, feeling out the market.

You made an error? It may be a short-term error. The essence of your decision is to buy top quality that sooner or later will, you hope, do as expected.

If I bought a painting by a fashionable painter and expect to make a relatively short-term profit (how foolish could I be), I will have to worry about the art market: Will it be strong next year or will it be weak? However, if I bought a painting of superb quality, one of those masterpieces that comes very rarely to the market, and I bought it with a long-term view, I have substantially less to worry about. The chances are if it really is a masterpiece, I will sell it in 10 years for much more than I paid, or my grandchildren or my favorite charity will sell it in 50 years for many times my cost.

❊

What to buy? Let's summarize. We want to find companies that meet four criteria:

1. Very fast growth
2. Some protection against competitors
3. Some protection against the fluctuations of the economy
4. Modest following on Wall Street

We are thrilled if we find—in addition to the above—that the companies also have:

5. An ever-growing repeat-order rate
6. A cookie cutter factor.

❉

We know from experience that some recession-resistant companies are actually *countercyclical*; when the economy is good they do well, and when the economy is bad they do even better.

How is this possible? These companies are generally *in the business of saving money for their customers.* They may save money for insurance companies by arranging discounts on medical service or hospital bed rates, or they may save money for corporations by supplying them with computer software that saves on payroll expenses, or they may help law firms by lowering the cost of telephone service.

❉

I have to be very emphatic about the following: *All these companies have to be checked regularly! If their backlogs stop growing, their stock has to be sold just like that of any other company!*

There is nothing wrong with buying a stock with the *hope* that you can hold it forever, but it is naive to buy it with the *conviction* that you will hold it forever. Every month, or even more frequently, you have to check the trend of incoming orders, and when the orders stop growing, you have to get out! And if the management is not telling you the incoming order numbers, then you have to rely on the data you get from their suppliers, customers, and printers.

Don't fall in love with *any* stock!

Eleven hundred years ago, a Chinese general, Wang Yang Ming, in a book on strategy for the imperial army, wrote as follows: "To know and not to act, is not to know."

In plain English there is no greater sin in warfare—or in investing—than having the facts and not using them.

And Carl von Clausewitz, almost a thousand years later, emphasized in *On War*, "Original plans are not as important as flexibility, as the ability to react to new facts."

I do not believe in investment miracles. I do not believe that all my stocks will turn into superwinners. I do hope, however, that some of them will make enough profits to compensate for the losses in others, and that, as a package, they will do exceptionally well.

No promises, no guarantees; use your own head.

And *keep checking!*

6

Never-Ending Research

When I joined my present firm and started our fairly independent division, neither Maureen, who by now was running our show, nor I knew much about hiring or managing a staff. She was in charge of transferring all our accounts to our new shop; I was trying to upgrade sales and research.

In the beginning I made some bad mistakes. Because computer stocks were becoming such an important part of our business, I hired, as my only analyst, a bright young man who had vast computer experience, but no experience whatsoever as a securities analyst.

It was a disaster. He tried his best and I tried my best, but it just didn't work. At one point he got so enthused about one of the companies we followed that he ended up borrowing money to invest more in his favorite stock.

When the stock collapsed, it was more than embarrassing for him: it was a financial loss he couldn't cope with. He quit: he lost his money—and I lost him.

❉

At one point, before we developed our criteria, we placed an ad in *The New York Times*: "We need a securities analyst who is an expert in biotechnology." Among the résumés we received, one came from a young, out-of-town doctor. He was an amazing fellow.

He had a degree from one of the top medical schools in the country and an MBA from one of the top business schools. It was beyond question that he was brilliant—and beyond question that he knew it: "I was top of the class whatever school I went to—from kindergarten to medical school, to business school."

"Why would you give up a medical career?"

"I have been a dermatologist for two years and I'm totally bored. Wall Street would offer a different challenge."

"How much do you make a year?"

"This last year, my second one as a physician, I made $115,000."

I didn't want to hire again someone who was a newcomer to security analysis, someone who didn't know the basics of how a Wall Street research department works. How could I turn him off politely?

"We are a very small division. Whenever we make some money on your recommendations, you get paid extra, but *the base salary* would be only $25,000."

I was pretty sure he would laugh in my face. Instead, he put out his right hand: "Done!"

I hired him for $25,000 *and incentives.* By the end of his first year, he was making money at an annualized rate of $96,000!

A Different Way of Finding Winners

Every morning I mark up the *Investor's Business Daily*, highlighting those companies about which I would like to see a chart, a so-called O'Neil *Datagraph.* I generally mark some stocks on the list of the "100 Stocks With Greatest % Rise In Volume," some in the article describing the previous day's over-the-counter activity, and some on the "NASDAQ Stocks In The News" half page.

I mark companies that I think we should take a look at, because some of them might meet our criteria. Occasionally I mark a few companies in the "Companies In A Leading Industry" column too, but only if the industry is one that meets our parameters.

A research assistant will get the charts. He will also go through the "Company Earnings News" and select from the "Best Ups" tables those companies that report a "Last Quarter % Change" of 30% or more. He will skip all the companies that are well known, sell over $30 (they've probably already been discovered), or obviously don't meet our criteria. Some days there are no companies left; some days there are several. He gives me a chart on each one; and I take a look at them and decide whether we should investigate them.

We have a bias. We prefer to invest in *service*, rather than *manufacturing*, companies. I watched for decades how even the greatest manufacturing growth stocks collapsed. Polaroid, for instance, first rose from near zero to 149, and then, in a year and a half, lost 90% of its value.

Some of the greatest *service* companies, on the other hand, seem to continue growing almost without end.

❈

I find the *Datagraphs* very helpful. They give a rather detailed fundamental and chart picture of the stocks—and they help to save time.

William J. O'Neil, founder of *Investor's Business Daily*, wrote a very interesting book—*How to Make Money in Stocks**—and he and one of his supertalented associates, David Ryan, recorded several tapes and gave an endless number of lectures to acquaint Wall Street with their approach.

All in all, the approach is brilliant. Even if I don't accept much of what they say about charting, in other

---

* McGraw-Hill, 1988

respects I have to give them credit for *bringing a breath of fresh air to security analysis.* These *Datagraphs* save endless hours because, in addition to the bar charts, they also contain an overwhelming quantity of fundamental data, figures that are updated every week.

What Data Do We Look for at the Very Beginning?

At the start of our research, we look at the following data:

1. A description of the company's business.

2. We prefer to investigate companies that are over the counter; most listed ones are already somewhat better known. Naturally, we have to be careful, because there are a great number of over-the-counter companies that *have already been discovered.*

3. Next to the stock's symbol, the *Datagraph* indicates the industry: if it is cyclical (money rate sensitive, commodity oriented, or such—*most* companies *are* cyclical), we automatically reject the company. You can make a lot of money in cyclicals, but they are a minefield, and we prefer to stay away from them.

4. The ideal company should have fewer than 20 million shares outstanding and a *public float* of under 15 million.

5. We stay away from foreign companies: the information we get is less than what we need—and generally almost impossible to check.

6. We look at the annual earnings record and prefer earnings that have been *steadily increasing.*

7. The estimate columns give Wall Street's earnings expectations for this and the next year. We like those companies most that grew not only in excess of 30%, but also show an acceleration.

84

8. We prefer *Alphas* of over 1.0; the best are *way over one.**

9. We seek an *Earnings-Per-Share Rank* of over 80, preferably between 94 and 99.†

10. We look at *Relative Strengths*. We like them high.‡

11. We look at the name of the company's investment banker. There are some who do their homework better than others, and we pay more attention to the companies that they sponsor.

12. The page includes a list of recent research reports about the company: who published them and when? We like those companies that Wall Street isn't aware of yet; there should be *few, or no* reports when we start to buy.

In the past, when the stock got discovered by major brokerage firms or institutions, we stopped buying. Re-

---

* This and the two following definitions are from O'Neil's "How to Read Datagraphs" found in the back of every set of charts O'Neil publishes. "ALPHA expresses how much the stock would have appreciated or depreciated on average every month over the past five years, assuming the S&P 500 Index was unchanged during that period. For example, an Alpha of 1.0 means the stock's price would have appreciated at the rate of 1% per month over the last five years, assuming an unchanged S&P 500 Index. A negative Alpha (e.g., –1.0) means the stock would have depreciated by the rate of 1% per month for the last five years."

† "EARNINGS PER SHARE RANK (EPS RANK) measures a company's earnings per share growth in the last five years and the stability of that growth. Four different factors (percent increase in the most recent quarter versus the same quarter a year ago, percent increase in the prior quarter versus the same period a year ago, the 5-year growth rate, and stability) are ranked separately and weighted according to a proprietary formula. This result is then ranked on a scale of 1 to 99. A rank of 70 means the company had a better earnings record than 70% of all companies."

‡ The RELATIVE STRENGTH NUMBER "measures the stock's price change over the past year compared to all other stocks. Extra weight (40%) is assigned to the latest three month period (with each of the other quarters receiving 20%). All stocks are arranged in order of the greatest price change and assigned a percentile rank from 99 (highest) to 1. A value of 70 means the stock outperformed 70 percent of all stocks."

cently, we changed this policy. A really outstanding stock can be bought for a long time. As long as the incoming orders are increasing (and as long as we are able to keep a good grasp on the incoming orders), we continue to add to our position.

There are very few superb quality companies around—we call them our *Rembrandts*. The parallel is probably inaccurate in many respects; all we are trying to point out is that the stock has to be of *ne plus ultra quality*.

We look at the sales for the last nine quarters. (No special reason why nine; just a habit that we developed and that has served us well.) Under the *Sales* line the chart conveniently shows how many percentage points the sales changed each quarter, up or down, compared to the previous year's identical quarter. We concentrate on this line rather than the actual sales. We prefer companies that, in each of the last nine quarters, *increased their sales by at least 15 %. We will make an exception as long as the growth* in the last several quarters was visibly *accelerating*.

The third line prints the quarterly earnings. Again, we go to the line below this, which points out the percentage changes in quarterly earnings, compared with the identical quarters a year before. On this line, we prefer companies that reported in each of the last nine quarters at least *a 30% earnings gain*. If they didn't, we would like to find companies that, in the last few quarters, sharply *accelerated their growth rate*, and we prefer those that in the last quarter or two reported an unusually high percentage gain.

13. The bottom of the page describes how many mutual funds, investment advisors, banks, and insurance companies own the stock. We like those that are not very widely owned yet.

Our biggest winners sooner or later become very much "institutionalized": the bottom of the page becomes totally covered with names of the funds, banks, and others who own them. We worry a lot about this; an unpleasant surprise could destroy the stock's price. If all these elephants start a stampede to get out of the compound, we can get crushed.

Our answer today isn't to abandon the stock: our answer is to try to do even better research, and one even more geared to our main indicators—*backlogs, incoming orders,* and *inquiries.*

❄

There are endless additional data on the *Datagraphs;* we will need them when we go into detailed analysis of the stock. The ones I just mentioned are only the few that help us in our very preliminary review.

I know that by explaining every step in detail I made this first, "get acquainted" glance at the company sound rather cumbersome. After a while, it becomes an extremely fast process: In a few minutes you will find out enough to know whether you want to continue.

(If you would like to know more about the *Datagraphs,* write to William O'Neil & Company, 11915 La Grange Avenue, Los Angeles, CA 90025 or call 800-545-8940.)

Calling the Company

When we decide to investigate a company, the head of my small research department will either assign the company to one of our analysts or, very often, call it himself.

Our criteria, as you know, are so stringent that sometimes for several days we don't find a single stock worth investigating—and even at the times when quarterly reports turn into an avalanche, it is a rare day when we have more than three. Not three that we want to *buy*; three that we want to *investigate*!

Our analysts will call the company, talk to the president, and ask him a long list of questions.

Figure 6.1, "Analyst's First Call," presents a worksheet that we use. Some of the questions are in a kind of shorthand: they are not necessarily obvious—but the worksheet provides you with the gist of the inquiry.

We also have an "Analyst's Follow-up" sheet, a questionnaire that gets completed every single month.

If there is anything even slightly unusual happening to the company or its stock, we will call it at irregular, and sometimes frequent, intervals, but if nothing special is happening, we will still contact management at least once each month.

The analyst expresses his opinion in a rating ranging from 10 (best) to 0. If he rates the company 6 or below, we reject it. At 7 it goes onto the back burner, and we make a note in our rotating file (our manual time trigger) and also on my Wizard (a pocket computer): When do we plan to take a second look at the company? This could be in a few days, or as much as six months later.

If the analyst rates the stock 8 or 9 (he never rates it 10 on the first conversation; we want to know much more before the stock gets the top rating), we will investigate the company.

Meeting, or a Telephone Conference

It is very important to meet "the man who moves the mountain" in person. If we cannot arrange that right away, we will set up a telephone conference. We try to have it immediately. This telephone conversation, in addition to the president, generally includes one or two of his associates, more often than not the financial vice president, sometimes the chairman. The person in whom we will have very much interest later, the marketing manager, does not participate in these first conversations.

The telephone conferences are mainly for my benefit. In addition to getting as many facts as possible, my goal is to get a general feeling for the quality of the management.

Figure 6.1
Analyst's First Call

COMPANY: NEXT STEP:
SYMBOL: WHY?
ASSIGNED: /   /   @ $
RELATIVE STR: EARNINGS STR:
SALES LAST 12 MONTHS: (>$15M?)
SALES NEXT 12 MONTHS: (<$250M?)
NEXT Q EARNINGS +%:

DATE: / /
CONTACT: ANALYST: CALL AGAIN:
TITLE: RATING: SEND #26?:
PHONE: BOOK: DOCS ON US?:

---

144 Blocks: How Much?:   When?:

Business:

Special:

Negatives:

Recession Resistant: Service: % Repeat Order: %

Dominates Industry: Cookie Cutter:

Estimated Sales growth this year: Next 3 - 5 year average: (>15%?)

Estimated EPS growth this year: Next 3 - 5 year average: (>30%?)

Covered on Wall Street by: Has company lost any customers
                                    in the last six months?:

Figure 6.1 (cont.)

Competitors:

National?:
International % of rev:
Same Store sales:

Estd Penetration of current market:
Customer > 10%:
Backlog:
Proposal Activity:
Dependence on single supplier?:

Seasonal?:

Cyclical?:
R&D as % of rev:
Areas of emphasis:

New product intro schedules:

Expansion plans:

Acquisition plans:

Legal Problems:
Quality Problems:

Boobytraps:

Est. size of mkt:

National:
Internl:
Est. growth of mkt:

Focus of marketing strategy:

Changes in marketing strategy:

Total Salesforce: Next yr: Last yr:
% of sales direct:
Total Employees: Next yr: Last yr:
Turnover:
Unions?:
Strikes?:

Auditors:
Switched?:

Balance Sheet and Income Statement
Capd Expenses & Goodwill:
Cash & Equivalents:
Working Capital:
Long Term Debt:
Current Ratio:
Writedowns/Adjustments:
Anything Odd?:
Tax Rate:

Figure 6.1 (cont.)

Margins - Goals:

Gross:

Operating:

Pre-tax:

Shares Outstanding:

Fully diluted:

Warrants:

Converts:

Options held my management:

Insiders control %:

Float:

Retail float:

Institutions hold:

Blue Sky Problems?:

Management Experience:

(Name, Title, how long there, options held)

1.

2.

3.

Investment Banker:

New reports pending:

Meetings w/ Street:

IPO

When:

Price:

Shares:

Warrants:

Secondary planned?:

Debt offering planned?:

AAA QUESTIONS: NO EXCUSES!

Banking Help?:

Advisory help?:

Do you know any company
    that wants to go public?

Aunt Sally:

1.

2.

3.

Shorts:

1.

2.

3.

Can I get a really good picture of someone in one conversation? No, but I get a first impression. I have to trust that this impression is more often right than wrong. Yes, I do make errors, but, naturally, the longer I have been doing it, the more the validity of these impressions increased.

When I get off the phone, the analysts stay on and explain to the president what kind of help we need from him, to analyze—and maybe recommend—his company. We need the help *urgently*, within the next few hours.

Why urgently?

During the last few years too often while we took our own sweet time investigating a company, its price ran up. That's a luxury we can't afford.

We ask for a relatively extensive list of the company's suppliers, a very extensive list of its most meaningful clients, and the names of its printers. No, not the financial printers, but those who print the promotional and marketing material, the brochures and the boxes. (Figure 6.2 is a sample of our request form. Many of these questions were inspired by the O'Neil organization's research.)

Major companies probably would not cooperate, but these young companies are eager for our help. We have relatively meaningful buying power, and we do very wide research. In addition, we have a decent following, not only among our own customers. Friends and the media ask us from time to time: What do we like? It helps a young company if it can tell everyone that we investigated it, and we came to the conclusion that it probably has a bright future.

All-Around Research

The head of the research department does most of the work. He checks the balance sheet data and all those ratios that we want to know about, even though they do not play the most important factor in our decision. They

Figure 6.2
List Sample Request Form

Company Name: _____

Please fill out this form and return it as fast as possible. Our fax is (212) ...-....

Management		
Name	Tel.	Fax #
Chmn:		
Pres:		
Fin VP:		
Mkting mgr:		
Sales mgr:		
Customers		
Company	Contact (and title)	Tel. #
1.		
2.		
3.		
4.		
5.		
6.		
7.		
8.		
9.		
10.		
11.		
12.		
Suppliers		
Company	Contact (and title)	Tel.#
1.		
2.		
3.		
4.		
5.		
Printers		
Company	Contact (and title)	Tel. #
1.		
2.		
Architects & Contractors		
Company	Contact (and title)	Tel. #
1.		
2.		

are the background material, not the crucial fact that tips the scale.

My other analysts will start right away an "all-around research" project. This process consists of calling everyone whose name the company supplied and, more important, whose name the analysts can pick up from the prospectuses, annual reports, and all other literature we can put our hands on.

The analysts will ask everyone about their experience with this company. The most important question we ask them: "Who else do you know who is a supplier or customer or has anything else to do with the company?" We do not want to limit our investigation to the friendly people whose names the executives supplied; we want to get "referrals" from them to other people who may see the management from a different angle.

※

A few years ago, one of the most popular magazines in the United States sent out a reporter to interview me. I found him very interesting; his questions were well selected; he was obviously quite bright and had an intriguing personality.

A few weeks later, I had a problem and, on a whim, I called and asked for his help. "I just finished a meeting with a company and I don't think they're telling us the truth. They claim that they have several contracts with one of the largest companies in the world and that they are also negotiating several contracts with Arab countries. Unfortunately, the numbers they give us just don't add up."

"Andy, give me the name of the company; I'll be back."

He called the next day. "These people have eight contracts with that giant corporation. I talked to all eight department heads."

"What do you think?"

"Every department head told me the same thing: they don't plan to give them any business again. Ever."

"How about the Arab countries?"

"The company had no telephone conversations with any Arab country. At least not for the last two years."

"How do you know?"

"Well, I know they had a conversation *with you* last February 12, from 3:00 to 3:15, and again on March 6 from 9:12 A.M. to 9:18 A.M., and . . ."

Yes, first the numbers didn't add up—then the stories didn't add up.

We sold our position and sold the company short. The stock went down.

❊

Many of my clients are surprised: "How come these suppliers, customers, and printers talk to your analysts?"

They don't just talk; many are *eager* to talk. They probably go home that night and brag to their spouse: "Wall Street called me today!" Most of them were never asked before. They feel flattered and talk in great detail; they enjoy their own importance. Remember: we generally don't investigate companies that sell to IBM or AT&T. Those probably have in their suppliers' or printers' contract a provision not to give out information. The people we ask aren't bound by any similar limitations. Very, very rarely, one source might say: "Please don't use my name." But the overwhelming majority doesn't even ask us for anonymity.

❊

When we finish talking to someone in the management of the target company—or someone during our "all-around research"—we try to get ideas from him about other companies we should investigate. This is our so-called "Aunt Sally question."

This is the way it goes:

"Thanks for all the information. I have a few concluding questions. Do you have any children?"

He is surprised: "Two boys and a girl."

"Just imagine that your Aunt Sally passed away and left $2 million to each of your kids. This is the way her will reads—and please concentrate, it is important that you understand the will. You have to invest $2 million for each of your children *within a month* in a company that: (1) is not your own; (2) has a manager whom you admire (we are looking for brilliance—so we don't care if this man is a supplier, a competitor, or someone you know through some business, social, or other activity); (3) has sales of between $20 million and $250 million; (4) is publicly held. (5) It can be one company or several. (6) If you don't invest the money within a month, Aunt Sally's inheritance will go to the Girl Scouts.

The man grins, scratches his head, and either comes up with some good ideas—or he doesn't. But it is worth a try. If these executives even occasionally produce something attractive, all our clients will benefit, and so will we.

We also ask a "negative Aunt Sally question:" "Whom do you know who is such a dummy, such a bad manager, that you can't understand why his stock is selling so high?"

If he names his closest competitor or potential competitor, we disregard the answer. If he names anyone else, we investigate. Actually, kicking a competitor is something that we consider a *negative input about him.*

❄

Because some of these companies aren't very widely traded, we ask the president to find out if any of the sizable holders (insiders, venture capitalists, other investors who bought very early) are interested in selling us a block. If yes, that would help us against the danger of pushing up the stock before most of our customers bought a decent position.

How much is a decent position? Generally, right at the start, we try to buy 5 to 15% of the public float. Later, we might accumulate as much as 25 to 30%.

This flies in the face of the principle of trying not to acquire more than what we can sell in a hurry. True. But there are very few "Rembrandt" quality stocks out there, and we want to own a sizable position in them.

Our approach demands that *we try to do substantially better research than others.* We should get caught as infrequently as possible with flat or declining sales and earnings. We should put all our effort into *picking up flat incoming order rates* early and selling while everyone else is still impressed by the *rising sales and earnings.* We should *try to sell into strength!*

As you are very well aware, the most important thing about investing is not buying, but *knowing when to sell! Never buy on someone's advice, if you aren't sure that he will also tell you when to sell.*

❄

Our analysts regularly go to so-called road shows, meetings where companies, which plan to go public, explain their prospectus. The first thing to do about a new issue is to read the summary page of its prospectus. We will probably reject the overwhelming majority based on their summary page. But if this is the one rare prospectus that is intriguing, our analysts will read it further and decide whether it is intriguing enough to go to the road show, where they can meet the management.

Although at these meetings, according to the law, the management isn't allowed to say anything that's not in the prospectus, the audience gets a reasonably good picture of whom it is dealing with. If you trust your impressions about people, these road shows can help a lot. This is very important, because, according to the same law, the management will not be able to come visit—or accept your visit to their headquarters—during the next month (except, again, to recite for you the prospectus).

If the analysts come back from a road show with the impression that they found a gem, they will go through the prospectus with a fine-tooth comb and collect the names of all those outsiders (customers, suppliers, whoever) who may give us information about the company. It is a very tough approach, but more than once we hit pay dirt. If we can get a good enough grasp on the company without management's help, we may decide to buy the stock right after the offering, whether the investment bankers gave us a few shares or not. (Mostly they give us very little, or zero.)

❈

Our research group has a rotating call list, which assures that every company we have interest in gets called at least once a month. Another list contains those companies in which we just became interested and we're trying to reach—as fast as possible. The third list is of those companies about which we completed the part of the research that involves management; we want to do additional, *all-around research* on them to decide whether we should get involved. And, finally, a fourth list contains the companies that are ready to be bought, but haven't been bought yet.

❈

When we analyze what were the main problems with our research in the past, we find two. In the beginning we may have asked too few outsiders about our selected companies; we ended up with a picture that wasn't wide enough. In the recent past, say during the last year and a half, our main problem was totally different. We did much broader all-around research, but *we moved too slowly.*

A while ago we decided that, because we want to accumulate stocks while they are still quite unknown, we should establish an arbitrary price where—if we did not start to buy the stock yet—we will stop doing research. We will admit that we missed it!

During a bear market, that limit used to be $20. In the bull market of last year, since October 11, 1990, we gradually raised that limit to $30.

Our problem was that if I found and assigned a stock to my research group at 16, sometimes the analysts waited till I assigned them a few more—and then another few. They accumulated 10 or 12 of these stocks and did a little bit of work on this, and a little bit of work on that, rather than *focusing on a single company*, on the one that seemed most promising.

Very often this lack of concentration in a "hot market" allowed a stock to move up to 24 and then to 30, without our participation. At that point the analyst, who took too long to develop an opinion, concluded: "It's out of our price range. Let's cross it off the list."

Obviously, we had to add to the approach *a sense of urgency*.

The solution: if the analysts develop an idea within three days from the time when I assigned the stock, *they will get a bonus*. During these three days, they talk to several people in the management; make sure that I talked to the chief executive—except if the offering was less than 30 days ago; do extensive, all-around research (reach over 20 people); and supply me with a summary of the analysts' collective opinion about the company—a summary good enough and short enough so the salesmen can use it when explaining the company to our clients. The analysts also have to supply us with a list of quotations from their interviews with the contacts and with an "earnings page," which shows sales and earnings and also estimates; fill out our so-called research checklist; supply the salesmen with all data necessary to set up files so the information should be at their fingertips; discuss the stock with the traders (find out who are the most important market makers and what seems to be their present position); and so on.

Yes, it means 16-hour days for three days, but the rewards to our customers and all of us can be very substantial.

❈

Figure 6.3 is a checklist that we use in our research. I think it is self-explanatory. *Many of these questions were inspired by the O'Neil organization's research.*

I keep emphasizing that *selling is a much more difficult and much more important decision than buying.*

If there is a potential danger, most of the time I run for the hills. Occasionally, we live to regret it, but I don't think we have much of a choice.

In the past, I often waited too long. I was convinced we knew the correct answer and the sellers were wrong. We should have redone our research in a panic, and if we found anything potentially wrong, we should have sold. We learned our lesson.

Our duty is to make sure that the customers' capital isn't exposed to imminent danger. It shouldn't even be exposed to too much uncertainty. Now we generally try to sell on the first whiff of *potential bad news.* And more often than not, this saves our skin.

The reverse happened in one of my favorite health care companies. (I must reiterate that in this business there are no permanent rules. Some approach will work so often that you develop a knee-jerk reaction. At that point, the *reverse* will start to happen.)

The chairman of the board of one of our favorite companies sold a *very substantial part* of his holdings. The president sold *all* his holdings. The executive vice president sold *more than half* of his holdings. Too much insider selling worries me. In this case I concluded that we would probably hear some very bad news during the next several months. I suggested to all my clients that they should sell their shares. Most of them did.

At the next meeting, the directors awarded the chairman a substantial amount of new options. What this means is that *he took part of his profits*, but then ended up with a rather *high number of future shares again.*

In addition to the insider sales, we also worried that the firm might develop a bottleneck in supplying its main service. The company confounded us and continued doing much better than expected. It seems we jumped the gun.

Figure 6.3
Research Checklist

Company Name: Date: /   /
ANALYST:

Please check every new idea against this list *before* you spend any meaningful time working on it. If the idea does not meet most of the criteria, don't spend any additional time before discussing it in detail with Andrew!

1. Character of management? _____
2. Does the company dominate an indusry, a niche, or a geographic unit? (which?) _____
4. Were the last 12 months' sales between $15 million and $250 million? _____ Amount: _____
5. Were the sales growth rate over 15%, earnings growth rate over 30%? _____ , _____
6. Are quarterly earnings accelerating? _____ From the previous quarter they are up _____ % From last year's identical quarter up _____ %
7. Is the relative strength greater than 70? _____ It is _____ .
8. Did the relative strength increase from last quarter? _____
9. Is the pretax profit margin positive? _____
10. Is the number of shares outstanding less than 20 million? _____
11. Is the price within 15% of the two-year high? _____
12. Is the *Datagraph* rating greater than 55? _____ It is _____ .
13. Service: _____ % Manufacturing: _____ %
14. Does it have ever-growing repeat orders? _____
15. A cookie cutter factor? _____
16. Three quarter estimate rating = _____
17. Next three quarter estimate rating = _____

Please check every single criterion and make notes. Give the notes to Andrew. Then, after discussing, let's proceed or put the idea into book 2 or book 3.

Unfortunately, if a similar situation develops again, I'll probably have to carry on the same way. Missing some profits is not as bad as exposing everyone's funds to a more than tolerable risk. The proceeds of the sales were reinvested in a number of ground-floor-stage companies and *statistically* the switch worked out very well. Which does not change the fact that it did not work out as planned.

There are very few "perfect games." *We were lucky*— and no one protests when the results are better then we deserve.

❄

The *lack of focus* is not the only major problem with a substantial part of the analyst community. I find that many, even some of the best ones, lack the degree of discipline that would be commensurate with their talents.

There is a "romantic" aspect to this profession. Analysts fall in love with stocks; they romance its strengths and forgive its weaknesses. They pay too much attention to vague hopes and too little to immediate negatives. I found many times that even the best research people have at least one of these "romantic" relationships, without which their results would be substantially better.

❄

Let me quote a memo from our senior analyst. This is how he summarized our research:

> We begin with criteria that are too rigorous for 99% of the brokerage firms—starting with earnings growth of at least 30% per year.

> We react quicker than most to deterioration in fundamentals. Often we discover it long before the Street in our all-around research.

> We know how to stick to our winners and have a number of companies with incredible appreciation.

102

Most analysts become apologists for a company's earnings shortfall. We gracefully exit and search for the next idea.

❄

We try to get newer and newer sources of information. Naturally, we do go back to the same people for information, but we don't want to do it *frequently*. We need a large stable of contacts.

Wild fluctuations, rumors, and announcements: they have to be investigated. It's okay to find ten false alarms, but we have to be prepared for the one that will be real!

Customers are grateful for good buy ideas, but, sooner or later, they become like the man with a wonderful wife: he does appreciate her but, at the same time, he starts to take her for granted: "Okay, they are good analysts. Great! That's why I'm doing business with them."

Some will get upset over the occasional failures; others are intelligent enough to realize that *if we didn't make mistakes from time to time, we would become marked men: no one would do business with us!* If we were always right, then the person trading against us—buying from or selling to us—would be automatically wrong. He would be nuts to consider doing business with us or our customers.

❄

The one move that even the most jaded customers appreciate, and give you credit for, is *getting them out before a stock collapses!*

Sometimes we are able to do it just as we hoped. Sometimes the stock starts down before we make our move; in spite of thorough research, we will never find all potential booby traps.

If the stock started down, we have to reexamine the whole situation. And do it as fast as possible. If we find that our expectations were wrong, that there is a reason for the slide, we have to sell, shamelessly, several points below the ideal level. Being stubborn, being proud, would

103

be counterproductive. We have to take the loss and get out and try to recover it in a better situation.

Thank God, recently, in most cases, we did not have to take a loss from the puchase price, only from the peak, from the point where someone was smarter, or better informed, than we and started selling before we did.

In this business you can't even hope to shoot for perfection—but if, in spite of talking to so many people, we don't pick up the "bad vibes" of something starting to move in the wrong direction, it will bother us, annoy us, shame us.

What can we do? Not much else, but *analyze the mistakes*, every time, *and try to learn from them.*

❄

Our experience is that the more frequently some phenomenon recurred, the more probable it is that now, when almost everyone expects it, it will not happen again. As some Wall Street sage said: "The market's main ambition is to shame the majority."

There are excellent books and endless numbers of almanacs that record events that routinely recur on Wall Street. There are theories about *which* hour of the day, *which* day of the week, *which* month of the year will normally result in *what* action. There are all kinds of wave theories about the longer and "even much longer" time periods. They are all very interesting, but somewhat less than reliable and not very useful. Most probably cause more damage than good!

❄

There is one theory that—although repeated to death and known by everyone—has some basis in reality. (And now, after I hold this one up as a shining exception, it probably won't work either!)

I'm talking about the *Presidential Cycle Theory.* The essence of our economic life comes from the essence of our political life: *each administration wants to get reelected.*

The president's first duty to his party, and to his fellow party members, is to get reelected.

If you check economic and stock market fluctuations during the last 20 presidencies, 19 of them had a meaningful number of similarities.

The president knows that before the next election he will need a substantial period of improving economy if he wants to get reelected or pick his successor. This knowledge becomes one of the main building blocks of his four-year program. If there has to be a recession, let it be relatively early!

The market projects what it expects to happen six to nine months later in the economy. (Caveat: None of this should be considered as more than a vague projection.) On the average, the good market of the preelection and election time continues until the middle of the first postelection year; then the market becomes weaker and weaker and stays depressed until—in expectation that within the next six to nine months the administration will pull out all stops trying to create a better atmosphere for the next election—it starts to go up again.

The only president during whose administration this pattern didn't work at all was Jimmy Carter. Carter, as an individual, is an admirable man, but he was not a professional politician on the national level. Carter probably hoped that he could go through his whole presidency without a recession. The reality was most unpleasant: just before and during the election, the economy was in such bad shape that it hurt him.

Although I do think that the "the more things change, the more they stay the same" principle applies surprisingly well to the successive presidential cycles, to count on it would be inviting disappointment.

Remember what the sage said: "The market's main ambition is to shame the majority."

※

There are several organizations that print so-called *"144" lists* that tell the world what insiders registered stock for sale. Insiders have a month to report to the SEC, and these publications generally take from a few days to a month to print the announcements. The information the public gets is not as fresh as it should be.

We subscribe to a system which gets the information relatively soon after the prospective or active selling stockholder registered it with the SEC. If there is massive insider selling, we do our best to investigate it. And if our findings are not conclusive, we will probably reduce or sell the position.

The standard opinion, that insider selling is always a danger sign, is not necessarily correct—and it certainly does not work well with very young companies. The key members of management are, more often than not, the founders. Other than the stock, they have no assets. Their investment banker may have talked them out of selling any personal holdings when they originally went public. Now, any major expense can push them to sell some shares, because *they have nothing else to sell.* A new home, a major educational expense, or anything else legitimate could force them to reduce their position.

We always want to check what percentage of the holdings are they selling, and did they sell any substantial quantity recently?

Insider sales can be misleading. One should always consider it as *only one piece of data,* and not always the most decisive one.

❊

Let me tell you about our newest tool. We started to use it only a year ago. *Since its introduction, our results have become incomparably stronger.*

It is simplicity itself; I call it our kindergarten approach. The essence of this approach is to estimate (and the estimates have to be good; otherwise, the "garbage in, garbage out" principle prevails) the earnings for the next four quarters and express them, so they should be comparable, not in dollars and cents but in percentages: How many percentage points do we expect them to improve (if we *do* expect them to improve) from last year's identical quarter?

We give more weight to the nearest quarter, average to the second, and a lower weight to the third quarter. Then we adjust the result for some of our qualitative criteria (very few of them can be expressed numerically), and, as a result of these computations, we end up *assigning a number to each company.*

We list all stocks in declining order of these numbers. In our experience, they generally range from a maximum of 27.5 down to zero. This listing expresses how much the stocks should move relative to each other—assuming that anyone on Wall Street will pay attention to them.

Expecting that they actually will follow this pattern would reflect an abundance of naiveté. Our experience, though, is very much better than what we hoped for. Wall Street actually does look at earnings estimates, and the companies with the highest visibility of near-term growth *do end up moving substantially more* than the slower-growing ones. We also work out an identical number for the nine-month period starting not with the present, but with the next quarter. This is for our longer-term guidance. We were Doubting Thomases, but this "kindergarten approach" made us substantially more profits than expected.

Figure 6.4 provides a detailed description of how we come up with these numbers and an example of how the finished list looks.

I don't blame you if you think the approach is not sophisticated enough. I thought so, too, until I saw the results.

Figure 6.4
Description of the 3 Quarter Estimate Rating Method

To calculate a 3 quarter estimate rating for our companies, we first determine the expected growth rate of the company's earnings per share (in the form of percentages) for the next three quarters (versus each comparable quarter a year ago). We then give each number a rating. An earnings change from negative to positive results would rate a 75% increase. A positive to negative change would be considered a 0% increase.

A. If the expected percentage gain in the next quarter is
    greater than 100%, it gets a 9;
    between 65% and 99%, it gets a 6;
    between 35% and 64%, it receives a 3;
    less than 35%, it receives a 0.

B. If the percentage gain two quarters out is
    greater than 100%, it gets a 6;
    between 65% and 99%, it gets a 4;
    between 35% and 64%, it receives a 2;
    less than 35%, it receives a 0.

C. If the percentage in the third quarter from now is
    greater than 100%. it gets a 3;
    between 65% and 99%, it gets a 2;
    between 35% and 64%, it receives a 1;
    less than 35%, it receives a 0.

After assigning three numbers to each company (one for each of the next three quarters), we add these three numbers together. We then multiply this number by either 1.5, 1.25, or .667 depending on what type of company it is. If it is a repeat order/cookie cutter company, it is multiplied by 1.5. If it is a repeat order business, but not a cookie cutter, it is multiplied by 1.25. Finally, if the company is a manufacturer, it is multiplied by .667 (divided by 1.5).

BUY LIST
as of 3/19/1992

Company	3 Quarters	Next 3 Quarters
VIEWlogic	22.5	22.5
Surgical Care Affiliates	22.5	18
Quantum Health Resource	21	13.5
Premier Anesthesia	27	27
Ross Systems	22.5	20
Medisys	21	24
BMC Software	17.5	11.25
Platinum Technology	10	11.25
Medaphis	16.5	13.5
Rotech Medical	9	9
HealthCare COMPARE	5	10
InterLeaf	20	17.5

7

Big Winners;
And How to Find
Them Early

No, this is not a chapter of tips, nor even a chapter of high-quality investment ideas about stocks that you should run out and buy.

In line with the old saying, "If you give someone a fish you will feed him for a day, but if you teach him how to fish you will feed him for a lifetime," I am going to look at five companies that produced enormous profits and will try to identify those characteristics that a present-day investor should look for when searching for new super-growth stocks.

Two of these winners have already become major blue chips, and some of the others are becoming very well known. What we want to find are the future blue chips, those companies of the highest quality that we can buy at the ground floor.

❊

I plan to write about a number of men whom I love and admire—men whom even the cynics of Wall Street love and admire.

I think you will understand why.

AUTOMATIC DATA PROCESSING (ADP)

The Highest Possible Degree of Work Ethics

We have set a record in profits since the first week
we were in business in 1949. There was never a
down quarter in the history of ADP.

—**Joe Taub**, Co-founder

One of the most spectacular corporate growth stories in
history was created by the most modest person I've ever
met: **Henry Taub**, founder of the company:

*I was a Depression baby. I have been working since I was 12
years old. At 15, I operated a billing machine for 55 cents an hour;
I was in the middle of a clerical production line requiring very
stringent deadlines and coordination of activities.*

*I graduated from high school at 16 and went to NYU to study
accounting. After school every day I worked for a CPA firm. Let me
give you an example: They would send me up to a luggage
manufacturer that had 50 people on its payroll. I would do their
billing, deposit their checks, balance their receivables, pay the
bills, do the general ledger, and experience all the problems of a
small business—meeting cash flow, dealing with the union, and
with help not showing up on time. It was really a management
experience at a very small level.*

*I graduated from NYU at 19, but I couldn't take my CPA exam
until I was 21. For a while I worked with a large accounting firm
and then with a friend: I took over his company's Accounts Receivable and Payroll Processing Departments.*

*Preparing the payroll started to become complicated. In the
past, if someone worked 40 hours at $1 an hour, the owner just
reached into his pocket and gave him two $20s. But now there was
Social Security, it was the beginning of the federal income tax, the
beginning of disability . . . ; it started to become a burdensome
accounting operation. We had to compute withholding tax, state
unemployment, the union checkoffs, and things of that type. Meeting a deadline became critical—and not easy.*

AUTOMATIC DATA PROCESSING, INC.
Summary of Financial Statistics, June 30, 1963–1991
(dollars in millions, except per share)

Years Ended June 30	Revenue	Pretax Income	Earnings Per Share
1963	$ 1	$ X	$ X
1964	2	X	0.005
1965	3	0.6	0.010
1966	5	1.1	0.015
1967	5	2.0	0.02
1968	16	3.0	0.03
1969	27	4.6	0.04
1970	39	6.6	0.05
1971	49	9.2	0.06
1972	62	12.8	0.07
1973	90	16.7	0.08
1974	112	20.5	0.10
1975	155	27.2	0.12
1976	188	35.0	0.16
1977	245	46.0	0.20
1978	299	54.0	0.23
1979	370	64.0	0.28
1980	455	76.0	0.31
1981	558	90.0	0.38
1982	677	106.0	0.43
1983	753	115.0	0.47
1984	889	133.0	0.54
1985	1,031	155.0	0.62
1986	1,204	185.0	0.73
1987	1,384	222.0	0.88
1988	1,549	255.0	1.10
1989	1,678	272.0	1.27
1990	1,714	285.0	1.44
1991	1,772	300.0	1.63

My idea of a payroll service developed out of this experience. Three of us started a company called Automatic Payroll. We borrowed $6,000, but the progress was much slower than expected, and after a while I became the sole owner and the sole person responsible for the debt.

My younger brother, Joe, joined me. The business was not capital intensive, but it required a lot of effort because we were steadily facing deadlines.

Figure 7-1 Automatic Data Processing Chart from 1977–1991

Courtesy of William O'Neil & Co., Inc.

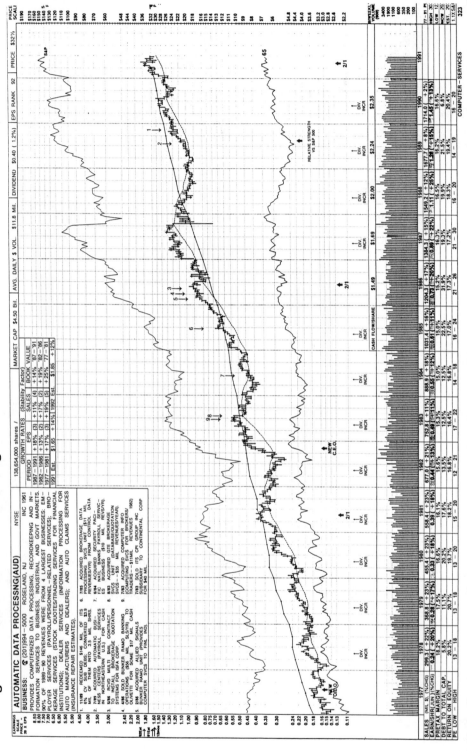

Figure 7-1 (cont.)

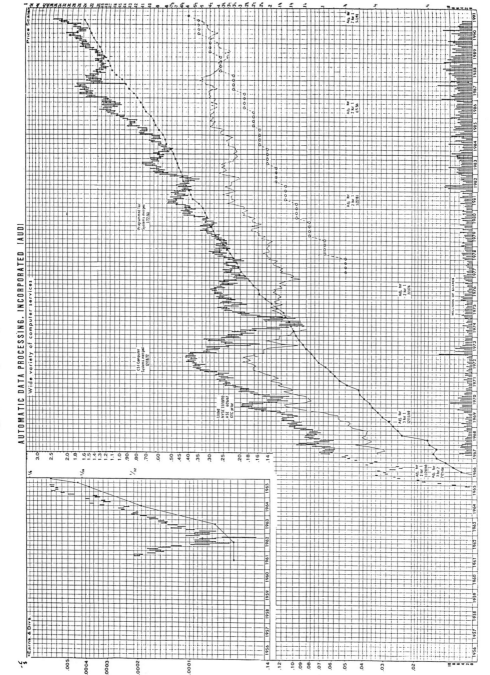

115

AUTOMATIC DATA PROCESSING, INC.
Income Statements
for Years Ended June 30, 1957–1961

	1957 (unaudited)	1958 (unaudited)	1959	1960	1961
Operating revenues	$149,719	$224,663	$284,956	$339,424	$418,937
Operating expenses	129,906	188,048	219,242	263,231	312,791
Selling, general, and administrative expenses	18,436	22,415	34,811	45,256	68,913
	148,342	210,463	254,053	308,487	381,704
Earnings before federal taxes on income	1,377	14,200	30,903	30,937	37,233
Federal taxes on income	413	4,260	10,300	10,300	12,000
Net earnings	964	9,940	20,603	20,637	25,233
Pro forma adjustment of federal taxes on income	—	—	250	250	1,900
Pro forma net earnings	$ 964	$ 9,940	$ 20,353	$ 20,387	$ 23,333
Pro forma earnings per share based on 362,000 shares of common stock presently outstanding	$ 0.003	$ 0.027	$ 0.056	$ 0.056	$ 0.064

Source: Automatic Data Processing Annual Report, June 30, 1961.

We were working in an office building in Paterson, New Jersey, and became friendly with a young insurance salesman in the same building: Frank Lautenberg.

His activities were mainly in the evening, visiting people. He would see us working day and night and he thought he could help. We liked the idea: "Why don't you try and sell our services?" He became very successful at it; Frank's skills and energy were fundamental to our expansion from a most modest revenue base.

❊

You have to envision this operation: the time cards came in, people analyzed the cards; at the next station somebody put in the rate; at the next station people calculated the card. If it was a piecework payroll, we had women with comptometers—remember those key-driven devices? We really had a paperwork factory.

By '57, our shop had several hundred payroll accounts. We were missionaries in a service business.

Our main advantage was the knowledge of the marketplace. There were many men smarter and much wiser in terms of the technology, but we always recognized that we had to know more about the marketplace and about the customer's business than the customer himself. We didn't dare rely on him to tell what he wanted; he was never that certain.

In 1957 we went through a terrible ordeal in converting from manual systems to automated procedures; it almost put us out of business. Luckily we never gave up our manual production line; it took a full year to complete the conversion which we planned to do in a month.

❊

In 1961, we went public. This glorious company of ours, after being in business for 12 years, was doing only $419,000 in revenues, $23,000 after taxes.

I liked to sell accounting firms and tax attorneys because they would lead to additional clients. One of these firms was impressed by the fact that we would deliver when it rained, when it snowed—it didn't make any difference—and the figures were correct! In the late '50s they suggested that we get involved with some of their brokerage firm clients, doing so-called back office work. We were not ready for it.

117

One of our clients was Oppenheimer and Company, a brokerage firm. They knew us as "those nice young guys in Clifton, New Jersey, who would do the payroll regardless of conditions." They thought that we might go public and directed us to potential underwriters.

Frank used to commute to New York with a young associate of Paul Weiss. We needed a law firm for the underwriting, so we went to them. We didn't know they happened to have been, and still are, among the most prominent SEC specialists on the Street. They were laughing; this was the smallest firm they ever assisted in an underwriting. But they did help us.

Half of the offering was for us, the principals, so we became independently wealthy. We divided approximately $130,000 among ourselves and had an equivalent amount to invest in the business.

Oppenheimer invited us once again to get involved in the brokerage back office business. By this time we were better prepared, and I assembled a team of knowledgeable back office people.

We have always been grateful for Oppenheimer's support. Their confidence in us helped to create our Wall Street segment, which by now has grown into a $750 million service.

We were slowly, but surely, making the transition from manual, to punched cards, to electronics, to communications. The operations at ADP today are as sophisticated as you will find anywhere in the world. The fact that we managed through these transitions is what really tells the story.

The cost of developing systems was a very difficult one to control. If all we did was to sell software to our clients for a fixed fee, then we would be like the rest of the industry. One of the things I liked about payroll is that it is repetitive, in the sense of being weekly, biweekly, or monthly.

After we went public, as modest as the offering was, we understood we had a stock at a high multiple that could be a vehicle for acquisition. We undertook to find partners across the country who would take advantage of our systems development work and our marketing approach, and would slowly disengage from being a general service bureau and change into our specialized business. Most of the acquisitions were for stock, and maybe a little cash.

Some of the new people, like Arthur Kranseler, who came from Boston, and David Perlman from Miami, joined us 25 years ago and contributed to our business in a very significant way. In Boston, Arthur ran a shop that did a lot of statistical work for Harvard and MIT and some engineering firms. It was a challenging business, with very sophisticated equipment.

We said to him: "Arthur, if you want to win a Nobel prize, keep doing this work. But if you want to make some money—each time we produce a paycheck we make a nickel—if you want to make a part of that nickel a check, and keep selling more and more checks, then you should join us." He did.

A competitor, a company called Brokerage Processing Center, was run by a very experienced fellow named Joe Rosen. One night we got a call from our IBM representative:

"This guy Rosen really has a problem; his equipment is down. You have the only 360 capable of processing his work. If you don't want to help him, I understand. If you want to help, you are a taking him out of this clinch."

We discussed it among ourselves and decided to do the right thing. We let him come in and we ran his work. A couple of years later, we merged the two companies.

We have found outstanding partners in over one hundred acquisitions, large and small. Great people who helped us toward reaching our potential.

❄

One other thing: I'm really proud of our people in terms of their involvement in the community. In 1974, Frank was invited to become general chairman of the United Jewish Appeal. It meant a real serious commitment in terms of time. I said:

"Why not accept it? You have good people behind you, they will rise to the occasion—and we will have a more seasoned middle-level management."

That's the way it works. Management at the top has to be willing to give rein to those in the middle level; let them make some decisions. You have to learn to let people make mistakes. You have to let go, but you don't delegate and forget.

When we started, it was totally beyond our imagination to be late delivering the payrolls, or to be less than 100%—or very, very close to 100%—accurate. Nothing changed.

Frank Lautenberg, the first salesman, first sales manager, and later the president and chairman of the company, is in his second term as a U.S. senator from New Jersey.

My father was a warper; that's a blue-collar job in a silk factory. He died a young man.

During the war, my mother got a job with a major insurance company because an agent had been called off to war. You can't imagine my sister's and my pride in her. She had a white-collar job, and in a sales force of 90, she became the third or fourth most successful agent. When the man returned from the service, my mother asked the company: "How about another territory?" And they said: "We don't give these jobs to women." Can you imagine? And it wasn't a century ago, either. She moved to Boston, went into the retail business, and she became quite successful.

In 1949, I graduated from Columbia University and, on my mother's suggestion, I joined the Prudential Insurance Company. I became modestly successful, but didn't like calling on people at their homes at night.

Henry and Joe's office was in the same building. I began to meet them regularly in the men's room; once in a while in the coffee shop.

I became fascinated with their idea and volunteered to try and sell the product. At that time, they had about ten accounts, doing maybe $35,000 a year. I came in with three new accounts very quickly.

At the beginning of '54, I joined the company full time, with a handshake and the understanding that one day, if things went well, I would become a partner.

I don't think any of us were geniuses. We were hardworking, very committed—and our dedication overcame whatever short-comings we had in planning. We were no visionaries. And we weren't hoping to become millionaires.

Henry had an incredible maturity of focus. Joe and I would sometimes grow weary and feel like checking out early—but we stayed, because Henry stayed. We worked like slaves. It was a good combination. I was always the salesman, Joe had a facility for putting together a team, and Henry was the one who kept us all together.

We offered exceptional value. For a small company, finishing the payroll preempted all other things. You couldn't go out and do sales, process orders, or collect bills if the payroll wasn't under control. That was the one thing that people had to have at the end of the week—no delays!

If I approached a company where the bookkeeper spent two days a week preparing the payroll and she made $150 a week: we offered an immediate and substantial saving, charging them only $25 per week. We would also process the quarterly payroll taxes, the year-end W2s, and all related records. There were no extra charges. It was a basic service, and we threw in pick up and delivery.

We introduced tabulating equipment from IBM in '57 and the first commercial computers in 1961. The 1401 was a relatively fast processor—and that's when marketing really came into its own. We had the chance to offer a standard product anyplace in the country. Our productivity went way up—and that's when the boom started, as far as ADP was concerned.

At the time of the public offering, we changed the name from Automatic Payroll to Automatic Data Processing. We became generic to the industry, like Kleenex in facial tissue. ADP is common terminology for data processing. Many managers say: "Yeah, this is my ADP department."

❊

We started an acquisition program. In '66 I went out to find small companies already in the computer service business that, with some help, could grow faster. Most of them became profitable within a very short time after the acquisition. I think we did over 100 of them, with a total volume of about $100,000,000.

We had one big acquisition, it was a time-sharing company in Ann Arbor, Michigan. Then there was an automobile parts service business that we bought in Portland, Oregon. Most of the others were pretty small. We started to grow so rapidly, we were barely able to control the business.

One day I got a phone call from a guy called Josh Weston. We had hired an executive away from his company, and he wanted me to know that he didn't like it. Josh and I ended up having lunch, and I was impressed. He ran a catalog company, a company that had lots of transactions. It was a business that, like ours, required follow-up: the order would come in, cash would come in, merchandise would have to be sent, and records would have to be estab-

lished. Their number of transactions was enormous and there was a great similarity between our businesses: quality control, lots of manual intervention, the realationship with the customer—all those things fit.

He was my kind of guy: hard-nosed. The principal owner of the company had moved out West and Josh was running everything for an OK salary, but with very little equity. We made him an offer that he found impossible to refuse.

Joe Taub left us in 1969; he had other interests. By the mid-'70s, Henry also decided that he wanted to be less active. The character of the company had changed a lot. It had become much more impersonal; a giant organization.

We were three kids from the streets of Paterson. Our instincts about people were good. We had a mission: to make sure that we keep productivity levels up and that we keep the customers' satisfaction level up. If we got stuck with a complicated situation late at night, we would call the salesman and he would come in. Even at 3 o'clock in the morning. There was no question in anyone's mind that the job had to be finished, and will be finished, on time.

I became chairman in 1978, and we made a number of additional acquisitions. I also became a commissioner of the Port Authority of New York and New Jersey and got involved in a number of other public projects. I enjoyed public service—and in 1981 decided to run for the U. S. Senate seat in New Jersey. No one believed, including me, that I could succeed. But I did get elected.

By this time, the company was doing very, very well. The acquisitions gave us a dominant position; at all these locations, we had the same marketing, standardized products, standardized pricing, and standardized training manuals. We didn't have to develop something new in every market.

Regardless of the economic conditions, there is always a work force that has to be paid—that's what gave ADP its first opportunity. Then we diversified: in 1963 we developed our back office business, and, in the '70s, we added a parts inventory business and also timesharing. It gave us some balance. We were able to increase sales and earnings even during recessions by continuing to gain market share. We kept growing because of the sheer power of our total commitment to the customer.

The repeat order was automatic; it didn't require a contract. The only thing that could cause us to lose an order would have been poor performance. Actually, occasionally one or another customer bought his own computer to do the payroll in-house. Very often, they found it more trouble than they asked for—and came back to us.

※

Since Frank Lautenberg's election to the Senate, **Josh Weston** has been chairman. He is an exceptionally strong strategist and something of a corporate philosopher.

On March 11, 1991, Weston wrote a memo "to every ADP associate:"

Since December 1972, Kidder-Peabody has been issuing a monthly list of the 50 companies on the NYSE with the highest P/Es for that month.

In these past 217 months, ADP was "Top 50" 194 times. Of the other firsts still on the list, the next longest record belongs to Merck, with 162 times. Then comes Wal-Mart with 158. No one else was on over 125 times.

The company's results are beyond comparison. Today ADP is the largest independent company in the United States dedicated exclusively to computerized transaction processing, record keeping, data communication, and information services. In the 1991 fiscal year ended June 30, it completed 120 consecutive quarters of double-digit growth in earnings per share. No other publicly owned company in America can match this 30-year unbroken quarterly record!

H&R BLOCK (HRB)

The Magic of Combining an Ever-Growing Repeat-Order Rate with a Cookie Cutter Factor

We hope that when our clients leave our preparer's desk, they will voluntarily say: "Thank you. That's the best job of tax preparation I've ever had."

—**Richard Bloch**, Co-founder

This is a company that took a "mom and pop" industry and became its leader. Today H&R Block totally dominates the market.

The company supplies a service that fulfills a recurring necessity; it helps customers complete their tax returns. This is a high-volume business, charging fairly, based on low cost and on a reputation for doing the finest possible work. H&R Block stands behind its work. If a client is called to visit the IRS, a Block representative will go along at no extra charge.

❄

Henry W. Bloch, founder:

The very beginning? It happened in 1945, right after World War II. At the Harvard Graduate Business School I read the transcript of a speech which Professor Sumner Huber Slichter gave to insurance industry executives. His message was: if insurance companies really wanted to help the country, they would invest some money in business, particularly in small business.

I made an appointment with Slichter and asked him what he thought of the idea of starting a business to help small business. He said it made sense.

My brothers and I put together a plan. One idea was to prepare customers' income tax returns; another one was to keep their books. We rented an office for $50 a month and went around to a number of small businesses trying to sell our services; some 50

H&R BLOCK, INC.
Summary of Financial Statistics, 1962–1991
(dollars in millions, except per share)

Year Ended	Revenues	Pretax Earnings	Earnings per Share
Year ended July 31			
1962	$ 1.4	$ 0.3	$0.001
1963	2.3	0.4	0.004
1964	3.5	0.6	0.004
1965	6.4	1.4	0.009
Nine months ended April 30			
1966	9.9	2.2	0.014
Year ended April 30			
1967	16.3	3.2	0.02
1968	25.1	5.0	0.03
1969	37.4	8.3	0.04
1970	55.5	13.3	0.07
1971	63.2	16.4	0.10
1972	68.3	13.6	0.08
1973	80.7	22.6	0.13
1974	98.4	29.1	0.16
1975	114.1	35.0	0.20
1976	123.9	39.4	0.22
1977	146.0	47.2	0.27
1978	161.3	49.4	0.29
1979	198.1	55.2	0.33
1980	229.6	60.6	0.35
1981	287.8	70.0	0.39
1982	318.7	70.5	0.39
1983	342.8	73.1	0.41
1984	419.1	88.0	0.47
1985	497.0	101.9	0.54
1986	615.1	115.0	0.60
1987	722.3	130.4	0.72
1988	812.6	144.6	0.86
1989	899.6	161.6	0.95
1990	1,052.7	200.5	1.16
1991	1,190.8	225.6	1.31

Courtesy of William O'Neil & Co., Inc.

Figure 7.2 H&R Block Chart from 1977-1991

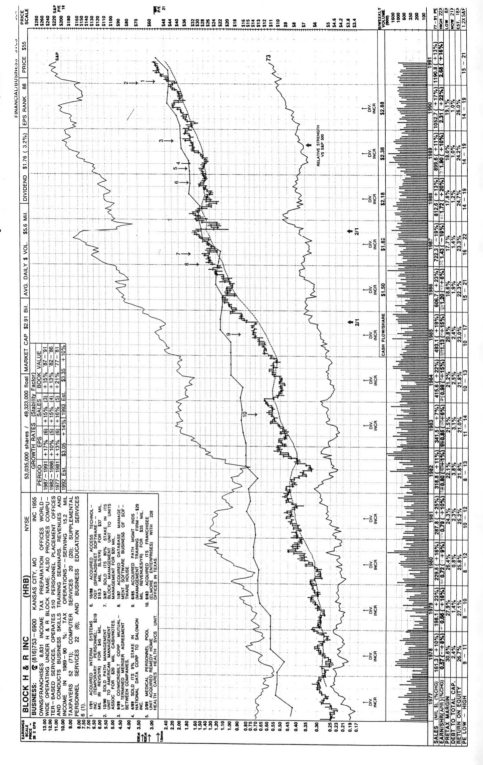

126

H&R BLOCK, INC.
Income Statement
for Years Ended July 31, 1961–1965, and April 30, 1966

H&R Block, Inc., a Missouri corporation, operates and franchises others to operate a nationwide system of offices engaged in the preparation of federal and any required state or local income tax returns for individuals, utilizing the systems and procedures which it has developed. On April 15, 1966, there were 1,190 H&R Block offices in operation in 43 states, the District of Columbia, Puerto Rico and Canada, of which 370 were owned and operated by H&R Block, Inc., or one of its wholly owned subsidiaries and 820 were owned and operated by independent franchises.

	Year Ended July 31					Nine Months Ended April 30, 1965 (unaudited)	Nine Months Ended April 30, 1966
	1961	1962	1963	1964	1965		
Revenues							
Tax return preparation fees	$484,258	$787,815	$1,334,070	$2,242,554	$4,148,758	$4,113,922	$6,571,501
Franchise fees	125,847	155,859	168,596	228,766	461,492	459,655	736,033
Interest income	716	4,335	5,862	13,173	21,280	9,581	23,713
Other income	144	10,523	5,581	19,279	202,259	75,810	164,842
Total Revenues	$610,985	$958,037	$1,514,049	$2,498,722	$4,838,789	$4,758,918	$7,496,089
Operating expenses	426,904	686,824	1,167,321	1,858,288	3,687,040	3,449,027	5,589,666
Earnings before taxes on income	$184,061	$271,213	$346,728	$640,484	$1,146,749	$1,309,891	$1,906,423
Taxes on income							
Federal	81,505	120,044	155,917	284,402	510,500	588,700	835,150
State	1,389	3,164	4,787	10,804	21,475	25,600	52,700
	$ 82,694	$123,808	$ 160,704	$ 295,206	$ 531,975	$ 614,300	$ 887,850
Net earnings	$101,367	$147,405	$ 186,024	$ 345,278	$ 614,774	$ 695,591	$1,018,573
Net earnings per share	$ 0.012	$ 0.14	$ 0.18	$ 0.34	$ 0.60	$ 0.68	$ 1.00
Cash dividends per share on common stock	$ —	$ 0.03	$ 0.18	$ 0.22	$ 0.20	$ 0.20	$ 0.30

Source: H&R Block prospectus,* August 11, 1966

*Here and in various places in the book we have pulled data from prospectuses, annual reports, and so on. We believe that the selections represent how the company viewed itself at the time.

different services, like temporary help—this was way before the day of temporary help companies—also window dressing, decorating, advertising, insurance, legal work, and all kinds of investments; all types of help that they might need around the company.

I thought we could subcontract this work once we had the clients. We were very young and every time we got close to signing somebody, the potential client said: "Well, would you give me some references? I would like to know what kind of a job you do for your other clients." Of course, we had no other clients. We had no clients whatsoever. So they would say: "Well, when the business gets bigger, come back and see us again."

We had no capital at all, so we decided to visit a wealthy great-aunt in New York City. She donated a lot of money for all kinds of charitable projects, and my brother Dick and I went to her to ask if she would give us $50,000 to start our new business. We met with her thinking that she was so wealthy—she lived in the Waldorf Astoria Tower, had an entire floor there—that she would be happy to help us.

"No, I won't give you $50,000—but I will loan you $5,000, if your father co-signs the note." This was back in 1946. Dad signed, and we started a little company in Kansas City. It was only my brother, Leon, and me. We had no business, we had no customers. Leon said: "I just can't see that we're ever going to make a living out of this business. I'm quitting and going back to law school."

He asked me: "What about our aunt's $5,000?" We decided to return it. We were able to return the money, not because business was booming, but because we played a lot of bridge, and we put our bridge winnings into the company. Leon quit the business; he's a lawyer today. Our father was a lawyer, too.

Eventually someone called and said: "I have a brother who has a hamburger stand. Would you be interested in helping him with his bookkeeping?"

And that's what got me started. At once I was in the bookkeeping business—nothing else. Through word of mouth some other people got interested; I went out and called on these little companies—and kept picking up bookkeeping until the business got to be more than I could handle by myself.

I told my mother: "I have to hire somebody else; I'm going to run an ad in the newspaper." She said, "I know whom you should hire!," and I said, "Whom?" and she said, "Your brother, Richard." "I can't afford to hire Dick, he's married." I was single at the time. "I couldn't pay his salary." She said, "Well, I'll pay part of it." "Oh, I wouldn't let you do that." Dick joined me, and about a year later we became partners.

In addition to the bookkeeping, we were also doing a lot of the small businesses' employees' tax returns. We were in a high-rise office building in Kansas City, and the owner had asked us to put a sign in the lobby, that we would do income tax returns for people in the building—and we ended up doing so many income tax returns that we had no free time left. We worked seven days and seven nights a week. By this time, we had a few women working for us, doing the accounting work.

The business kept growing until nine years later, in 1955, we decided to quit preparing tax returns. We wanted to get out of the income tax business, because at this time we were so busy with our accounting work, doing corporate and partnership returns and sales tax and excise tax and monthly financial statements, that we didn't have time to do individual tax returns for non-clients.

There was a client of ours, John White, who worked with the Kansas City Star, the newspaper here, as a display advertising salesman. We had done his tax return for years. He suggested that before we get out of the tax return business, we try to make a business of it. Exactly the reverse of what we planned!

He came up with an ad, two columns by 5", saying we offer income tax preparation for $5; that's all we were charging at that time. I asked him how much the ad would cost, and he said $100. I thought "Well, gosh, we'd have to do twenty returns just to get our money back." And then he said, "No, you'd have to run at least two ads, because one ad won't prove anything." "Well then, we'd have to do 40 returns!" Dick said, "Oh, let's take a chance, what can we lose? We could only lose $200."

So we ran those ads and business came in immediately. In fact, that first day, while I was picking up our clients' checkbooks, Dick called me and said, "Get back as soon as you can; we have an office full of people." We made about $25,000 in 1955, our first year.

We were very lucky; our ad appeared at exactly the right time—near the end of January, when W2s came out. If we'd have done it two weeks earlier or a month later, we might never have stayed in the business.

The next year we decided that it worked so well in Kansas City, we ought to go somewhere else; we talked about cities around

Kansas City like St. Louis, Wichita, Omaha, Springfield, Missouri, and so on—but finally we decided to open up in New York City. We opened seven offices there. We borrowed all the money we could to go to New York City—and we broke even the first year.

We broke even, but we decided to sell our New York operation. It was a tough place to do business, and we figured to make it work, one of us had to move to New York—and neither one of us wanted to leave Kansas City.

We put an ad in The New York Times to sell the business and two CPAs answered the ad. It was the only answer we got! But they didn't have much money; only $10,000. We were determined to sell, so we said: "We'll give you the New York City operation, we'll also give you Connecticut and some additional territory in the state of New York, and you give us your $10,000 and agree to pay us a royalty on any business you do." Back in 1956 nobody, including us, thought the business would grow like it did. And that move put us into franchising. It probably was the very beginning of franchising. We had never heard of the word franchising at that time.

When the two CPAs agreed to pay us a royalty, neither of us dreamed of the trend that we were starting.

The move didn't work out too well; we were not happy with the way they ran the offices. A few years later we bought them back: for over $1 million! That's how fast the company grew.

This experience gave us a new way of expanding. We took all our profits and plowed them back into opening company-owned offices and when we ran out of money, we would franchise other cities—like we did New York. Franchises cost us no money, because the franchisee paid most of the expenses. So, by opening both company-owned offices and franchised offices each year, we often grew by a thousand offices a year.

We had a lot of lucky breaks! We even had a lot of bad things happen that turned to our advantage. The first lucky break was the ad that I mentioned. The second was that we didn't want to live in New York, and as a result we discovered franchising. The third was that in 1961 we tried to go public and we didn't succeed—which ended up a blessing.

As you know, to go public you need an underwriter, you need a lawyer, and you need a CPA. We had picked the three biggest ones in Kansas City. And about halfway through the process, one day the accountants didn't show up. When we called, they told us that they were pulling out. They weren't going to audit our books, because they had received word from national headquarters in New York that we were competing with the accounting fraternity. We tried the other members of the Big Eight, and, quite obviously, they all turned us down.

After that, the lawyer backed off and the underwriter backed off, so our underwriting fell apart. In the meantime the company grew tremendously. We were growing at a 100 percent rate or more a year. So we put the offering off, and when we had our public offering a year later—February 13, 1962—we sold just a small part of the company. We did what they call a "Reg. A" (Regulation A) filing, where we sold 75,000 shares at $4. And we kept most of the company to ourselves.

Canceling that first underwriting made my brother and me a tremendous amount of money. Letting us keep most of the company and also keeping it for another year was our third big break!

If you had bought 100 shares at that initial offering at $4 a share, back in 1962—we paid a nickel a share dividend that first year—for that $400 investment you would have received $67,000 just in dividends since. If you had invested $10,000 in our stock, when we went public, the total value of the stock and dividends together would be over $12 million today.

We had eight splits so that you would now have 120 shares for each original share. We've raised our dividend every year—actually we doubled it in the last four years—and we think we've got a lot of growth ahead.

Our top line has kept growing since we have been in business—never a single down year. The total sales of the company, including our franchises, last year reached $1.98 billion. That's counting all revenues. Our profits have grown every year but one, and that one year, in 1972, our profit went down about 17 percent. But we've made money every year, including that one. And that decline turned out to be good news, too. There aren't many people who can look back at their only relatively weak year and say: "It's the best thing that could have happened to us."

We opened over a thousand new offices that year, 1972. A gentleman named Johnny M. Walters was the commissioner of Internal Revenue. He made a statement recommending that taxpayers should fill out their own returns, and if they had any questions they should contact the IRS. And he also stated that the tax forms were very simple to fill out and that even a fifth-grader could complete them. Many schools around the country tried to teach their fifth-graders that year how to fill out a tax return. Well, the kids couldn't do it, of course.

The reason Mr. Walters suggested that people should not go for tax help was that this industry was unregulated. There were a lot of preparers who shouldn't have been in it. Anybody could put out a shingle and offer to fill out your tax return. He didn't have to be able to read or write. There was no regulation. Today it is a regulated industry. I think he did the right thing.

Because of his suggestion, most of the people in the industry went out of business. We ended up pretty much being the whole industry, having all the business to ourselves. So even though we were temporarily hurt, the long-term result of the 1972 drop in earnings was a steadily growing flow of future earnings.

We did not end up dominating the industry—we ended up being the industry. Today we do 13.7% of all the returns in the United States. If you ask me who is the second largest company and how much they are doing, I don't know. The gap must be enormous. In Canada we do, I think, about 12.3% of all tax returns, so we have a similar position in Canada.

There are companies that do computerized tax preparation for the accounting industry, but that's a totally different business.

We're going to computerize half of our offices in 1991-92. In the past, we've always done the returns by hand. We've done surveys among our customers: Would they prefer a computerized return or one done by hand; they have no preference. However, we think it would be an improvement to computerize.

Income tax is normally the largest expenditure in a person's lifetime. And one thing we know about our clients: they want to file a correct return; they don't want to be audited by the IRS. They don't want to get into any trouble, and they feel that it's good to have somebody else's name on their tax return. It's too easy to make a mistake, to forget something.

Then, of course, you have the tax laws, which keep changing. We have a House Ways & Means Committee, and it has a mission: its mission is to change taxes. If they never changed the tax laws, they wouldn't be doing a good job.

Every time Congress "simplifies the taxes," it helps our business. They've been changing them so much and so often—and then changing them back again—that the average person gets confused. Let's look at long-term capital gains: the holding period used to be 6 months. It was then changed to 9 months, 12 months, and back again to 6 months. Another case in point is the investment tax credit. It has been changed 10 or 15 times.

Our business has many advantages. We have a low charge and we have a very wide geographic spread, because we're in every city of 5,000 or more. We have no accounts receivable and we have no inventory. Another one of our main advantages is that we get a lot of repeat business from old customers.

When we look for a company to acquire, we won't buy one that doesn't have a repeat business. I think that's the most important thing.

We ask every new customer, when he comes to our offices: "What attracted you to Block?" And he will say that he saw our sign or our ad on television or that his neighbor recommended us. A very substantial part of our new business comes from referrals. And each year at the start of the tax season we send our clients a letter that encourages them to return.

Many businessmen feel sorry for us, because we are seasonal. Actually, it's one of the biggest advantages we have. We begin January 1 and we finish on April 15. After April 15, we start to call meetings, a lot of meetings: we get our people together, we look at last year and discuss what didn't work well, what were the mistakes, what needs to be improved. This office should be moved, those supplies should be changed, and so on. We have the luxury of being out of business for eight and a half months; we can examine our company and make improvements. We start a new business every year—and each year can bring a lot of improvements.

We get ideas from all over the country. A very simple one comes to mind; it happened 20 or 30 years ago. At one large meeting we were discussing the problem that our clients were mailing the federal return in the envelopes addressed to the state, and vice versa. Somebody held up his hand and said: "Why don't we print the state envelopes in green? So we could tell the people: mail your state return in the green envelope." Little things like this.

We know that when you start filing your tax return you're generally in high school or just out of high school. So we give gift certificates to high school graduates at Christmas time, which is right before income tax time, and we say: "We will prepare your return free of charge." We do over 100,000 high school seniors' returns. Their return obviously very simple, but doing it with us gets them into the habit. Having your tax returns prepared by a professional is a habit. If you don't start doing it yourself, you probably never will.

❄

We've had 36 great years. Where do we stand now? In the past year that ended in April '91, despite the slowdown in the economy, our company registered an increase in both revenues and earnings. The number of taxpayers served worldwide is over 17 million. We filed over 5 million returns electronically.

There are some proposals circulating in Congress that could result in tax law changes, some of which are designed to lessen the burden of middle-class income taxpayers and others of which are aimed at stimulating the economy. In the past, tax legislation has generally created taxpayer confusion and thereby helped our business.

One reason for our success is that H&R Block charges relate solely to the number and complexity of forms and schedules in the return. The charge does not vary with the size of the client's income, his tax refund, or the time involved.

Since we have been in business, the average charge for income tax preparation worldwide rose from the original $5.00 to $49.60.

We have close to 9,000 offices around the world, nearly half of them company owned; the balance are franchised. In the United States, Canada, and Australia we are the largest participant. In most other countries—for example, in Europe and in the few offices we have outside of Europe, like the Far East, we are primarily preparing U.S. returns for citizens living abroad.

There is a lot of room left for future growth. We diversified into a number of other, successful businesses, and as far as our tax business goes, some 53% of U.S. taxpayers still prepare their own returns!

We are not as interested in the returns already being prepared by CPAs and attorneys. Our question is: Who is there to provide superlative service to the millions of taxpayers who get their help now from local, less experienced, mom and pop shops, and, mainly, to the millions who still prepare their own income returns? We would like to do it!

134

✳

H&R Block's first public offering was in Kansas City. When on August 11, 1966, the company had its second, larger offering on Wall Street, very few people recognized its attractiveness. The size of this second offering had to be cut back from a planned 300,000 shares to 200,000.

Most analysts and potential investors were disturbed by a company that earned all its income during a three-and-a-half-month period and lost money during the rest of the year. They did not understand that the loss simply meant more money spent on organization, preparation, tax schools, and improved procedures for the next years.

One customer told me that if I annualized the last nine months' losses, I'll find that the stock is selling at 40 times losses!

There is only one fallacy bigger than figuring a growth stock's price/earnings ratio on the basis of past earnings, whether that be fiscal year, calendar year, or last 12 months, and that is trying to annualize a seasonal business. A growth stock's price/earnings ratio should be figured on an extremely well-researched estimate for the next 12 months (or, in a very few cases, on even longer-term estimates). My customer doubled the error: not only did he use past figures, but he also tried to annualize a seasonal business.

✳

What did we learn about H&R Block? Let's summarize:

1. Although very few investors recognized it, H&R Block was that relatively rare company ripe enough to be bought when it first hit Wall Street (first major offering, even if technically a "secondary").

2. Its growth record was totally unbroken: up to the offering, every year produced all-time-high sales and earnings.

3. In a mom and pop industry, the company created one well-organized corporation. Ever since, it has dominated the industry.

4. Although its management does not consider the company recession resistant, it has an enviable record—36 straight years of sales growth, all but one of which also reported increased per share earnings.

5. The company is the classic example of the "ever-growing repeat-order factor." Historically, of every 100 clients, an average of 72 return the following year. As a number of them bring along a few friends and relatives, and as 72 of every 100 friends and relatives return and bring their friends and relatives, the possibility for continued growth is almost endless.

6. The company is also a perfect example of the "cookie cutter factor." Two brothers started a service business in Kansas City, established in it a well-thought-out routine, and found that they could repeat the same routine in New York City; in Columbia, Missouri; and in Topeka, Kansas. What works in 4 cities may also work in another 40 or 400 or 4,000 locations.

❋

What did I personally learn from my experience with Automatic Data Processing and H&R Block?

I learned the fallacy of Wall Street's "You Can't Go Broke by Taking Profits" principle. These stocks ran up sharply and I took a little profit; when they ran up again, I took a little more profit; and so on and so on, until I totally sold out both positions.

Cashing in on your winners makes you feel good, but keeps you poor—especially if, at the same time, you let your losers run.

As a young broker I was eager to take profits—and there was no one to explain why I shouldn't. It needed substantially more than a decade of additional experiences, of additional mistakes, to realize that as long as a company's incoming orders keep growing and as long as it meets our other criteria, I should hold on to it.

❄

From the H&R Block Scrapbook

A very-well-dressed woman came to the Block Executive Tax Service in Denver and tried to convince our consultant that her first three husband-hunting trips to Europe should be deductible as gambling losses. To be fair, she said, she didn't plan to deduct the fourth trip, since it was successful.

In Boston, our tax consultant received the shock of his life when his very pretty young client asked him sweetly if she could take off her clothes. It turned out that she was an airline hostess and was thinking of deducting her uniforms.

In Pine Bluff, Arkansas, a couple said they were entitled to a $400 deduction for home repairs, and an additional $187 for medical expenses. Seems their outhouse collapsed with a neighbor inside!

SURGICAL CARE AFFILIATES (SCAF)

Try to Please Everyone!

For the first four years the stock had its ups and downs—more downs than ups. In early 1986, it dropped to below $.80, and, at the bottom of the 1987 collapse, it dropped again to the equivalent of $1.29 (adjusted for all subsequent splits). By late October of 1991, SCAF moved to $43.25. In roughly four years: up more than 33 times!

Using traditional measures, the stock seems to be totally overpriced—but by those same measures, it seemed overpriced when it was selling at a quarter of today's price.

How did this happen? For explanation, let's turn to one of the most engaging businessmen you will ever meet.

Joel Gordon, founder:

My father was a Polish immigrant who came to this country in the early 1900s and served in the American Army in World War I. He ended up settling in Crofton, Kentucky, a small mining community in western Kentucky with a population of 650 people and no paved streets or running water, where he operated a general store. It wasn't a big business. He and my mother ran it seven days a week, from 5 in the morning till 9 at night—and the most business they ever did was $65,000 per year. That wasn't what they made; that was the most business they ever did in a year.

I was an only child, and attended Crofton High School that had only 55 students totally in grades 9 through 12. My graduation class numbered 12. All during my high school days, I had to work in the store on weekends and after school.

I happened to be a pretty good athlete, and on graduation was offered a basketball scholarship to the University of Kentucky. At Kentucky I earned a B.S. in management. In college, one of my close friends was Robert Fraiman, who later had a major influence on my life. He became a member of the New York Stock Exchange, a member of the Board of Governors—and a partner in a specialist firm.

Bob kept suggesting that we should go into business together. He thought he could raise the money if I came up with the idea. We decided to enter the nursing home business.

I recruited two associates and we incorporated General Care Corp. A public offering to build and operate nursing homes was scheduled. Ladenburg raised $1,800,000 in February of 1970. General Care built five nursing homes, but after a couple of years we realized that the nursing home industry was a much less attractive business than we had thought.

I had several physician friends in the medical community in Nashville, and they encouraged the company to convert its operations to acute care hospitals. The physicians suggested that we should convert the Nashville nursing home with 250 beds into an acute care hospital—and they wanted to be equity owners in the hospital.

This was the beginning of joint ventures with physicians. Doctors had owned many hospitals previously, but General Care was the first public company to joint venture hospitals with doctors. The physicians owned 49 percent and General Care owned 51 percent. We managed the business operations and the physicians directed the medical decisions. It took us about 15 months to convert the nursing home to General Care's first acute care hospital. The converted West Side Hospital in Nashville was an immediate success.

The reason the hospital performed so well was that the physicians had the ability to determine the type medicine they wanted to practice, the type of equipment needed, determine who were the best personnel to hire—and they were totally involved in structuring and operating the facility.

The company sold the remaining nursing homes and over five years built 11 acute care hospitals in Tennessee, Alabama, Georgia, and Florida. In 1980, General Care Corp. was acquired by Hospital Corporation of America (HCA) in a transaction with a value in excess of $100,000,000. The stock had traded as low as $2 in 1973—and when acquired by HCA the comparable price, after splits, was $117 per share.

That format served General Care very well, and I developed a lot of expertise in working with doctors. After HCA acquired General Care, I began to look around to see in which direction health care was headed and determined it was going to an emphasis on

139

outpatient care rather than inpatient. I decided to enter a new arena: outpatient surgery.

I got together with Andrew (Woody) Miller, who had been the president of Hospital Corporation Management Company, a subsidiary of HCA, and Woody and I formed Surgical Care Affiliates. We acquired three outpatient surgery centers and used the format that I've been successful with before; we decided to have joint venture limited partners in each of our facilities.

The company was incorporated in October of 1982. SCA began to look for facilities to acquire that had physician involvement, had been profitable, and represented quality medical care. We located two in Kentucky and one in Texas—and in June 1983, we acquired the three centers.

Thomas Frist, Jr., founder and chairman of HCA, was a good friend, and HCA invested in Surgical Care. It guaranteed a $6,000,000 line of credit and invested $2,000,000 start-up capital in the company. HCA owned 17% of Surgical Care Affiliates after the public offering—but sold their interest in 1988, when management took the company private. Nashville venture capitalist and HCA co-founder, Jack C. Massey, came in for another 10%.

I invested $240,000 in the original capitalization of SCA. I was making a venture investment at the time and planned to be chairman of the board, but did not want day-to-day responsibilities. It didn't work out that way. I got more and more involved on a full-time basis, and it has been a most rewarding and satisfying experience.

With Ladenburg, Thalmann's help, SCA raised about $15,000,000 in January 1984. Much of the credit must go to Carl "Buddy" Erpf, then chairman of Ladenburg, who was most supportive of our efforts and helped me develop the idea of an outpatient surgery company.

In SCA centers, the surgeons are able to reserve a block of time to schedule operations to follow other cases; their schedules aren't interrupted by emergencies, as they are sometimes in the hospital. Patients like the atmosphere because it is much friendlier. The payors like it because the cost is substantially lower than in the hospital.

SCA helps control health care expenses by offering a rare combination of high-quality medicine and lower costs. We charge less than the hospitals do for either an inpatient or an outpatient. Most of the procedures are nonemergency, low-risk, low-cost surgery, but during the last two years more complex surgical

SURGICAL CARE AFFILIATES, INC.
Summary of Financial Statistics, December 31, 1983–1991
(Dollars in thousands except per share)

Years Ended December 31	Revenue	Pretax Income	Earnings per Share
1983	$ 1,689	$ (550)	$(0.06)
1984	5,219	(568)	(0.02)
1985	13,267	(779)	(0.03)
1986	22,977	480	0.01
1987	35,049	1,959	0.05
1988	52,968	5,407	0.11
1989	82,157	10,111	0.19
1990	123,770	19,156	0.32
1991	170,295	33,672	0.57

procedures are moving to an outpatient setting—surgery that was not offered on an outpatient basis until recently. New medical technology will help SCA grow even faster.

Daniel E. Bruhl, M.D., eye surgeon, Fort Worth, Texas:

We put together a surgical center with 20 to 30 doctors. I was the president. We didn't have any financial people helping us; we just kind of muddled our way through. We financed it with an industrial revenue bond, obtained a "Certificate of Need" that was required in the state of Texas, and got the building finished.

We were ready to open our doors and start operating—and out of the blue, Joel Gordon gets wind of this through some friends of his and calls one night at ten o'clock:

"Hi, I'm Joel Gordon in Nashville, Tennessee. We've got this idea—the same as you—that this is a timely concept and we have two other surgery centers in Louisville and Lexington. They have been developed similarly to yours. We are soliciting your center: let's put the three together, along with some venture capital—and form a company that we can later take public."

That's the way it started.

Joel Gordon:

We don't want to go to New York or Massachusetts because it is extremely difficult to obtain a "Certificate of Need," and we don't

141

Figure 7-3 Surgical Care Affiliates Chart from 1987–1991

Courtesy of William O'Neil & Co., Inc.

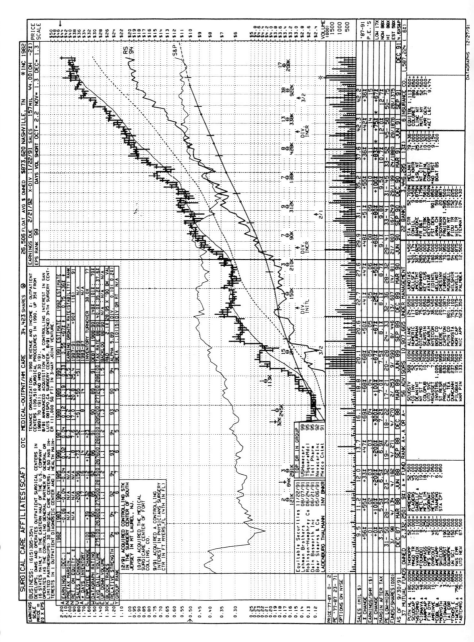

142

plan to go to Montana, the Dakotas, and other places where the population is so small—but other than that, we intend to open in about 40 states. We can be successful in any town that has 75,000 in population or more.

We get a lot of repeat business—from the doctor, from the insurance company, and from the satisfied patient—but our most important source is the doctor. We will keep growing for a very, very long time. Back in 1983, 4% of all surgery was performed in free-standing centers. Now it is about 20%, and because we are doing more and more rather complicated surgery, the procedure cost and the profit potential are moving up.

SCA has produced sequentially 24 straight quarters of increased earnings. And now we plan to move into the recovery care area. These are attached to our surgery centers and help to provide the setting for new, less invasive surgery.

SCA is one of the two largest companies in the industry. By now everyone wants to get into the business—which is good because it stimulates, from the acquisition point of view, a lot of interest from physicians who want their centers to be acquired. We are comfortable with the way things are going for us and expect to add eight to ten centers a year. I would think in five years we will be a $500,000,000 company.

Ken Melkus, president:

I was developing a health maintenance organization in Nashville. In 1984, Joel Gordon and Woody Miller, the two founders of Surgical Care, called me and asked for a meeting. I guess it was kind of love at first sight. They invited me to join their company and extended me an offer to have some of the founders' stock. I was flattered and accepted.

If you go back and track our record, in 1986 and 1987 we slowed down, because we realized that we didn't have the kind of operational systems and discipline that would generate the earnings we needed. It's one thing to create units and another to develop and operate them profitably. We needed to focus on the latter. Taking the time and developing the discipline really benefited us: if we acquire a center now, we can integrate it into the company and teach them our methods without a hitch.

The industry is booming—and the competitors are not the other public companies in the business, or any private companies that

143

intend to get into surgery center business: the competitors are the local hospitals. And the hospitals continue to be plagued with problems, with inefficiencies, with administrative slippage. This provides us with an opportunity: we can take advantage of the fact that we offer higher quality at a lower cost. And as long as we're able to do so, we will continue to grow.

The hospitals are still doing the majority of outpatient surgery, but we are becoming far more appealing to the insurance companies and managed care companies that shop for the business.

Another thing that is working for us is the fast development of technology. It allows physicians to expand the number of procedures, doing more surgery and more complex surgery.

The third thing that helps us is that when we have been in existence in a community for several years, people start to consider us a mainstream player in the health care system: they realize they don't have to worry about whether the facility is going to be there in the next several years.

All these factors contributed to our steady growth, along with aggressive marketing of our centers. We work very hard to be physician friendly, to let each one know how he or she can benefit from utilizing a surgery center and how his or her patients can benefit from using the surgery center. When we bring in new physicians, they are absolutely amazed at the efficiency and at the environment that we offer their patients and their patients' families. This cannot be replicated in the hospital environment.

We have developed a very effective prototype: we have spent tremendous amounts of time and resources to make sure that the way the surgery center is laid out, the patient flow, the physicians' workplace area, the access to the sterile areas, and the way in which patients are discharged should be functional, but also efficient, warm and personal. We are now able to roll that prototype out and to do it in a very cost-effective way. We make very few changes when we go from one market to another, because we have a physical structure and an equipment program that have been proven successful.

We also standardized all our administrative systems; the average days of revenues in accounts receivable are an unbelievably low 35 days, which I would challenge anybody in the health care field to match.

❊

The amount of business, in terms of the procedures that can be done, ambulatory, is rapidly increasing. You've got a situation where—from an economic perspective—each unit is like a hotel or an airplane. The more rooms you fill, the more seats you fill—in this case, the more procedures you perform—the closer you get to the break-even point. Sixty percent of the costs associated with a surgery center are nonvariable, so the situation is highly leveraged. When you get above the break-even point, your earnings expand rapidly.

You've got restricted entry into the industry, because in most of the states where the company operates, you have to receive a "Certificate of Need" to open up a facility. This is a difficult and time consuming process.

Surgical Care Affiliates meets the present-day guidelines regarding physician ownership. Now just try to imagine a bunch of doctors who own a facility, and own too high a percentage of it. They don't meet the guidelines. They probably will decide to sell the surgery center—and guess who is going to be there to buy it. There may be more and more units coming to the market ready to be acquired. SCA has the capital, the systems, and the management team to complete the transaction, integrate the center into SCA, make it grow, and improve its performance.

Unless the fundamentals change a lot, SCAF should continue to do very well.

❄

After Mr. Gordon's first company, General Care Corp., went public, the stock did not do well. But he was up to the challenge and developed the company to a point where, at its acquisition by Hospital Corporation of America, the stockholders had an enormous profit.

When Surgical Care Affiliates went public, many investors remembered the General Care Corp. experience. Joel Gordon had a lot of admirers, and a lot of credibility. Investors were clamoring to get the stock.

It's easy to say in retrospect that the stock was overpriced at $14. After the offering, it dropped to $7.50. The revenues did grow, but the earnings were less than spectacular. Then, by the end of 1987, management learned how to run the company and the leverage started to kick in. During the first quarter of 1988, sales increased 56%, the following quarter 33%, and the next quarter 47%. In the same three quarters, earnings tripled, went up 143%, and then 121%. For the full year, revenues increased 51%, earnings 166%; facility operating margins increased from 24% to 31%! For the second consecutive year, the board of directors approved a five-for-four stock split. (It doesn't cost the company anything, but stockholders like it.) SCAF announced that it is accelerating the development and acquisition program. Two new centers were ready to open during the next six months, and SCAF held negotiations with several acquisition candidates.

The stock started to fly! During the months since the November 1987 collapse, the price had already nearly doubled. Now it really went wild. How many other companies do you know that have seen their price increase roughly 33-fold in four years?

❋

Where does Surgical Care Affiliates stand now? It doesn't stand. It is moving—fast. During 1991, net revenues increased 38%, net income 80%, per share earnings up 78%. During the last quarter of 1991, the respective increases were 37%, 89%, and 89%—with surgical cases growing 25% over the previous year.

Industry analysts project that outpatient surgery will grow to approximately 60% of all surgery performed, while freestanding centers should continue to develop faster than hospital-based units.

❋

Should you buy SCAF?

I'm still nibbling at it, but that means adding to an already sizable position. I am buying some of it for new clients, too. Obviously, I think for the very-long-term investor there is still a possibility for substantial appreciation. For the short-term player; the stock has been overpriced for a long time. And if you are a short-term player, I can't help you anyway. That is not my business.

And yes, there is always the danger of stricter legislation. Trying to please everyone—and actually pleasing everyone—worked well. Up to now. But the "I wouldn't want a procedure done in a center that's partially owned by my surgeon" principle may win in the long run, even if it's not always logical. Whether it is or not, sooner or later the emotional issue may be decisive.

As always, rather than putting substantial amounts into companies that have been already discovered—and Surgical Care Affiliates certainly has been discovered—I think you should analyze the example and then go out and try to find the next Surgical Care Affiliates.

HealthCare
COMPARE Corporation (HCCC):

How Not to Lose Customers!

HealthCare COMPARE Corp. is America's leading independent provider of healthcare cost management
services. Our COMPARE division provides medical
services utilization review and our AFFORDABLE division negotiates fixed price contracts with medical providers in order to develop and maintain preferred
provider networks for the exclusive use of our clients.
Together, we achieve significant healthcare cost savings for our clients... without compromising the quality of care, or freedom of choice of healthcare plan
participants.

—1990 Annual Report

That quote is quite a mouthful, isn't it? But it is easy
to translate it into very simple English—"utilization" review
means saving very big money for insurance companies,
self-insured corporations, and giant unions. "Fixed price
contracts" means saving even more money for the same.

Since the 1987 stock market collapse HCCC's price
is up 20 times. Why? If you save your customers money,
most of them will stay with you practically forever. You
sign up more and more customers; you spread to more and
more states.

Does this sound like Automatic Data Processing and
H&R Block all over? You bet! Again: the combination of
the ever-growing repeat-order rate and the cookie cutter
factor.

❋

What do you do if you are a 60-year-old physician
with a terrific practice in a highly appreciative community? You probably decide that it's time to take it a little
easier and play more golf. At 65 you may even retire.

HealthCare COMPARE Corp.
Summary of Financial Statistics, June 30, 1982–1991
(dollars in thousands except per share)

Years Ended June 30	Revenue	Pretax Income	Earnings per Share
1982	$ 0	$ (183)	$(0.03)
1983	0	(304)	(0.05)
1984	39	(664)	(0.12)
1985	1,354	(828)	(0.15)
1986	5,535	576	0.05
1987	11,603	1,988	0.09
1988	20,829	3,794	0.13
1989	31,458	4,079	0.08
1990	42,238	8,234	0.23
1991	70,910	20,292	0.50

Not if your name is Dr. Bob Becker! He believed he saw serious flaws in the way medicine was being practiced, and he decided to do something about it. At age 60, Dr. Becker took everything he owned and put it on the line, starting a new company that he believed would help to correct the flaws. And at age 65 he took the company public.

Robert J. Becker, M.D., founder:

I was an allergist in Joliet, Illinois, for 26 years. It grew into a very successful practice with a lot of employees; we practiced good medicine. I got bored, so I became involved in many different medical societies and associations. I didn't think physicians were terribly cost efficient, nor very cost effective; they were not accepting the idea of accountability, and I felt that was wrong.

In California there were a couple of foundations that had contracted to do utilization reviews—inpatient, and outpatient—a concept that was new and innovative. I started a similar foundation in Joliet, but we didn't get too far.

I recognized that the health care industry had a major problem and that was the lack of cost efficiency, and the general philosophy that more is better, that more medical care is better! As a physician I know that that is not always true. First I tried to address the

Figure 7-4 HealthCare Compare Chart from 1987–1991

Courtesy of William O'Neil & Co., Inc.

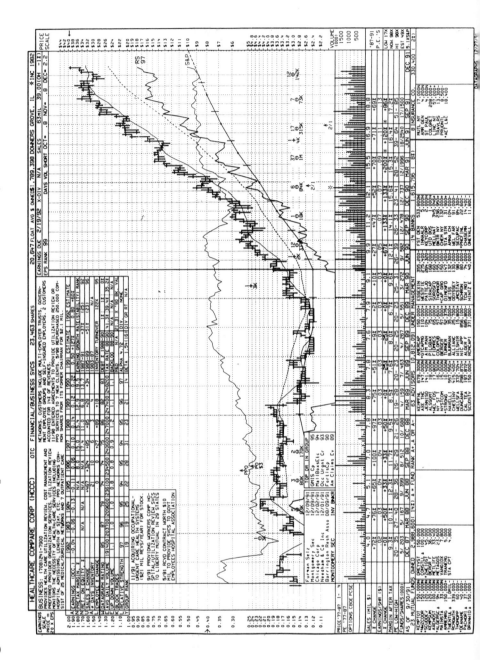

150

problems through several organizations, but in the early '80s I decided that what had to be done was to look at it privately, personally, with my own effort. On June 1, 1982, I started Health-Care COMPARE—two days after my 60th birthday.

I sold my practice and I sold the building. Everything I had—my IRA, my Keogh plan, mortgaged my home, used up all the securities I had. And the bank that lent me the money even asked for the key of my safe deposit box. I gave it to the vice president who approved the loan. Next day, the bank president tells me: "There are two keys to this box. I want the other key, too." I learned very fast what an entrepreneur is: a person who exchanges security for total insecurity.

The big problem in health care at that time was the expense of hospitalization. So we started with a process of preadmission hospital review. There were some major horror stories, where physicians owned nursing homes and took patients out of the nursing homes into hospitals to do hysterectomies and other surgical procedures, took them back into the nursing homes again, and charged a great deal of money. They took advantage of the patient, and they wasted Medicare and Medicaid dollars. Health care was consuming at that time about $400 billion, about 8% of the GNP, and no one seemed to have any idea how to control it and how to reduce the costs.

The equation, as always, was: price times volume equals costs. If HealthCare COMPARE was to be successful, we had to address all those issues. But we had to do it a bite at a time. The first step was the hospital review, the preadmission review—to which we added continued screen review and second opinion. The second part of the equation came in later.

Nobody knew what utilization review was. We had to explain to them and convince the potential customers that we can save them money and, meanwhile maintain the quality of the care. It took us a year and a half to sign up the first client—CNA Insurance Company.

One of my first clients spent about $150,000 and saved $7,000,000 the first year.

Didn't save that much in subsequent years, because the utilization review creates a "cop and radar" situation. You establish the radar and you catch a lot of speeders—but after a while you catch fewer and fewer speeders; what you are doing is maintaining the fact that everyone has to obey the speed limits. That's exactly what *happened. We caught a lot of speeders; we had to correct a lot of bad practice habits. What we do now is that we make sure that the good habits continue.*

Physicians have on the whole modified their practice patterns. They became much more efficient and effective. Not perfect, but much better.

A few years ago physicians claimed that practice patterns are local. What is appropriate in one part of the country in medical care is not appropriate for the rest of the country. Well, that attitude has changed, and we have been one of the forces that have driven home the concept: the same medical care is appropriate everywhere. Standards of medical care became nationalized—which has given us the opportunity to replicate our services all across the country.

But I am getting way ahead of myself.

What an entrepreneur needs in addition to guts is persistence. I put in $900,000, that was everything I owned after 26 years of practice. We had to find some venture capitalists to back us. Most venture capitalists told us that they do not want to invest in services; they needed inventory, products, not services. That was in '83 or '84.

At one point it got very rough. In February of 1984, I was having difficulty coming up with a payroll, never mind coming up with payroll taxes. I mentioned it to a friend called Mel Garb. Mel knew what we were doing and lent me $100,000, simply on my signature. When you talk about the success of a company, people like Mel don't get mentioned—but where would we, or many other young companies be, without the Mel Garbs? Today he is a member of our board and his $100,000 was converted to common stock. He has done very well.

A very good lawyer friend of mine, Ron Galowich, worked for the Pritzkers. He introduced me to them.

Tom Pritzker, chairman; president of Hyatt Corporation:

One day we had a meeting regarding Hyatt's health benefit costs. They were growing at an unacceptably fast rate, and when I asked what we can do about it, no one had any good ideas. It was very frustrating. A day or two later, I got a call from Ron

152

Galowich, one of our lawyers, and he suggested that I talk to a friend of his, who is in the utilization review business; I didn't know what utilization review was.

I met Bob Becker several times, and he described the business. For the time being he was doing it as an individual, financing it by putting a mortgage on his home and so on. I came to the conclusion that if we were going through this increase of medical expenses at Hyatt, everybody else had to be going through the same. If we would get involved in this business, we could save some money for Hyatt—and in addition we would make enough money so I wouldn't have to feel guilty about how much we were spending here.

I told Dr. Becker that he should find a partner for operations. And for sales. He came back with Jim Smith—and Jim Smith returned two weeks later with a plan. He had a $2,000,000 budget. After a few meetings, we put together our share of the amount and off we went. We got very lucky; it worked well.

We had a good combination of skills. Bob Becker thoroughly understands every angle of the medical part; Jim is a very disciplined, capable businessman.

Deep down I think that Bob and Jim are real heroes: they've seen a great demand and they built from the ground floor a way of solving, of answering that demand and creating a great business.

Dr. Becker:

A group of people put together $2,000,000. I think a quarter of it was equity, the rest was a loan. Half of the total came from the Pritzkers. The venture capitalists let us, that is, Jim Smith, Ron Galowich, and me, retain 38% of the company—which I think was very generous.

We were in the right place at the right time. That was the beginning of all the rumbling about health care costs. Our first employees were in their late twenties or early thirties, with some experience in health care. Some were nurses. We had also a number of sales and marketing people who had an understanding of health care. A great percentage of those employees are still with us.

Things went well, but we needed additional funds. We went public in the spring of '87. The underwriting was on my 65th birthday. Really, life begins at 65!

153

In 1989 I decided to retire. My personality is that of an architect rather than of a contractor. I enjoyed the challenge, the kind that I used to get at COMPARE, but now it had become a much larger company.

Leaving the company gave me the opportunity to face some interesting challenges, find some new opportunities out there. Maybe at 75 I'll start another company. Or maybe before.

Jim Smith, president and chief executive officer:

I had just sold a group of businesses and decided to take a year or two off and go sailing. Ron Galowich, a business friend, asked me if I would do him a favor and meet a friend of his and help him put together a business plan, so that they could raise venture capital.

I met Bob Becker, spent a few days with him and the people he had working for him, and pulled together what I understood to be the business possibilities into a plan. And then went back to prepare my sailing years.

A couple of weeks later Ron called and indicated that they had shown the plan to some venture capital folks, who seemed to be interested—but wanted me to come and explain the numbers. So I did, and while explaining it, I got really more and more drawn into what looked to be a promising business. Some of the venture capitalists also told me that they would like me to stick around and run the business.

The Pritzkers decided, sort of at the last minute, to come in, but their investment was the key because it helped us get off the ground. They've always stayed in the background, but provided us help, advice, and support whenever we needed it, and have been wonderful partners.

The original plan was that we will provide hospital review services. When we started to get a bit of business in that, we broadened the scope and added a utilization review service, which focused on just about every major medical provider segment in the marketplace.

Utilization review could be defined as a series of activities, which, on behalf of the payers, oversees provision of medical services to the patients. Hospital review is one of those services.

154

A major unnecessary expense is admitting the patient too early or keeping him in too long—and doing procedures which don't have to be done in a hospital at all. We supply second surgical opinion, management for long-term cases, chiropractic review, and pharmacy review. We try to reduce the cost everywhere.

Initially, the greatest concentration of business available to us came from small- and medium-sized group health insurance companies. We signed up 27 or 28 of them; they provided our growth the first couple of years.

We became highly regarded as a service institution—and we turned our focus on developing opportunities on a more direct basis. We started selling to Fortune 500 companies and to large self-insured unions. At that time it wasn't uncommon for an employer who had something like 900 hospital patient days for 1,000 covered people to see that average get down with our help to less than 600 days per 1,000.

In addition to Fortune 500 companies and large unions, we also went after federal employees. We focused heavily on these three areas and we succeeded very well. The first major federal employee group we had was the Mail Handlers Benefit Plan.

We knew that although we're doing a good job and supplying a good set of cost management tools, we weren't providing to our clients a total solution. In addition to controlling the volume, we also had to try to control price. We decided to look around for a good acquisition in the PPO (preferred provider organization) field.

We checked several companies and decided to concentrate on Affordable. It was a California-based company with an excellent reputation and was around longer than anybody else we found. We acquired it on June 3, 1988.

We were successful in cross-marketing the client base that we had in utilization review into PPOs.

Most of our clients said, "We like what they've done in California; if you go ahead and develop contracts for the rest of the country, you can count on us: we will use them!"

We went through a period of heavy development expenses which showed up as operating losses for that year. That was one year only. And the top line kept growing.

Affordable's in the business of negotiating fixed price contracts with hospitals, physicians, and other medical providers, which we then offer to our clients. For example, with a hospital we negotiate a single, fixed, all-inclusive per diem (daily fee). That includes all *the expenses that one is typically charged for during a stay in the hospital.*

We negotiate those rates based on the strengths of the business that we have amalgamated. Today that represents about $11 billion in medical charges on a national basis.

It's not enough to be a good negotiator and have all your data straight. You also have to have the power of business buying and to be attractive enough to the hospital administrator or the medical group or the physician or the other medical providers so that they want to make sure they get your business. We tell everyone how many people and how many dollars we represent in that marketplace, and we make it clear that we are prepared to assist our people to use one medical provider in preference to another one.

Obviously medical providers, when they offer us advantageous rates, do so because they want to increase their market share, or they want to protect what they already have. This includes hospitals, doctors, radiology centers, labs, and surgery centers, and we are now looking at pharmaceutical charges.

When we acquired Affordable, they were essentially in a couple of western states; we are going to be this year in 45 or 46 states. We will have roughly a thousand hospitals under contract. We established a national network of PPO providers, which puts us into a unique selling position when we approach anyone who is large and has employees or insureds scattered across the country. We generally have the only good solution for these folks.

In the last year and a half, we found that we could leverage our good rates and broad networks to interested workers' comp payers. It is becoming a very important niche.

❊

Our investor customers have a very substantial position in a company called Occupational Urgent Care Health (commonly known as OUCH from its NASDAQ symbol—OUCH, like the sound you make if someone pinches you), specializing in workers' comp. One week after this conversation with Jim Smith, we found out that the two companies had decided to merge. Obviously, the acquisition of Affordable gave great synergy to both companies, and I expect that the merger with OUCH will do the same.

＊

The greatest stimulus to the growth of our business is the rapid inflation of medical costs and the payers' desire to reduce that cost. We are doing well in good times and bad times, but it's quite clear that when the economy is poor, it provides even more of a stimulus to employers, insurance companies, and others to find a way to cut back expenses. They will reach out and find folks like us in any type of economy, but their search will get more intense when the economy is bad. So if anything, we benefit from a down economy.

HealthCare COMPARE has an exceptionally high client retention rate, and we are very proud of it. Our services are triggered by one of our client's employees, members, or insureds requiring medical service. Within a given population, there is a certain expectation how regularly that will occur, so from a year-to-year standpoint we have a built-in repeat-order factor. As long as we provide good service to our clients, we believe we will be able to retain most of them.

There are two dimensions to our nationwide growth. One is that we've gone from one market to the next and the next from coast to coast. We negotiated contracts with medical providers all over the country. The second dimension is that when sets of contracts are done—we define them as networks, for instance the Chicago network or the Dallas network—we are in position to sell that network to major clients. The fact that the population covered keeps growing gives us even more future negotiating power with the medical providers.

What ultimately can make us even more profitable is driven by our ability to sell the same network over and over again.

＊

Revenues and earnings in 1990 established new records in each quarter. Annual revenues increased 34%, net 183%.

Business Week ranked COMPARE as the best-performing over-the-counter stock in 1990. It succeeded in selling its PPO services to many of its large utilization review clients, expanded the hospital PPO network from 17 to 25, and expanded the outpatient care network into seven states. Its strategy has paid substantial dividends.

Many clients, which represent approximately 50% of the company's utilization review revenue, started to also use the company's PPO services. They include the National Association of Letter Carriers, State Farm Insurance, United Airlines, Montgomery Ward, McDonald's Corporation, American Postal Workers Union, and the Hyatt Hotels Corporation.

The company did exceptionally well during 1991. Revenues increased 68%, net income 131%, and earnings per share 117%. In the quarter ended December 31, 1991, the increases were 62%, 133%, and 113% respectively.

Not bad for a recession!

BMC SOFTWARE (BMCS)

You shouldn't get caught up in all of the gee-whiz technology that BMC has. Our basic business principles are not new and not particularly innovative on their own; they are innovative in that the mix of them works. Keep the profit motive: let the software author get some of it, let the salesman get some of it, and naturally the company deserves some of it.

Rick Hosley,
former president and vice chairman

BMC Software went public on August 12, 1988, offering 3 million shares at $9.

We considered it an interesting company with extremely fast-growing sales and earnings. But when we started our research, we ran into some problems.

1. Because of the high-tech nature of the business, the company's description included unfamiliar terminologies. We had to do some homework.

2. The per share earnings for the June 1986 quarter were flat.

3. The prospectus informed us that John J. Moores, the company's founder and chairman, was retiring from day-to-day operations and selling a substantial part of his holdings.

We didn't buy the stock at the initial offering. However, we did talk with the management several times and invited them to visit us and give us some education. After we learned more about the industry and after several conversations with management, we decided to start to buy the stock. We made our first purchase on July 25, 1989, and we had to pay $16 (adjusted for a subsequent split). Obviously, our delay was costly, but the reasoning,

I think, was sound. We didn't want to buy the stock until we really understood the company.

John J. Moores,

Software. Sugar Land, Tex. 47. Married, 2 children. Married high school sweetheart at 19; they went to law school together. Never practiced. Programming, marketing for IBM 1966–74. Started BMC Software 1980 to create systems software for IBM mainframes. Designed first few products himself. Key to success: "I guess I'm more in touch with my weaknesses or deficiencies than most people. I have an ability to recognize and admire people who are smarter than I am." Went public at $9 in 1988* recently over $50. Revenues rose over 50 percent in 1990, to $93 million. Homes: Colo., Calif.; collect vintage Corvettes, Ferraris, Mercedes. His 29%, other assets, worth $440 million.

Forbes 400, October 21, 1991.[†]

John J. Moores, founder:

I was 19 and took an aptitude test. The first thing I knew I ended up taking a course at IBM to become a programmer. I found out instantly that I liked it a lot; it was just fun. Programming came to me naturally and I ended up going to work for IBM.

When I was 26, I started law school. At IBM I was an instructor, a technical representative, a salesman. I had a broad background. I would have to say that I wasn't very successful as either a technical representative—what IBM called a systems engineer—or as a salesman. Writing programs, that's what I felt called on to do.

The sales background gave me one thing: working with customers gave me an enormous appreciation of the value of good

---

[*]Split 3 for 2 on 3/8/90.
[†]*Forbes'* list of the 400 wealthiest people in the United States.

salespeople, and it stuck with me. Without that, it would have been impossible to start BMC.

I left IBM in 1974 because they were not really happy with my going to law school. I joined Shell as a programmer. It was a great place to work: it gave me a chance to write lots and lots of programs there.

In about '77 a friend of mine, Bill Wise, a guy that I particularly admired, started a software company and he asked me if I had ever thought about writing commercial software. I said no. About two or three hours later—I remember driving down the freeway in an old truck of my father's—a little lightbulb went on. It hit me that in fact I did have a couple of ideas that should be very, very attractive to a lot of customers.

I went to the Shell management and told them: "Look, I want to write software and a friend of mine is going to market it. Do you have any problem with that?" Their response was: "Hey, we don't have any problems: we would just like to get a free copy of anything that you do." I said, "You got it."

Shell continued to get free products for a long time. They were quite happy with that, and so was I.

❊

I finally got my first product on the market: the 3270 Optimizer. An IBM 3270 terminal is a ubiquitous piece of office equipment. There are just hundreds of thousands of these things installed all over the world. Well, I figured out a way to shorten the time it takes to transmit a message from a mainframe computer to a terminal, so that if a response time at a terminal was 5 seconds, I could reduce it to maybe 3 seconds. The important thing to understand is that the product could be easily installed; it was transparent to the users and it had an immediate impact.

My buddy, Bill Wise, hired a salesman and we were fairly successful in selling the product to a lot of Fortune 500 kind of companies.

❊

In the summer of 1980, Wise decided to quit selling system software.

I started BMC Software, Inc., and instantly hired the oldest and best friend I ever had, a fellow I had known since I was a teenager:

161

Rick Hosley. He is one of the most remarkable guys I ever met. He was phenomenally successful as an IBM salesman and had incredible management instinct.

Hosley started recruiting salesmen who at IBM had sort of reached the peak of their career and didn't have anywhere to go. We had a better working environment; people could come in in blue jeans or shorts and get on the phone, contact 15 to 20 people a day, and end up making substantially more money than at IBM. He knew a lot of people and ended up recruiting no one but the very best, a staggering number of outstanding people from IBM.

They were selling the Optimizer. It had three important characteristics: (1) There was no competition. (2) It was intuitively obvious to the customer that there was a benefit to it: it will save him money from day one. (3) It was easy to install very quickly, so the user didn't have to do a lot of extra work.

We decided, if any new product didn't fit these three criteria, then we don't want to develop it.

When Rick Hosley joined us, we decided another thing. When we develop something new, it has to be a product that we can sell through the telephone and that we can support through the telephone.

Hosley handled the sales part of the business: he was very effective at recruiting and keeping a group of world-class salesmen with amazing performances; the turnover was very low.

I wanted this company to be the best company it could be. But somehow at the same time I never thought that it would become this successful. It was irrelevant. All I wanted to do was to work with the best people I could find. For a long time the last thing I thought about was taking the company public.

When we finally decided to do so, I gave every employee a stock option. It wasn't something that they negotiated for when I hired them. The reason that people came to work for us was sort of a quality of life issue, a chance to make much more money in a nice environment. The stock options that I gave them was a way of letting them know that we want them to participate in the success of the company.

Somewhere in 1987, it dawned on me that I probably shouldn't stay on as president and CEO; maybe somebody else could do a better job. So I talked to Hosley; I thought he was better equipped to do it than I.

＊

Rick Hosley worked very hard and he was very focused, which was fortunate for the company, because John was pretty loose—the creative guy. Rick was the type who was so focused that if he had a "to-do-list" there were probably only two things on it, but they both got done. The two of them were a good balance.

Max P. Watson, Jr.
president and CEO

Rick Hosley, former president:

BMC was started in the summer of 1980, incorporated in September of '80, and consisted basically of two people—John Moores, who was the president, and me, the first salesman, cook, and bottlewasher. We hired a secretary and a couple of programmers.

The first year's sales were under a million. When I left the company in October 1990, we had over 500 people, more than 100 of them in sales, and revenues were more than $100 million.

I figured out very quickly that I could make a lot more sales calls over the phone than in person. I didn't need to spend any more than 20 minutes with anybody describing the attributes of the product and how it would be installed.

We started calling people on the phone and trying to get them to install the product under something we called a "30 day free trial." In reality, it could last up to 6 months, as long as there was intent, on the prospect's side, to actually install and evaluate the product. It wasn't a stroke of genius; it was dictated by necessity. We just didn't have any money for me to travel, and I didn't want to allocate more than 20 minutes to anyone. This is how our telemarketing started.

A few years ago we did a study and took the most optimistic number we could get for a direct marketing organization that actually traveled door to door, and then we took the most pessimistic numbers for our sales force, and we determined we could make at least three times the number of telephone sales calls than direct, that is personal, sales calls. When we developed a 100-man sales force, we could effectively compete with at least a 300-man sales force doing direct marketing.

This approach limited the types of products we could develop—and this is one of the best things that could have happened to us. The product had to be almost immediately cost justified, user friendly (easy to install), and simple to describe on the telephone.

❋

We had a potential problem and that was the relationship between programmers and salesman. They are natural enemies. We were trying to figure out how to get these two groups to cooperate. We put in place a commission scheme that took care not only of the salesmen, which is typical, but also the software developers. The developers could earn an unusual amount of money, but only if their products sold. They had to get as close to the salesman as possible and stay attuned to what the customer wanted. On every program sold, the developer was paid a commission on a sliding scale rate over a six-year period: the first year 6% and the sixth and final year 1%. It kept their interest up—and their creative juices flowing.

❋

I always felt that we were the best company in the industry, because we did things differently. Our telemarketing approach enabled us to become a very powerful company in terms of sales call volume. Also, since this approach was a lot cheaper than actual direct visits, we were able to take a large portion of the revenue and plug it back into our R&D: 25% of every revenue dollar was put back into research.

There was a study done by Business Week a few years ago, and BMC came up number 1 among all software companies and number 7 in a survey of 1,000 companies in the United States. It showed that the ratio of R&D spending per employee has an almost 100% correlation with corporate profitability.

Everyone, experts in the industry and analysts on Wall Street, told us that when we got beyond $20 million in sales, telemarketing would not work anymore. This program not only outlasted all industry predictions, but it became the most copied program among all the mainframe software companies in the world: including Europe, Japan, Australia, and so on.

The way you make a sales force use telemarketing is simple: give them no budget for travel and entertainment, none. And don't give them enough salary to sit on their butts and effectively do nothing. BMC salespeople all over the world are using it and they are all going great guns.

The best prospects for any software are the existing customers. We check the whole customer list and figure out who would be the best prospects for a new product and then ship them the product on a free trial basis, normally with a videotape that describes what the product does. We time bomb the product so that it would run only for, in many instances, 120 days. We put an introductory price on it, so if they buy it before a certain date we give them a discount, say, 10%

Three things happen with this approach. First, we get some instant sales that we couldn't have gotten that quickly if we went through the normal selling process. Second, we introduce the product and if they don't want it or can't justify it now, they became familiar with it and if they need it X number of months or years down the road, they are already aware of the product and may order it then. Third, if we have any competitors with a similar product, they never have a chance to show it to our customer; he's too busy installing and evaluating ours. It shuts the competitor out completely.

❅

After a few years I became convinced that the company could run without me. The research organization was in place, the sales organization was in place—both extremely successful.

I knew Max Watson, a salesman at IBM. He later worked for Wang Labs. The key to leaving anything is to make sure that you hire a top quality replacement, and I felt I had hired that replacement in Max. He is a very able manager and an innovative busi-

nessman. I retired from the company, and I think Max is doing very, very well.

BMC Software continues to get bigger and prosper—and the guidelines that we put in place more than ten years ago are still there.

Max Watson, president and CEO:

I came here six years ago, in 1985. Most other software companies were developing their sales forces. We decided to stay with our telemarketing approach.

The other companies were developing products that could become commodities. We call those fancy applications—and typically shy away from them. We prefer the ones that are extremely difficult to develop. When we face competition, we design a superior product and demonstrate the higher value of the product rather than get into a price war. We have the luxury of watching several sections of the software and hardware business, where price discounting and cutting became the way of life; over time no one wins.

We have always had the attitude of product differentiation, investing heavily in the products and in moving them along. We like those that are very deep in technology, that require a unique skill to develop.

❄

Right now the economy is not very strong and the world economy is not much better, but our business keeps growing. Our products can return the customers' money in savings in a 6- to 12-month period, so it is easier for them to justify the purchase even in bad times. We always write software with a very quick and demonstrable payback.

We have diversified enough across the globe: when one country is down another one is doing great. The fact that we have wholly owned subsidiaries helped us to insulate ourselves to some degree from individual country fluctuations. We have direct contact with the customer, rather than acting through an agent or third party; as a result we are more in control of our destiny.

166

The customer's perception is that we will save him a lot of money. Just think about some of those large computer systems—for instance, airline reservations systems or major banking systems. If these systems are out of service for a while, the cost to the parent company is staggering. We have products to help companies avoid outages, and even if the system has a hiccup and somebody has to reload the computer, we have tools that will make that happen much faster. And we also save them money, because we enable them to cut back on hardware purchases. When the software budgets get cut, BMC's products are the last ones to be cut out. Ours is necessary stuff: it gets inside the guts of those large IBM mainframes and makes them run better and more efficiently.

❈

People view us as a niche company. Our view is, as to the size of the niche: it's about the size of the Grand Canyon. Probably somewhere in the $6 to $8 billion range.

Most other companies have taken the view that the mainframe market is very small, not a big business opportunity. It keeps many potential competitors from coming in.

We see it as a very vibrant market that needs new products—and we will continue to develop these new products, and our salesmen will continue to exploit them.

We do not customize these products. Once they are working, our stuff gets shrink-wrapped, not customized. After we develop it, try it, and know that it is going to work, the extra cost of each copy is probably $20, and that includes putting it in a box with some manuals and putting a stamp on it. If we send out three packages at $20 each, and one of them gets bought for between $50,000 and $200,000, that's not a bad return.

Geography is no barrier, language is no barrier; in every country, we employ nationals of that country. The only barriers are in the places where there just aren't any mainframes.

In the future we may go into some nontraditional markets; that will be non-IBM equipment, and maybe some mini and PC-level products at some point; our market will continue to grow bigger and bigger.

For a talented and creative person there is no upper limit in this company. In some years, one or another of our software writers

BMC SOFTWARE, INC.
Summary of Financial Statistics, March 31, 1984–1991
(dollars in millions, except per share)

Years Ended March 31	Revenue	Pretax Income	Earnings per Share
1984	$ 5,851	$ 617	$0.04
1985	9,348	(189)	(0.01)
1986	17,966	1,998	0.13
1987*	27,083	5,653	0.17
1988	38,544	8,977	0.25
1989	56,985	14,574	0.44
1990	87,088	25,001	0.69
1991	130,112	38,229	1.02

*Figures are restated as of 1987 to reflect a change in accounting policy.

makes more than a million dollars. I regularly tell our people that they should try to make more money than I—and some of them do.

❋

The figures BMC has produced are nothing short of incredible.

The company is financing its international expansion and product development program internally; it has a strong balance sheet, a strong cash flow, and no long-term debt. For six straight fiscal years—1986 through 1991—BMC's revenues and net earnings have risen at an annual rate averaging 50% and 74%, respectively. And for the fourth quarter of 1991 alone these increases were 50%, 125%, and 113% respectively.

Unfortunately, for those who would like to buy the stock now, the company doesn't meet one of the criteria: it isn't unknown anymore; 350 institutions own it, and a long list of major investment banking firms and brokerage firms recommend it.

I feel about BMCS just as I do about SCAF: somewhere out there is another John Moores and another Rick

Figure 7-5 BMC Software Chart

Courtesy of William O'Neil & Co., Inc.

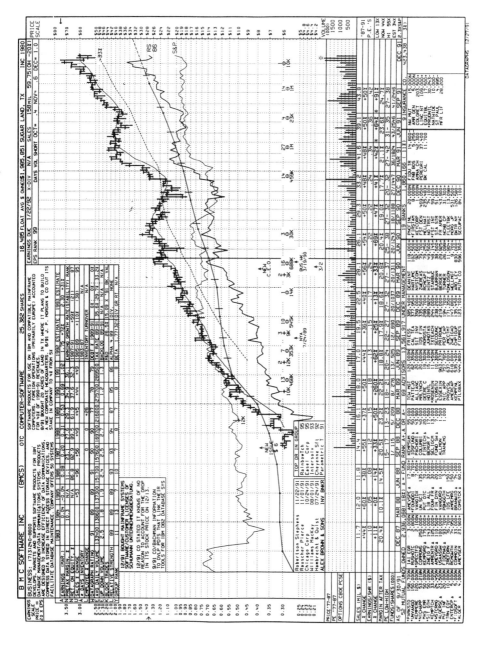

169

Hosley starting another BMCS. The circumstances are different, maybe the industry is different, maybe everything is different—except the creativity and the determination to produce something better than anyone else in the world.

Find it, investigate it—and buy it!

8

A Look Inside
Our Shop

In Chapters 8, 9, and 10, I plan to explain our sales efforts and how our division works. *Let me warn you: if you are not a broker, or a customer who would like to have more information about how a brokerage unit works, these might be chapters that you want to skim, or skip,* and continue with Chapter 11.

Every morning all the salespeople and I look at the charts: what happened to the stocks up to last night's close. We use the so-called *Bridge System.* Its screen can give us monthly, weekly, daily, and intraday charts for our stocks, and for about every average we may be interested in. It can also add moving averages to each chart. Some other of its "pages" supply sales and earnings figures, and almost endless other up-to-date data.

For these morning meetings, we generally use the so-called "2 by 5" charts: they depict a two-day moving average line and a five-day moving average line. When the more volatile two-day average pierces the slower five-day average going up, the subsequent part of the chart turns green, and when it penetrates it going down, the charts turns red.

Let me again emphasize, we look at charts, but we are not chartists! The difference is that chartists believe in the predictive ability of whatever graphic depiction they look at. We do not. An even more important difference: we only look at the charts of those companies that we previously selected after doing extensive fundamental research. We rearrange fundamentally attractive companies using technical signals. But the emphasis is on the fundamental advantages.

This approach gets the benefit of the medium- and long-term *fundamental and* also the short-term *technical considerations.*

❄

We have a short buy list, a list of about 10 to 15 stocks that we expect to act best. We call it our *Hit Parade.* We consider even the lowest-rated stock on this list attractive.

Every week we have a meeting: analysts, traders, and salesmen discuss the latest information about all of these companies, and we adjust our model portfolios. During these meetings, the analysts bring all team members up to date on every single stock we own. The traders will fill in the analysts and the salesmen on the trading action of our favorites. We will jointly decide what stocks to add to, or eliminate from, the model portfolios, or which quantities to change, whether up or down.

❄

By the way, let me explain why we created a "model portfolio."

Prospective customers, mainly those who up to now invested in mutual funds, keep asking: "What is your performance record?"

We have to explain to them that only those investment professionals who handle *discretionary* money are allowed to publish their performance records: bank trust departments, mutual funds, investment advisors, and others.

Individual brokers, on the other hand, handle *non-discretionary* money, and are not allowed to publish a track record. Why? Because the record is always *the joint record of the customer and the broker.* If I recommend a stock at 10 and the customer buys it right away, then I recommend it to a second customer who will "watch it" till it reaches 15 and then he finally buys it, and to a third customer who will not buy it at all: whatever happens to the customer's portfolio, *it is not my making alone*; the end result depends *at least* as much on him as on me.

The standard reaction to this explanation is that the potential customer rephrases the question and repeats it: "Yes, I understand, but if I would have invested $100,000 with you ten years ago, what kind of annual return would you have produced for me?"

Again the same, "mutual fund evaluation" mentality.

We became quite frustrated and decided to set up a "model portfolio." Figure 7.1 is an example of our model portfolio and how it looked on December 31, 1991. Obviously, it was an unusually good year for us. Our model portfolio was up 99.30%. During the same 12-month period, the Dow Jones went up 21.38%, the Standard & Poor's 500, 27.76%, and the NASDAQ industrials 57.54%.

Please pay special attention to the footnote on the model portfolio: *"This list of holdings should not be construed as a current recommendation to purchase at present prices and market conditions."* And this relates to every list in this book!

Why? By press time, our opinions might have changed on a number of the stocks listed. And, as always, don't buy a stock on someone's recommendation if you haven't a good reason to believe that he or she will also tell you *when you should sell it!*

❊

A while ago my second wife, Anika (after being a bachelor for 24 years, I remarried a year and a half ago), came up with a brilliant idea.

She asked me to describe my typical day. She wanted to know whether I spend my time well or waste a big part of it. When Anika found out that I spent several hours

Figure 8.1
Model Portfolio

MODEL PORTFOLIO   Tuesday closing prices   12/31/91

Market Value Order

Current Holdings		Total Return On Investment		+/-		Annual Rate
Total Cost	$2,507,913.24	Realized G/L		$ 220,309.60		
Market Value	$3,836,437.50	Combined G/L in last 12 months		$1,243,128.44		+ 99.30%
Unrealized G/L	$1,328,524.26	Combined G/L previous 12 months		$ 305,705.42		+ 117.09%
Unrealized G/L	52.97 %	Combined G/L since 10/19/90		$1,548,833.86		+ 102.37%

#	Ratings	Shares	Symbol	Weighted Cost	Price Now $	% off High	Value Now $	$ G/L	% G/L	Annualized Yield	[Purchase Dates] First	Last	% of Total at Market
1	9R 17 4/	10,000	HCCC	13.44	39.50	3.07	395,000	260,569	193.83	299.12	10/19/90	07/26/91	10.30
2	9* 12	7,000	TKOS	26.94	45.00	2.70	315,000	126,428	67.04	141.78	03/25/91	10/02/91	8.21
3	9* 25 4/	6,750	SCAF	21.22	43.75	3.31	295,312	152,098	106.20	173.83	10/19/90	08/07/91	7.70
4	9* 13 4/	15,000	MEDA	14.61	18.25	6.41	273,750	54,584	24.91	112.96	10/09/91	10/16/91	7.14
5	8R 21 2/	4,000	BMCS	37.11	66.00	11.70	264,000	115,548	77.84	125.05	10/19/90	07/30/91	6.88
6	9* 9	15,000	ROTC	12.52	16.50	14.28	247,500	59,764	31.83	165.71	10/17/91	10/30/91	6.45
7	9R 16 2/	20,000	ROSS	9.99	12.25	18.33	245,000	45,242	22.65	51.64	07/09/91	08/14/91	6.39
8	9R 6 2/	10,000	GMIS	17.95	24.00	4.95	240,000	60,457	33.67	424.11	12/02/91	12/02/91	6.26
9	9 9	12,000	INSUA	12.74	19.88	3.64	238,500	85,646	56.03	121.27	04/25/91	10/02/91	6.22
10	9R 13 6/	20,000	PCHM	10.24	11.25	15.09	225,000	20,228	9.88	38.92	08/14/91	12/23/91	5.86
11	7* 21	6,000	OSII	21.14	36.50	3.31	219,000	92,182	72.69	128.10	05/15/91	07/18/91	5.71
12	9* 25 4/	9,000	QHRI	17.01	23.88	3.54	214,875	61,762	40.34	70.64	05/15/91	07/18/91	5.60
13	0 0	10,000	VIEW	17.45	19.50	0.00	195,000	20,486	11.74	857.54	12/26/91	12/26/91	5.08
14	8* 12	8,000	FORT	11.55	23.50	6.93	188,000	95,572	103.40	232.00	07/09/91	08/14/91	4.90
15	8* 13 4/	20,000	HICI	6.98	8.75	4.11	175,000	35,287	25.26	112.08	10/02/91	10/30/91	4.56
16	4* 9	2,000	HRC	31.42	52.75	0.00	105,500	42,669	67.91	105.04	05/02/91	05/16/91	2.75

                        Average Position Size   239,777

Small cap emerging growth stocks are only for those whose investment decisions are based on KNOWLEDGE, DISCIPLINE and
PATIENCE. Given their small size and market factors, these stocks often exhibit high volatility.

The Model Portfolio is composed of hypothetical transactions which assume our recommendations were followed.
All trades include standard commissions. This list of holdings should not be construed as a current
recommendation to purchase at present prices and market conditions. The period covered was one of a strongly
rising market. Past performance naturally does not mean that the future record will match it: it could be better
or worse. Please also consider that most of the companies we recommend have modest floats -- so
purchases, if the recommendations are good and the market is with us, could be executed at higher, sometimes
substantially higher prices. The reverse problem may occur when selling. Since inception, the account has
been involved in multiple purchases and/or sales of 31 stocks. There were 90 closed out recommendations
of which 57 advanced and 33 declined. Over the past 12 months, there were 83 closed out recommendations,
of which 53 advanced and 30 declined. Closed out recommendations are available upon request.

every day explaining to each prospective customer *what we are doing* and *what makes us different from other analysts and other brokers,* she said: "Why don't you make a videotape or an audiotape and send it to every prospective client? How much time would that save?"

"Probably at least 40 minutes per prospect."

"Try it."

As time management goes, her idea was brilliant. I asked the two assistants, sitting at my side, to keep track of every question prospective clients ask over the next two to three months, tabulate them, and give me those that are the most frequent inquiries.

When their notes were in, we wrote a script answering the questions and adding some color and humor. I asked a very successful and very likeable couple, who specialize in giving financial information on TV and radio, to help me do the recording.

We rented a TV studio and Ken and Daria Dolan posed the questions. They did a very nice job, and we started to send out the videotapes to everyone who seemed to be a potentially sizable client.

❈

Up to about a year ago, we refused to publish our investment ideas. We had enough buying power to accumulate a substantial percentage of the public float in the companies we selected. Also, we did not want to create competition for ourselves while we were accumulating. But the demand for reports kept growing, and we finally decided to publish a few, somewhat irregularly, say, one report roughly every second or third month.

❈

In addition to our printed or verbal reports and to the individual reports connected with a recent or planned purchase, we also send our clients a monthly mailing consisting of general and up-to-date information regard-

175

ing the stocks they own *or should own:* the stocks on our recent or present buy lists.

This monthly mass mailing, which from time to time goes out to our prospects, too, is a combination of reports from the companies and about the companies and clippings from the press, or any and all information that we think customers would find interesting. Occasionally, it includes some humor, too.

✳

Your broker should have a relatively sizable administrative team.

You can expect that he will do almost anything to keep you happy. If you have a problem, comment, or complaint, he should make sure that someone tries to satisfy you right away, whether within the division, or with the help of the firm, or with the help of outsiders. Answering your concerns with *a great degree of urgency* should be part of the broker's discipline.

The head of our administration assigns the problem to someone right away and then checks whether the problem was solved. If it wasn't, he gets involved personally. If it was, he calls the client, and inquires whether it was solved *to his satisfaction.*

Another key point in our client relations is the way we handle trade confirmations. Whenever someone opens a new account, we promise him that the same evening, or next morning, one of my associates will call and give a verbal report on the stocks we bought: how many shares of each, at what price, and so on. (He decided what to do—and we want him to know, way before the mail arrives, how his orders were executed.)

Not every firm gives a new client this courtesy. We find it not only helpful in customer relations, but it also helps us avoiding errors—or, occasionally, correcting them.

✳

176

It is very important for a customer that his broker like him. Being a *broker's pet* can put money into your pocket.

If the broker accumulates issues that have a relatively modest float, the first purchasers might have an unfair advantage. The stock that they bought at 10 could be at 13 when the last client buys it, and if the broker decides at 20 to sell the stock, the favorite clients probably will sell at 20 and the last one at 16. One made 10 points, the other one 3!

Whom does the broker call first? Like any good businessman, he calls the most important clients first, the ones who generally give him the biggest commissions. But the second most important consideration is: *Whom does he enjoy doing business with most?* He will mix his favorite medium-sized or smaller clients right among the largest ones.

How do you become your broker's pet?

1. Be nice to him! He should enjoy talking to you. I used to have a French customer whom I always called when there was some tension; he was smiling, he was cheerful, and he relaxed me.

2. If something positive happens in your account, call him and tell him that you appreciate what he is doing. *Say: "Thank you!"*

3. If something negative happens in your account, call him in a friendly way, discuss the problem with him, and *if there doesn't seem to be a real problem then have patience* till, we hope, everything works out the way the two of you expected.

4. If you know what industries he's interested in, and you happen to get some information on that industry, call him and tell him. Brokers appreciate any input that can help their research.

5. Know your own mind. No one likes clients who say: "I want to discuss this with my accountant, my second cousin . . . , my . . ." If you trust

him, follow him. If you don't, find another broker. You want the best, you're paying for his services.

I sometimes ask clients "Does it really make sense to pay for a very expensive dog and do the barking yourself?"

6. The one thing that will always put you on the broker's best side: get him new customers. If he is that good, you should mention him to your friends and associates. If he is that good, they might appreciate it.

If you send your broker a new customer, he will make sure to say "Thank you" by moving you to the very top, or close to the very top, of his list.

❄

What about the client who is a chronic complainer, who questions all executions, who questions anything that our analyst, broker, trader, or administrator does? There is only one thing a broker can do with this kind of client. He has to protect his team from the person who abuses their time or tries to abuse them.

He has to fire the client!

In this business, we have to keep a cool and level head. Our *other* clients deserve from us all our talents.

We politely ask the troublemaker to tell us where we should transfer his securities. If he doesn't supply another firm's name, we will be happy to ship the certificates to his home. (If he happens to have a margin account—that is, he has been borrowing money from us—that complicates the situation.)

What you *do want* from your broker is high-quality service. Among other things, he should get you *all possible information that you can't get yourself.* What he does not owe you is frequent answers to frequent calls about: "How is the market doing today?"

If the client happens to be a trader, *he probably should do business with someone else.* If he is a long-term investor, he can get quotes and summaries of the market action from tomorrow's newspapers. The time that he wastes with these inquiries prevents us from doing more research, doing more constructive thinking, *prevents us from making him more profits.*

❋

As I get older, my outlook on life is becoming simpler and simpler. By now it can be summarized in two sentences:

1. Be nice to everyone.

2. Have fun right now; not in a week, not in a day, not in an hour—but now!

It is important to define what we mean by "being nice to everyone." Yesing people to death, forgiving all their weaknesses, or catering to their neuroses does not constitute being nice. What being nice really means is: *trying to get them to perform according to their best talents,* being nice means bringing out of them the maximum they are capable of, helping them to the pleasure and satisfaction of a best-ever performance.

What does this mean when it comes to clients?

If a client calls and places an order that, in our opinion, is not to his best advantage, we have to explain why he should *not* do it. We have to use all our knowledge regarding the company, regarding its short- and long-term prospects—we have to share with him everything we know.

We will say: "We make our living by getting commissions from you. *This is one commission, that we would prefer not to make.*"

If for some reason the client insists in proceeding, we will politely say, "Thank you for the order. With your permission, I'm going to mark it: 'Unsolicited.' Just so the

179

record shows it was your idea, not mine. *You are the boss. And my conscience is clear."*

I never had a client who got insulted. And on the occasions—and I hope very rare occasions—when the client's hunch was better than our research we didn't end up being stubborn and doing damage.

Anyway, refusing his order would be rude and destructive to our relationship.

❇

We never spend any time with a client on chit-chat, discussing the weather, sports events, certainly not discussing politics.

Without wasting too much time, we do want to show our interest in his personal life. We send every client a birthday card or a modest, but, we hope, original gift and on his birthday, we call to express our hope that "today starts the best year" of his life.

We remember clients during the holiday season, again with a card or modest gift. If there is sickness or death in a family, we write. If a client mentions anything special, be it a daughter's piano performance or a son winning an important tennis tournament, we send a very, very short personal note saying that we were delighted to hear the good news.

Most key people in the division have simple social stationery and use it to make clients know that we participate in their pleasures and pains. They are part of our family. They are *part of our team.*

❇

Whenever we open a new account, we send the client a simple, inexpensive mug with my caricature and our phone number on it. (A new client called to thank me for "the mug with your mug on it.")

A favorite close friend of mine, Francis Robicsek, a top-flight heart surgeon in North Carolina, got into the habit of giving his patients, the morning after the operation, a small stuffed animal. He's convinced that the fuzzy little creature accelerates the healing process.

We stole his idea and recently sent several hundred of our clients a little stuffed lion—cuddly, fuzzy, and cute—wearing a T-shirt. You guessed right: it has the caricature and our phone number on it. (I would have preferred a stuffed bull, but there was—no pun intended—no *cheap bull* available.)

Whenever a client takes his first profit, he gets a T-shirt with the inscription "I Love Profits!" The back of the T-shirt has the same caricature and phone number.

All these gifts are very, very inexpensive and even in combination add up only to a modest number of dollars. But people *love* to get gifts, even nominal ones. Everyone likes to be remembered and appreciated.

❊

We teach our brokers to divide their day into three equal parts:

1. Make cold calls (that is, call total strangers).
2. Follow up and try to open established leads.
3. Do business with customers.

After a young broker starts to make a reasonably decent living, he will almost automatically spend more and more time with his clients and less and less with prospects. Even the most disciplined one will decide: "Oh, today I'll speak to customers only, I'll prospect tomorrow."

Cold calling is very tough work, and trying to open accounts is not much easier. When the discipline of doing *all three every day* disappears, the broker starts to stagnate. His commissions will go up for a while, but they will sooner or later start to level off.

❊

Being associated with a high-quality firm like Ladenburg, Thalmann, which is not a major wirehouse, has two advantages for us: we can do our own research and we can advertise. The advertising creates leads for our brokers—gives them someone who expressed an interest, someone to call.

People, especially doctors, lawyers, corporate executives, and residents of affluent neighborhoods, have been harassed by hundreds of cold calls. Their reaction is negative—except if the caller makes them smile, or if he sounds so exceptionally pleasant that he can tempt them to listen to a few sentences . . . during which they *might* become interested.

We advertise a lot. And the person who has read, heard, or seen our ad on TV and made the effort to call us or write us is automatically a better prospect than an irritated stranger.

We are playing the numbers: say, on average, we have to make *500 cold calls* to land a good quality customer. We may achieve the same result by following up *50 leads*. And if the lead is from a prime source, say, a top metropolitan newspaper's financial section, the conversion rate could be higher.

Advertising does not sell, it only presells. It is still the quality of our approach, the quality of our literature and, above all, the quality of our presentation that turns the information seeker into a client.

Because we want to waste as little time as possible with callers or writers who are not potential customers, on the advertising coupon—or at the time of their first call-in—we ask several questions, to *qualify them* as far as their potential for meaningful business.

I am convinced that the two most important items in a broker's budget should be the money spent on research and the money spent on advertising. It is important to spend, on these two, a higher percentage of our revenues than our competitors do.

Just spending naturally is not what counts: as always, the *quality how* you spend is what matters.

❄

We want brokers who are self-motivated, brokers who can get excited by a good idea and burn to share the idea with the rest of the world, brokers who love to talk to their customers and future customers and who like to explain the ideas *intellectually*, like to "turn on" the client or the prospect *emotionally* and enjoy the moment when the client agrees to take some positive *action*.

You probably recall the old theory: a person, in addition to his body, consists of three parts—mind, soul, and the ability to act.

A salesperson has to address all three. We want brokers who concentrate on facts, not on hype. Being emotional is terrific, but it has to be a deeply felt, honest emotion—not a cheap copy of it.

❋

The analysts' time and the salesmen's time is a very limited asset. We want to offer top quality—and we want to be fully paid for it.

We do not give discounts to clients when they buy any of our ideas. We expect everyone, including our biggest clients, to pay full commission. If they don't want to do that, we don't need their business. We offer discounts only if the client asks us to execute one of *his* ideas: we do the execution out of courtesy; we have no research expense. The only other occasion for a discount is when one of our ideas didn't work out and the client takes a loss of more than 10%. In this case, the client automatically gets a discount, generally without even knowing it.

❋

If it is possible, we want the salesman to spend every second of his time with a customer or a prospective customer, not with telephone operators or secretaries.

Let me describe how this works in my case. On my left side sits Kevin, my assistant handling customer calls. Every morning, he takes the "Bread and Butter List" and marks those people whom he wants to get in touch with:

183

clients who should make changes in, or additions to, their accounts.

This lineup is based on our discussions as of the same morning. "We should get out of this and this company," or "We should start to accumulate that and that stock," or "Now that it's September, we should check all those stocks in which anyone has a loss; tax selling time starts soon and many stocks that are down at the end of September have a good chance to go even lower by year end. This year everyone had major profits: let's take the losses, eliminate part of the taxable gains, and in the last few weeks of the year, we can decide whether we want to buy any of these stocks back."

Obviously, we would like to have our cake and eat it too: we want to reduce the taxable gains and hope that, at the year end, we can buy back some of the stocks at a lower price.

This last point is only the secondary consideration.

The primary consideration is that if the stock does not look to us to be a winner, we have to eliminate it. In December we will redo our research and decide whether the situation became substantially better. Is the improvement enough to consider buying the stock back?

It doesn't happen too often.

Kevin's job is to help in deciding what are the priority calls. One of the priorities is to alert all those clients whose stock ran up more than 30% in a short time and give them an opportunity to take a one-third profit. *We do this only once.* If the stock goes up another 30% or 300%, we will not suggest a second profit on the same position. At the first occasion, we "took out insurance." After that, we hope that he will hold the stock until he is 95 years old, or till the company's incoming orders slow down. In the latter case, we will call and suggest that he sell.

The next priority is to find out which clients have cash in their account and call them so we can invest it. The next one: get in touch with every client to whom we haven't spoken for two weeks or longer.

When we have a brand-new idea, we call our clients right away, rather than wait the usual two weeks.

In addition to arranging all calls in order of importance, Kevin also has to listen to the conversations and make sure that neither the customer nor I make decisions that are in conflict with the stock list, cash, or margin position. He does not make the decisions, but helps to start the motor and then serves as a safety valve.

He will make notes about almost everything the customer and I discuss, recording what we want to sell, what we want to buy, what monies we want to spend, or, inversely, what monies we want to use to reduce the exposure or the margin position.

The next step: when I want to buy a stock that a few customers already own, with our computer department's help we produce a *negative cross-reference list:* who should, but still doesn't, own that stock.

When we decide *to sell* a stock—again with the computer department's help—within a minute or two we are able to produce a cross-reference list of all those who own the stock—customers whom I want to call and alert to our changed attitude regarding this company.

I learned long ago that there are two ways to delegate a job. You can give all the details to the person whose assistance you need. Or you can trust in the person's experience and creativity—or "street smarts"—to plan and do the job himself or herself.

❄

On my right side I have generally a very young broker, or someone who I think that with good training could become a junior broker. My present second assistant's name is Richie. His duty is to get me on the phone with *prospective clients.*

Whenever we get inquiries (originating in interviews, or based on speeches or workshops I gave, or based on advertising, or on referrals from existing clients or prospects—from whatever source), Richie is the one who writes up the 3" × 5" card containing all the information we have on the new prospect.

We need the potential customer's name, address, phone number, *what moved him to call us,* and (sometimes a touchy question, but most of the time we get a reasonably good answer), what is the value of his common stock portfolio.

If this is a telephone call-in, the person who had the first conversation with the potential client fills out a card, with all details, and gives it to my prospecting assistant. Richie makes sure that the potential client gets a form letter which explains who we are and what we do. We send in each envelope a few of our own research letters—and also a few *Datagraphs* regarding the stocks that we find most attractive right on that day.

After the reports went out and another associate noted what the specific companies were and at what price they sold on that day, Richie puts these cards into our "rotating file," eight days ahead.

Every evening he takes out from the same rotating file those cards that represent the prospects to whom we sent literature eight days ago. Those who could become sizable clients (by this time we generally know something about their present stock holdings or their professional standing, or both) get called first and the rest are arranged in declining order of their assumed future importance. Richie starts to call these *prospects* at the same time Kevin starts calling the *clients.* Both assistants are going to feed me opportunities to talk to a person whom we know or who we expect will be interested.

The two assistants work simultaneously, and they try everything possible to make their work more effective. They will make notes during the telephone conversations, but will keep these notes on the side till the opportunity comes to add the new information to the client's or prospect's card.

During the conversation, both guys will step in, even uninvited, when necessary. They will ask the person on the other end for clarification of addresses, phone numbers, or any other data (business trips, vacation, etc.). The second the conversation is over, they dial again. When Kevin gets a client on the line, Richie has free time to bring all his notes up to date: condense them, copy them onto the prospects' cards, and put the cards in the "Please Mail!" box, from which the mailing assistants will pick them up for processing.

When we happen to finish with a client, Kevin can't start to call right away: he has to listen while I repeat the buy and sell orders to the order clerk—and make sure that the instructions are the same as those he heard during our conversation with the client.

❋

Each broker follows the same 3" × 5" card system and keeps on the cards identical records regarding what stocks he discussed with a client or prospective client: what day, at what price, and when were these reports sent out? (Probably the following day.)

If he is on another line or he's out of the office, any of the other salesmen can pick up his card, read and interpret his notes, and carry on a reasonably intelligent conversation.

❋

The approach to calling customers has changed quite a bit during the past 20 years. In the beginning, my secretary, assistant, and bookkeeper helped in dialing people I had to talk to. The next step was having one full-time telephone assistant to work for two brokers. Then one "caller" for each broker. As I just described, in our case, it's two callers for a broker.

In several major firms the system is getting quite involved. Some brokers have a registered assistant who in turn has several callers. The callers dial strangers from lists that the firm bought from mailing list houses or call published industrial or professional directories or any other source. If they find someone who is willing to talk, the registered assistant takes over and "qualifies" the prospect: finds out if he is interested and if he has the money to justify spending more time with him.

I know of a partnership of two successful brokers in which one is managing money and the second is opening accounts. This second one has several registered helpers, each of whom has several unregistered callers.

The approach may be getting out of hand.

9

Building a Team

We find that most of our associates become passionately involved with their work. No, not right away. But the challenge, the demanding atmosphere, and the special financial rewards are seductive.

How do we know how they feel? *We ask them*, in many different ways. We ask everyone, at about six week intervals, to write us a "5-15 note." What this means is that it takes them *15 minutes* to write and it takes each member of our small management committee about *5 minutes* to read it. The idea originated with a short article in *Inc.* magazine.

A well-written "5-15 note" consists of three parts:

1. What he or she accomplished since the last note and how is his or her morale

2. Advice to the management committee: what should be done differently, how we could improve the team's performance

3. Advice to several individuals he or she works with: what could each of them do, one by one, to grow and advance faster, and make more money for themselves and all of us.

❊

We have two other customs that I've never seen in any other brokerage firm:

Every three months (sometimes more frequently), we have a two- to three-hour team meeting over pizza and sodas, where everyone presents whatever ideas he or she has to improve our results. The top analyst will contribute, but so will the person who handles the mail or the copy machine. This is corporate democracy at its extreme. Most teammates get turned on: their friends in other offices are never asked about how they would run the unit.

We ask. And a substantial number of suggestions arc worth listening to.

Another thing that we have found very fruitful: about halfway in between two meetings, we go out, the whole team, to a restaurant for a strictly social get-together. No wives, husbands, girlfriends, or boyfriends. It's simply a good dinner, a few drinks, a lot of laughing, and an opportunity for everyone to let their hair down.

❊

All of us have a so-called "rotating file." What I plan to describe here may seem involved—but it is a hell of an organizational tool, whatever business you are in. We have six 3" × 5" inch dividers with the name of the days from Monday through Saturday in red and then, behind those, six identical dividers marked in blue—to cover two weeks. Behind those, the name of the 12 months, each of them twice: one card marked in *red*, "January," then one card marked in *blue*, "January," then the same for February and the other months. Each divider represents the first (red) or second (blue) half of the month. At the end of this section, there is a card marked with next year and another one marked with the following year; a card is marked "Specials" (things to do, when we have extra time and money to spend); and, finally, one marked "Miscellaneous."

If we decide that we want to do something next Wednesday, we place a 3" × 5" card, as a reminder, behind the "Wednesday" divider, and if we want to do something five days later, then we put another card behind the divider five days ahead. For simplicity's sake, there is a special 4" × 5" marker at the divider which represents *tomorrow*. This makes it easy to figure where the next week starts and where the following week starts. This special marker travels ahead every day by one divider. When we put it ahead, we take out all cards listing what should be done tomorrow and proceed to get organized to do it. The rotating file makes sure that whether some action had to be taken in a month or in seven months, when the time comes; there will be a reminder waiting.

My older son bought me a pocket electronic organizer, a Wizard. It is terrific! It serves, among many other purposes, the same function as the "rotating file." For the time being, we use them both. But after we become comfortable, probably all reminders will move to the Wizard and only the actual customer and prospect cards will stay in our "rotating file." And even those only temporarily. We already have a system on the computer that will soon replace the cards. This system will automatically arrange all clients' files each day so the most important clients get called first. When a client's turn comes, the computer brings up his portfolio on three screens, in *market value order* (biggest position first) and in *date order* (which positions were established first) and at the same time on a third screen shows his record: what stocks we recommended to the client recently, what day we sent him the reports, and what the price of each stock was on that day. The computer also *will call* the client. When he gets on the line, the broker has all pertinent information on hand.

❊

The size of our team grew substantially during the last year. From a sharply reduced 11 members, it grew in one year to 28. Every time we have an addition—or any kind of change in addresses, phone numbers, and so on—everyone gets a new "players' list," so that, in an emergency, we should be able to get in touch with each other.

❊

A small company hired a new employee by the name of Sexauer. They forgot to tell the telephone operator. The next day, someone called:

"Sexauer, please!"

"Whaaaaat?"

"Don't you have a Sexauer?"

"Sex-hour? Mister, we don't even have a coffee break."

❄

Whenever a problem has to be solved, we assign it a *time limit*. Whether it's a research problem, an administrative problem, any kind of organizational problem; when we assign it to someone, we give that person a date by which we want the project finished. It is important that these time limits should be reasonable, because nothing destroys their effectiveness more than extensions—especially regular extensions. Everyone has to accept the project as his or her personal responsibility and that *solving it by the day before the time limit* is also his or her responsibility. That gives one extra day to take care of emergencies and put the report into its final form.

The principle is: "A plan without a time limit is *a wish.*"

❄

We have a short *book list* which we give to the new teammates and encourage them to read as many of the books as possible. Here is a partial listing of the recommended books:

Successful Telephone Selling in the '90s, by Martin D. Shafiroff and Robert L. Shook.

The Money Masters, by John Train.

The Time Trap, by Alec R. Mackenzie.

Confessions of an Advertising Man, by David Ogilvy.

How I Raised Myself from Failure to Success in Selling, by Frank Bettger.

The Sophisticated Investor: A Guide to Stock Market Profits, by Burton Crane.
Common Stocks and Uncommon Profits, by Philip A. Fisher.

Other books that we recommend are:

The 30-Day Action Guide to Big Money Selling, by William E. Edwards.
The Intelligent Investor, by Benjamin Graham.
The Contrarian Investment Strategy, by David N. Dreman.
Reminiscences of a Stock Operator, by Edwin Lefevre.
Extraordinary Popular Delusions and the Madness of Crowds, by Charles Mackay.

We don't recommend these books because we agree with all of their principles and conclusions. We recommend them because they are interesting and thought provoking—and even those that we have conflicts with, are worth studying.

❄

All of us understand that *we get paid for results.* No one gets paid for coming in at 9, being here all day, and going home. *We want dedicated workaholics!* Anyone who does not fall in love with the challenge of this business will leave us very soon.

In October 1991, when I decided to finish this book, I asked the members of our team to write one or two pages: how do *they* see it, *what does out team do in a different way?*

I found the team spirit very high. Let me quote you from the notes of some of the members:

The profit potential here is boundless for everyone—or is bounded only by the drive, ingenuity, hard work, and ambition that motivate a team member.

We don't want excuses. We want results! Don't tell us about the problems: solve them! No stories! We work with an end in mind, with a game plan, with carefully formulated strategies—engineered with the finish line in mind.

There is discipline in our method. We try to do everything right by going down unproven paths. We don't ascribe to convention. We rewrite it.

The division has no patience with mediocrity, nor does it accept excuses. The operative word is: results!"

One of our young brokers wrote:

We spend hours talking clients out of selling; we want to miss commissions if the client is better off continuing to hold the stock. We help our clients relax; after a while they know that what they are getting is a list of facts and not hype.

❊

Whenever we decide that there should be some special incentive to the sales force, we throw the ball right to the salesmen. Let them decide what and how much the reward should be. They design it, show it to me, and I approve. There never yet was one plan that was excessive, that I had to cut back.

Somewhat similar is our approach to rewarding the research group, though, because the rewards come on so many different levels, the management committee had to get involved in this one. Analysts get extra for profits in the trading account for finishing a major research project both extra well and extra fast, and for the quality and the result of their recommendations—although this last one is mostly reflected in their bonus. We are working on a more direct rewards system that would be tied to the results in the customers accounts and/or the model portfolio.

The most difficult part was to make the administration participate in the financial rewards. We set a certain limit. If the team's commissions grow over a specific dollar amount for the month, a percentage of the commissions gets distributed among the members of the administration.

❊

Newcomers often find it difficult to adjust. *Sales representatives* in other sales departments are used to telling the customer, with great excitement in their voice: "I just came from a research meeting. We have a brand-new 'have to buy' idea! It is terrific!! Let's take a position in it." And then continue pitching a single stock with every possible superlative.

The size of the purchase is often not very large.

In our shop, they have to recommend a strategy rather than a stock and—at least when they are trying to open a new account— the urgency is never as direct as it was when they pitched one single stock. Now they are talking of buying at least four. They also are talking about long-term or *very-long-term* investing versus the proverbial fast buck. The size of the first order is not the customary "let's start with $10,000." Now, in addition to turning from stock jockeys into "strategists," from hacks to "philosophers," they also have to ask for a $50,000 minimum. Not an easy transition! (Since this was written, we revised the minimum to $100,000.)

Salespeople are generally eager for instant gratification. It takes some education to make them understand that taking fewer short-term profits and *letting the profits run* is better for their future than is making too many transactions. It takes quite a while before a new salesman starts to tell the client: "I would prefer *not* to do that sale. I don't think it is to your advantage! We think the stock could go substantially higher."

The salesman's future is built on three pillars:

1. Having superlative research

2. Being on the customer's side (refusing "strictly for the commission only" trades)

3. Opening many high-quality new accounts

It takes a while, but they learn it.

❊

With *new analysts*, it also takes a few months to make the transition, learning that we are not all over the place, but that we cover a tiny niche—the niche that we think is going to become the most profitable one for the customer, the analyst, and the whole team. It takes a long time *to focus on the best idea* rather than work on several at the same time. It takes a long time to develop a sense of urgency.

The greatest difficulty for analysts is learning to feel the immediate pain of a client or a salesman when a stock declines, to develop the spirit of dropping everything and calling the company and calling its customers—and calling our traders—whenever something unexpected happens. What we need is an *immediacy*, an *urgency*, a *refusal just to sit around, wait, and hope.*

The *new administrators* seem to have many problems, too. A number of them come from the relatively calm atmosphere of the back offices: margin department, transfer, and "cage" (securities vault). There are emergencies in those departments, but in our, sales-oriented office, there is an almost *constant sense of urgency*. It takes some time to adjust to it.

Part of their jobs are routine—but a meaningful part gets assigned day by day. We have an important rule about these tasks; we either assign them a *time limit*, or they have to be completed on the day of assignment. If anyone doesn't finish his project the same day, he has to give the administrative manager or me a 3″ × 5″ card with a valid reason for the delay. This card will make sure that the project doesn't get forgotten and "fall through the cracks."

To have an exceptionally well-functioning team, it is not enough to give it a spiritual goal. You have to give your teammates a financial goal, too. We expect that everyone will end up making substantially more money than their basic salary. Our hope is that everyone will become very much overpaid, priced out of the market—making much more than they could get from any competitor.

And when the lean times come—in our business they do come back, occasionally or frequently—the discipline and excitement of our work, the memory of big rewards, and the lure of future ones should carry us all through to the next bull market.

The last time we had a market collapse, almost everyone on the team volunteered to give up a percentage of their basic income to assure that our group would be around and alive when things turned better again. When the market did turn up, we figured out who lost how much during the bad market—how much in salaries, bonuses, other benefits. Then we paid everyone a few extra checks, to make up for their sacrifice.

This was probably the wrong thing to do. In the future we do not intend to make up for losses, but we intend to *raise the level of incentives on future accomplishments.* The more the team member helps us to bring the division up to the former, and then *way over the former level,* the bigger his reward should be.

❄

Each Monday morning everyone prepares an "A-B-C list." This prioritizes his or her weekly duties and goals. In the A column they list those parts of the plan that—come hell or high water—absolutely have to be done. The other important plans are listed under B, and under C come those that can be postponed until next week, without doing any major damage. On Monday, the team members will write out the following week's A-B-C list and also add some notes about what they accomplished from last week's program.

We are totally inflexible regarding these notes: they should contain no attempts, difficulties, obstacles, *only*

197

results. We don't want to read that: "I called Mr. Smith and he was out of town." Or: "I called Mr. Smith and had a chat with his assistant." We want to read: "I called Mr. Smith out of town, in his hotel on a business trip, and gave him a report regarding the question he asked us."

We dislike excuses, we dislike them to the extreme. Everyone on the team has to have the same attitude as its sales members: "If I gave the best pitch of my life, but did not make the sale, I will not get paid. I get paid for results only! We all get paid for results only. Attempts don't count! Excuses don't count! The only thing that counts: results!"

Naturally, there always can be a *vis major,* a *God's will* type of interruption. But if these appear too frequently, obviously they are just overblown excuses.

❄

In addition to the team members who have their well-designed duties, the research, the sales, and the administration each should have at least one well-trained floater who has a reasonably good grasp of the highlights of every job in that group. One of these floaters should be able to take over in an emergency as a research or sales assistant, an order clerk, troubleshooter, or in a number of these functions. These floaters have to be very bright, very well trained, flexible, and totally customer oriented.

We teach our team members both sides of the coin:

1. Be nicer and friendlier to the customer than anyone since his mother held him on her knees.

2. Never take any abuse.

Everything we do has to have a structure, has to have a discipline. We all heard about geniuses with cluttered offices and cluttered desks. I assume they exist. But I'm sure that this "romantic image" of creativity is mainly used by a bunch of slobs who are too lazy to put their lives in order and who would probably deliver substantially better performance if they would learn some discipline.

About five years ago I hired a bright and exceptionally pleasant young man, in his early twenties. For three years, Les was my assistant and then became a broker. He is just finishing his second year as an independent "producer" and is going to take home the kind of money that in other professions even star salesmen won't make till the very end of their career.

If anyone deserves it, he does. Les is at his desk at 6:30 in the morning, makes calls till 6:30 in the evening, and then goes to a postgraduate course to get his MBA. If anyone needs help, Les jumps. In an informal way, he is our small group's sales manager: he interviews potential brokers, sales assistants—or just anyone who is bright and hardworking. *We are always hungry for good new people.*

I asked Les what does he tell the other salesmen, especially the new ones.

I teach them to prospect with a strategy, not just hustle for a trade or a new account. Treat all prospects as if they were clients: give them the same high-quality service, and don't forget them just because they didn't do business right away; continue to send them mail and continue to talk to them from time to time.

We monitor insider trades; we use the 144 lists both for leads (they just sold some stock, they have investible money) and to see what our companies' managers are doing with their stock.

We tell our clients not just our opinion about the companies we recommend, but also the opinion of a great number of business-men who have a relationship with those companies.

We make the customers feel a part of our team. They are not just buying or selling stock with us: they are one of us.

When the market is bad, we don't just hold their hands: we try to convince them that after a great stock sharply declined—when it starts to go up again, they should add to it.

We do not hide under the desk if something bad happens. We'll try to find out the facts and call everyone who holds the stock and explain what happened and why.

Most brokers on Wall Street tell the client about sales and earnings; we try to tell them about backlogs and incoming orders that will create sales and earnings. We have an extraordinary number of analysts, computer experts, traders, order clerks, and administrators compared *to the number of salesmen they service.*

We prioritize everything, try to focus on what's the most important thing to do. We are extremely specialized, long-term oriented, with a lot of discipline and probably more patience than most.

We don't act because of our emotions, we act because of facts.

10

The Broker's Tools

When we talk to our customers or prospects, we don't want to depend solely on our accumulated knowledge, nimbleness, and verbal skills. We need a set of well-prepared levers and reinforcements that help to turn a dangerous and tiring performance into an easily executed routine.

Stock Summaries

After we finish all aspects of the initial research on a company, we write a summary of its main points. This summary is designed as an aid for the brokers in explaining the stock to their customers. It is called *the pitch*.

It requires an extremely refined form of art, a very special talent to *summarize the main points of a company in a short period,* say, in a minute or less. It has to be written in the simplest possible form, so a customer should be able to understand it immediately—and to react to it with some questions.

We tell the analysts: "Write it as if it would be for your 9 year-old-niece."

This short monologue will describe what the company's business is, why we think it is an attractive investment, and why the customer should consider it for his or her portfolio. After the last word, we switch to the figures: we read the customer the sales of the last several years, of the last interim period, and we give our estimate for the next year and the next interim period. When necessary, we round down the sales figures to the nearest million.

After this, we give the earnings record for the same years, for the last quarter, then the estimate for the next year and the next quarter.

Before starting the pitch, we always ask: *"Do you have a pencil or pen and some paper to make notes?"* Our old customers generally grin and say, "I *always* take a pencil and paper the second I hear your voice."

Between the pitch and the figures, we request again: "Please make notes!" While reading the figures, we stop at least once to ask: "Are you taking notes or am I too fast?" We want to ensure that the customer records the key points, both because this helps his understanding and because by putting some effort into it, he gets identified with the idea. It becomes a project in which he already invested some work.

Insisting that the customer make notes is the same basic principle that advises: never go to a customer's office; let him come to yours, or take him out to lunch in your neighborhood.

Why? The first reason: in his office you will be steadily interrupted by incoming calls and emergencies. The second: as long as he has spent some money on a taxi (or even on the subway), he already made an investment in the relationship, or in the stocks you are going to discuss. Psychologically he is more prepared to say yes, because he is somehow already part of the deal.

Presentation Sheet

Every salesman has an identical *presentation sheet* (see Figure 10.1) that is a shorthand summary of the key data of the stocks that we are buying. The minute we

Figure 1.3.1 Sample Presentation Sheet

8:45:56 PM   12/16/91

Tkr	Location Date/adj price	Institutions No.No.Shs./Insti %Float	Share Price Range 1989	1990	Common Shares (000)/ $Value (000)(2)	Public Float (000)	Year End	Sales ($MM) Oper EPS 87	88	89	90	91 E	92 E	Interim	LAST INTERIM REPORTED Sales ($MM) Oper EPS prev.	pres.	+%	Net Income prev.	pres.	+%	NEXT INTERIM ESTIMATES Int	Sales Est. ($MM) Oper EPS ($) prev.	pres.	+%	Net Income ($MM) prev.	pres.	+%
BMCS 21.25	Sugarland, Tx 19/88 @5.94	151	7,768 21 7/ 30.87%133 2/	8 15//18	25,163 11,465,745	115,000	Mar		28.0 0.19	41.6 0.32	57.0 0.44	87.1 0.69	130.1 A 1.02 A	185.0 1.70	2 Sep	29.3 0.22	43.8 0.42	49% 91%	5.55	10.82	95%	Dec	33.2 0.24	47.5 0.45	43% 88%	6.04	111.65	93%
CXIM 8.75	Milwaukee, WI 1987 @5.25		6,746 14 2/	1 6/	43,005	3,395	Jun			15.30 0.46	13.8 0.04	18.2 0.05	25.1 0.18	32.0 0.33	1 Sep	4.61 (0.01)	5.70 0.02	25% +	Dec	6.20 0.05	7.90 0.07	27% 40%		0.59	
ERS 6.25	Woburn, MA 8/90 @ 8.00	15	1,000 17,89%119 4/	6 6/	5,590 181,675	3,250	Dec		3.28 (0.11)	5.79 0.11	10.7 0.29	17.3 0.45	27.0 0.68	35.0 0.87	3 Sep	4.30 0.10	7.28 0.17	69% 70%	0.48	0.96	100%	Dec	5.30 0.24	8.20 0.24	55% 60%	0.80	1.35	69%
FORT 12	Irvine, CA 6/91 @10.00				3,887 80,655		Mar		5.8 0.13	9.6 0.09	12.3 (0.46)	20.3 (0.32)	28.9% 1.10?A	46.0 0.42	2 Sep	6.6 (0.05)	11.4 0.09	73% +	0.13	0.38	186%	Dec	7.5 (0.02)	12.0 0.10	61% +			
GMIS 7.5	Malvern, PA 7/91 @13.00		25 2/	13 1/	4,300 77,400	1,438	Dec		(0.24)	2.8 (0.45)	4.0 0.03	6.1 0.32	8.8 0.43	12.3 0.58	3 Sep	1.3 0.04	2.1 0.07	63% 75%	0.11	0.26	136%	Dec	2.5 0.23	3.4 0.23	35% 0%	0.68	0.99	46%
HCC 17.5	Downers Grove,IL 5/87 @ 5.50	121	9,400 37,633	4 1/ 10 6/	24,990 827,463	16,800	Dec		13.3 0.09	24.6 0.13	31.5 0.11	42.2 0.23	70.0 0.45	100.0 0.80	3 Sep	11.20 0.07	18.8 0.13	68% 86%	1.57	3.24	106%	Dec	20.0 0.07	20.0 0.14	65% 100%	1.88	3.58	90%
HIC 13.5	N. Miami Beach, Florida		1 7/ 3 1/		13,000 110,500	10,000	Dec		10.6 0.16	27.7 0.26	35.0 (0.29)	31.8 (0.45)	56 A 1.20 A	80.0 0.38	4 Sep	8.90 (0.13)	16.40 0.00	84% +	(1.19)	0.91	+	Dec	11.10 (0.05)	16.50 0.03	49% +			
INSW 9	Memphis, TN	113	1,354 11 4/ 17.36% 7 7/	6 7/ 2 3/	7,801 177,015	4,000	Dec		17.4 (0.10)	19.0 0.52	21.1 0.46	22.0 0.22	27.0 0.60	33.0 0.80	3 Sep	5.80 0.05	8.44 0.15	46% 200%	0.36	1.18	23%	Dec	5.40 0.04	6.70 0.13	24% 225%			
MEDA 13.5	Atlanta, GA 10/91 @12.00				8,900 164,650	2,300	Dec			14.7 (4.16)	26.0 (0.18)	41.6 0.24	57.0 0.44	80.0 0.70	3 Sep	10.7 0.06	15.5 0.13	45% 117%	0.38	0.85	124%	Dec	11.2 0.07	18.3 0.12	64% 71%			
OSI1 21	Valley Forge, PA 7/90 @ 16		765 10.28% 22 4/	12	7,500 217,500	3,500	Dec			16.2 (0.16)	22.8 0.10	21.4 0.30	57.5 0.52	84.0 0.90	3 Sep	9.23 0.06	14.8 0.15	60% 88%	0.56	1.17	108%	Dec	10.20 0.10	16.0 0.17	57% 78%			
OOCH 18.5	Sacramento, CA 6/83 @ 3	30	3,805 21 4/ 37.72%127 2/	5 4/ 9 4/	10,087 249,653	4,700	Dec		5.70 0.07	11.2 0.24	17.9 0.37	29.5 0.49	41.0 0.71	32.0 0.50	3 Sep	5.34 0.07	8.07 0.14	51% 100%	0.68	1.40	107%	Dec	5.90 0.08	8.00 0.15	36% 88%	0.26	0.52	100%
POHM 13.75	Menlo Park, CA 8/91 @8.50	5	2,000 10.00% 12	9	20,000 370,000	6,000	Dec		8.34 (0.22)	6.9 (0.20)	15.5 (0.26)	15.5 0.13	24.0 A 0.30 A	36.0 0.33	3 Sep	4.0 0.03	6.5 0.12	63% 300%	0.12	0.61	408%	Dec	4.4 0.06	6.6 0.09	50% 50%			
PLAT 5	Lombard, IL 4/91 @ 15	5	1,250 11.92% 16 6/	13 4/	10,490 237,336	4,250	Jun		1.36 0.01	12.8 0.03	40.0 0.12	73.0 0.43	95.0 0.67		3 Sep	3.57 0.05	7.40 0.07	107% 75%	0.62	1.41	127%	Dec	6.60 0.09	10.00 0.12	55% 33%			
ORSI 25.5	Orange, CA 4/91 @ 12.00		14 6/	6 6/	8,483 125,124	2,750	Jul		7.10 0.04	9.60 0.17	12.8 0.17	32.6 (0.87)	149.7% 1.14 ??	61.0 0.51	1 Sep	12.00 (0.08)	21.0 0.12	72% 300%	0.26	1.64	531%	Dec	12.70 0.06	24.0 0.14	89% 133%	0.56	1.86	232%
ROSS 16.25	Redwood City, 4/91 @10.00								35.0 0.05	53.0 0.11	82.2 0.19	123.8 0.33	169.0 0.56	220.0 0.80	1 Oct	5.03 0.10	15.30 0.02	28% +	(0.54)	0.18	+	Jan	NA 0.09	118.00 0.15	67%			
ROTC 9	Orlando, FLA 8/85 @3.00		930 13 3/ 15.00% 18 4/	1 6/ 9 3/	6,200 93,400	2,600	Jul					16.9 0.30	124.3 A 1.43 A	33.7 0.62	13 Sep	31.1 0.09	7.8 0.15	55% 50%	0.36	0.71	96%	Jan	5.50 0.10	8.00 0.14	45% 40%		0.14	
SCF 25.5	Nashville, TN 11/84 @ 7.00	131	7,026 17 4/ 19.38%111 5/	3 5/ 5 5/	36,254 1,377,652	124,750	Dec		35.0 0.05	53.0 0.11	82.2 0.19	123.8 0.33	169.0 0.56	220.0 0.80			42.2 0.15	36% 67%	3.06	5.36	75%	Dec	35.20 0.1	46.00 0.2	31% 78%	3.33	5.90	77%
TKOS 12	Santa Ana, CA 12/90 @ 12.00	145	4,000 25.54%116 4/	7 4/	15,662 563,332	10,000	Dec		32.4 (0.12)	48.5 0.05	62.6 (0.09)	75.4 (0.20)	112.0 0.78	145.0 1.08	3 Sep	20.2 (0.10)	30.2 0.21	50% +	(1.42)	3.44	+	Dec	21.5 (0.07)	33.0 0.23	53% +			

N.M. indicates a number that is not meaningful.
N.A. indicates a number that is not available.
A indicates that 1991 year end data is actual.
* indicates a management estimate in which we hold little faith.

1) Institutional data does not include shares held in mutual funds and should only be considered an approximation as shares may be double- and triple-counted by Vickers.
2) Closing prices are as of 11/5/91 .
*) SEPT FY prior to 1992E

approve a new stock, meaning that our salesmen may solicit and that our customers may—actually should—buy it, the junior analyst adds the new company to the presentation sheet. This is for us what the trumpet is for the cavalry brigade. We get into action.

Reasonably soon every trader involved in the stock on Wall Street will know that we are buyers, and they know from experience that our buying can be concentrated and substantial. We want to accumulate as big a position as possible, before other research departments and sales organizations become aware of the situation.

Earnings Pages

Earnings pages are forms that our analysts prepare for the salesmen. They indicate what the company's past and estimated sales and earnings were or are, giving the salesmen a record of how the company in the past did, or failed to, live up to its own and/or our expectations. These forms generally give several subsequent estimates and the reported numbers. In some companies the actual reported figures are much better than the previous (*usually growing*) estimates—and in some other companies the actual reports are weaker than the previous (*usually diminishing*) estimates. The trend of the changing figures gives us a degree of guidance, whether this is a company whose projections should be taken seriously—or if they should be taken with a grain of salt. It's not a perfect system; there always will be surprises—but it gives us some indication of the company's credibility.

Quotations About the Company

The next sales tool that, to the best of my knowledge, no other sales organization uses, is a list of the individuals among the target company's suppliers, customers, and printers whom our analysts interviewed, and also their business affiliations and functions (for instance, sells computers to the company, or uses the company's services, or prints their promotional material). Although the interviewed people generally don't mind if we use their names when we quote them to our customers, if we quote them *to the press*, as a matter of policy, *we don't give out their names* or affiliations.

We end up with long and detailed notes about what they said. The analyst doing the "all-around research" tries to select one or two of the most representative sentences of each interview and includes it in this "summary of quotations."

When we talk to a client, in addition to giving him (1) a thumbnail description and (2) a sales and earnings report of the company we suggest for investment, we also (3) read him a list of quotes from the people whom we interviewed during our all-around research.

Let me give you a sample of quotes (without the speakers' names) about one of our recently examined companies:

Rotech reduces costs to payors, keeps patients at home where they prefer to be, and prevents loss of fees by doctors. It seems a winning combination to me.—Dr. A. B. C., family practitioner, Clarksville, Tennessee.

We supply many home infusion companies. Those that match Rotech's excellence are precious and few.—John Doe, director of Rotech's account at one of the biggest drug wholesalers in the United States.

Their performance is outstanding. Rotech manages to keep costs down, serve patients well, and keep doctors in charge of their own patients. You can't ask for more.—Dr. X. Y. Z., internist, Orlando, Florida.

And so on. (Naturally, while quoting them *to the customer* we use the sources' real names.)

The reaction to these quotations is hard to describe. Clients are used, unfortunately, to a lot of hot air. What they get now is a short factual description, a listing of financial data (mainly sales and earnings), and *a number of third-party quotations from outsiders* who know the

205

company well and know it from several angles. By the end of our conversation there is no question in the customer's, or prospect's, mind that we're trying to do rather thorough research.

I ask them, "Did any of your brokers ever give you these kinds of details?" Most say, "No, Andy, no one ever."

New customers ask questions about *the balance sheet.* After a while they learn that if a company's balance sheet is not exceptionally strong, we prefer not to get involved. The questions cease, but we make sure that our customers get detailed financial data about the companies anyway. At the very minimum, we send them the last annual and interim reports.

Summary of Previous Public Recommendations

This is a list that we generally keep on our desktop, under the glass, with the dates *when* we recommended certain stocks, *what* stocks, and *at what price*—so, if anyone who listened to those recommendations at a convention or on a TV or radio interview or read them in a research recommendation or if the press happens to call, we should be able to bring him or her up to date. We will have a printed chart on hand (with data as of last Friday) about most of these stocks, and we can get charts on the Bridge system that are current practically up to the last trade. This way, if anyone asks us what happened to a stock since we recommended it, we can instantly answer his or her inquiry.

First Purchase List

Clients rarely ask, but prospective clients do: "When you did start to buy that stock and at what price?" We do want to have the answer on hand.

While supplying the information, we generally remark: "I am not sure that that is an important question."

206

We proceed to explain that the *"low"* *price*, the level where a stock comes from, is only important when you talk about a *cyclical company*. Cyclicals are supposed to go from 10 to 20, back to 10 to 20 and again back to 10 and 20 (I know this is an oversimplification) and investors would like to buy them at 11 and sell them at 19. Unfortunately, it never quite works out that way.

We try to buy *straight growth companies* in the hope that the best of them will go from 5 to 25 to 125 and further. (No promises, though, and certainly no guarantees!) If we are not convinced that they have a chance, at least a modest chance, for that kind of appreciation, we don't want to get involved in them. On the other hand, *if they are that good, the biggest mistake we could do is not buying them because they already moved.* The person who did not want to buy H&R Block because it had already doubled since going public missed a 50,000% gain from that doubled price. The person who didn't want to buy Automatic Data Processing because it already doubled missed a 90,000% gain.

If a client wants to know where a stock is coming from, he can call a very junior, freshly registered salesman, or even a sales assistant, who will probably give him the correct answer.

Customers and potential customers don't call me to ask for the past record. They call in the hope that, because of many years of experience, I might have some thoughts on where the stock may be going. They do not expect promises or guarantees, but they do expect that I and my associates will do some wide-based research and follow a list of demanding criteria.

Timely Quotes by the Press

Any time the press publishes something that we consider parallel with our thinking, we cut it out and supply it to all salesmen. These lines, quoted to our customers and prospects, coming from a third party, are often considered a much stronger argument than the salesman's own words.

Enclosures

We collect literature about all subjects that interest us, including quotations from the press about our own operations. We reprint and enclose them as part of the literature we send to people who inquired about us and also insert some of them into our monthly mailings.

Why? Because these too are third-party reinforcements of our approach and ideas.

Immediate Research Information

It is important that all salesmen receive—and digest—all research material as soon as it has been completed.

Whenever the management of a company visits us for the second time, in addition to the analysts all salesmen participate in the meeting. They don't just listen, but ask questions, get answers—become more knowledgeable about the managers. One of the keys to their success is the ability to say to customers: "I just spoke with Mr. Smith, the president of ABC Corp. and he said . . .", or, "We had Mr. Jones in our office last week and I . . ."

You Can't Bore a Client into Action

You have to make his conversation with you enjoyable. It is important that the salesman be a colorful speaker, that the customer or prospective customer should find his style engaging.

We occasionally distribute lists of sentences that the person on the other end of the phone may find interesting or amusing. These sentences have to be very short, not more than a few seconds each. We don't have time for anything that wastes the hours available. At the same time, we hope to give the people we talk to more than profits and intellectual food. We also want to engage their *emotions* and their *sense of humor.*

Let me give you a few examples:

A customer just remarked that he considers one of our favorites "a nice little company." Our response: "A nice little company?!? This is the English under-statement of 1992!"

The client said that this and this much quoted, but totally phony "expert," predicts that such and such will happen. "He wasn't right on *anything* since 9 months before he was born." (*Burton Crane*)

"How are you doing, Andy?" "Great! Probably much better than I deserve." (This one almost always gets a pleasant little laugh.)

A client has a very good portfolio, but he wants to make a few, in our opinion unnecessary, or actually damaging, changes. "If it ain't broke, don't fix it." (*Burt Lance*)

A client mentions that this is a dull market, we probably are wasting our time trying to find some company that will move; we suggest that he should *do some homework.* "If there is no wind—row!" (*Winston Churchill*)

The client doesn't like that we refuse "to predict" what the market will do. "I never make forecasts, especially about the future!" (*Samuel Goldwyn*)

We quote Murphy's Law: "If anything can go wrong, it will." Also Murphy's second law, "If one thing goes wrong, *everything* will go wrong." And Sullivan's cor-ollary: "Murphy is an optimist."

A quotation does not have to be humorous as long as it is brief and helps to emphasize the point.

"I find that it is better to be on the side of the *minority*, since it is always the more intelligent. (*Goethe*)

"If too many people agree with you, chances are you're wrong." (*Walter Lippman*)

"In order to be a great writer—or investor (our addition)—a person must have a built-in, shockproof crap-detector." (*Hemingway*)

"No wind blows in favor of a ship without a destination."

"To err is human; to really mess things up takes a computer." I learned this one from my older son, George.

"There is always an easy solution to every human problem—neat, plausible, and *wrong*." (*H. L. Mencken*)

About good stocks going down with the bad ones: "When they raid the hotel, they bring down the good girls with the bad ones."

"There is nothing so disastrous as a rational investment policy in an irrational world." (*John Maynard Keynes*)

"It doesn't pay to worry; if you went through last year's file marked IMPORTANT, chances are the only thing you'd keep are the paper clips."

We tell our brokers: whatever you say, it has to relate to investing and to the specific subject you discuss. And, please, don't make it a point to include any of these. Just reread them occasionally and let them pop up in your conversation at the right place.

"Closing" Tools

Other than advising clients regarding their investments, the most important thing for the salesman is his record of opening new accounts. New accounts are this profession's lifeblood, and *any salesman who doesn't open a steady stream of new accounts is not doing his job.*

Some clients move to a faraway country, pull out from common stocks for any logical or illogical reason, get sick, or die. If the salesman does not open new accounts regularly, his business will fade away.

❄

Opening an account, for both the salesman and the potential customer, *is the moment of truth.* It's a difficult point even in the average relationship, where the salesman tries to convince the client to buy one single stock for a few thousand dollars. He will do everything to turn the client on—and he will generally ask for a modest, sometimes very modest commitment.

Our people don't sell a stock. *They sell a philosophy, a strategy.* And they are asking now for a *minimum* of $100,000. Junior salesmen are allowed to open smaller accounts, but we expect them to make steady progress in increasing their minimum.

❄

There are a few sentences that were created by the best of our profession. Anyone is free to use them.

The salesman is supposed to say one of these sentences—and then wait for the reaction. If the reaction is positive, he opens the account—if it isn't, he goes to the second sentence and waits again. In a meaningful percentage of cases, before the list is used up, the customer will start to do business.

If he doesn't, there can be a legitimate reason—or the salesman hit on someone who is unwilling or unable to make a decision. This last category is someone we call "a Hamlet." If a salesman finds one of these prospects, he should abandon him as fast as possible. There is no sense wasting time.

Let me list some of the typical "closings." (We tell the salesmen: "Don't cuff them. Do them accurately! But, for heaven's sake, don't sound rehearsed!")

1. "I called you today because the right time to buy is today, not tomorrow!!" (You had better be able to explain: *why* today? This argument can change with news about the world, the economy, or the individual company, but it has to be a truthful, logical, convincing reason.)

2. "Would you agree that most of the time two things move stocks—*value* and *demand*? (Wait till he answers. Most of the time he will agree.) I am trying to show you *exceptional value* very early, in the hope that *when the demand develops* the stock will make a substantial upmove."

3. "Opportunity and correct timing equal very large profits!" (You can explain why the stock represents opportunity and refer to the current events to support your timing argument. We are talking about timing the individual purchase; as you know, we try to stay away from guessing about the general market. The salesman may mention an imminent earnings report, a corporate event, or something similar that he expects to be favorable.)

4. "These are compelling situations!" (Explain what makes them compelling.)

5. "You and I want to swim the English Channel, let's put our toe into the water." (This one generally gets a smile—and the smile sometimes breaks the ice.)

6. "I want to start a profitable relationship with you, right from the very first trade. I want to buy these stocks while they are still unknown."

7. "Let's buy them while they are cheap. I would like to own XYZ below this and this price and ABC below that and that price."

8. "There are three types of stocks: there are Honda (or mention any other very reasonably priced car), there are Cadillac, and there are Rolls Royce-type stocks. This one is a Rolls Royce that we can buy at a Honda price!"

9. If the potential client didn't decide yet, we go back and summarize our basic criteria again (market domination, resistance to economic fluctuations, fast growth, relative obscurity), and

10. We repeat what we feel our main duties to the client are: (a) suggest what, when, and how much he should buy, (b) suggest when he should add to or reduce his position, (c) suggest when he should sell all, because incoming orders turned flat.

11. We explain to the prospective client that we have on our computers a cross-reference, so that whenever the analysts change their opinion about a stock, we can get within a minute or two a list telling us who owns the stock and who should be called right away.

    When we need the cross-reference, we can call up the names in "Bread and Butter" order (major customers first), size order (biggest holders of *that stock* first), alphabetic order (clients come up in order of their names), and in cost order (cheapest stock first and then the more expensive stock; if a client bought the stock at several different prices, his name will come up several times in this cross-reference).

    The message here is: "When anything important happens, we can and will do our best to reach you."

12. If after a series of strong, even passionate, attempts at closing the customer still says: "I'll think about it and call you tomorrow," most of the time we answer: "That's fine. We will talk to you tomorrow. Have a terrific day!"—and let him go. This is totally at odds with the standard Wall Street approach:

"If you don't sell him today, you will *never* sell him!"

We did our best to convince the prospect intellectually and emotionally, but we *do not want to twist his arm.*

Many salesmen disagree. "Maybe we've let an almost 'closed' prospective customer go!" There is a point where you have to stop pushing. You should not get results at a price that the customer feels raped. *We want him to make decisions that he is comfortable with.*

"Bread and Butter" List

This is a list that we designed years ago and we update every month. It lists for every broker each of his clients in declining order of importance; how much business do we expect the customer will give us, based on last year's commissions and a dozen other criteria. The first page has the 25 most important clients in alphabetic order; the second, the next 25 most important clients, again in alphabetic order; and so on. Next to the client's name, we have data that we need at our fingertips: his time zone and state; who is his second broker (our salesman who will pick up if the customer's main broker is on the phone); the date when he opened the account; his family members', assistants' and secretaries' names; the number of all the accounts he controls; the number of leads he's sent us and how many of those actually opened accounts; and so on and so on.

Link Account Printout

The link account printout takes all the accounts related to one client (wife, children, trusts, corporations, etc.) and prints them as if they were one single account.

214

It helps us to understand the real size and relative proportion of his different security positions.

Cross-reference Lists

Which clients own the stock? The cross-reference list helps us when we want to add to a stock—or when we want to eliminate it. The list can also tell us who *doesn't* own the stock, who *never* owned it, or who *used to* own it, but doesn't own it anymore. Depending on the circumstances, we will need one type of a list or another.

Net Position List

We print out every week a summary of all the stocks that our clients own. This list helps us decide whether there are any of our favorites that are underrepresented (we should own more shares of them). Figure 10.2 is an example of a net position list. It shows our positions of a million dollars or over.

Other In-house Lists

We have a great number of additional lists that our computer people created in-house. They range from simple ones—bookkeeping records or capital gains records (which we send to the client and his accountant if they ask our help in listing all transactions for tax purposes)—to more complicated software that helps us in whatever business problem develops. The fact that most of the programs are written in-house gives us direct control over them. If we desire any new type of report, we make our own modifications, which allows us to produce results faster with relatively modest effort.

Figure 10.2
Sample Net Positions List:
Net Postions over $1,000,000
Closing Prices on February 13, 1992

Rating		Security	Float	Held	% Of Float	Present Price	Dollar Value
1	12.50	Health Care Compare	16,800	285,320	1.698	40.000	11,412,800
2	25.50	Quantum Health Resources	4,250	289,314	6.807	26.000	7,522,164
3	18.75	PharmChem	2,300	624,405	27.148	12.000	7,492,860
4	22.50	ViewLogic	4,025	339,280	8.429	21.000	7,124,880
5	25.50	Surgical Care Affiliates	24,750	158,511	0.640	43.750	6,934,856
6	11.25	GMIS, Inc.	2,000	274,645	13.732	25.000	6,866,125
7	13.50	Medaphis	2,300	317,845	13.819	19.500	6,197,978
8	9.00	Home Intensive Care	10,000	614,000	6.141	10.000	6,140,000
9	22.50	Ross Systems	2,750	436,355	15.867	13.750	5,999,881
10	9.00	Rotech Medical	2,600	311,110	11.966	18.250	5,677,758
11	20.00	Interleaf	6,045	376,145	6.222	14.125	5,313,048
12	17.50	BMC Software	15,000	72,033	0.480	68.500	4,934,260
13	22.50	Medisys	4,000	446,200	11.155	10.250	4,573,550
14	21.00	Orthopedic Services	3,500	131,956	3.770	33.250	4,387,537
15	16.50	Occupational Urgent Care	4,700	103,395	2.200	37.000	3,825,615
16	3.00	Tokos Medical Corp.	10,000	101,390	1.014	37.000	3,751,430
17	6.00	Criticare	4,482	375,225	8.372	5.750	2,157,544
18	5.00	Platinum Technology	6,000	67,230	1.120	20.750	1,395,022
19	6.00	Fortis	1,700	74,370	4.375	17.750	1,320,068
20	9.00	Health South Rehab	15,000	32,406	0.216	31.500	1,020,789

Total Dollars in Top Twenty Positions: $104,048,165

We can handle special requests from the analysts, brokers, or other members of the division and do the programming almost immediately.

More Help for the Brokers

In addition to the analysts and the administration, the broker has a number of other helpers:

The order clerk will help him figure out the details of complicated orders and will place them with the traders.

The traders, in addition to executing the orders, are watching for unusual market activity and doing their best to find out what is the reason for it and reporting the reason to the sales manager and to me. If it seems important, we immediately ask the analysts to investigate. If it's not important, we want to be well prepared anyway for the ringing phones: some clients will want to know what is going on and why.

Computers: When I started my career, one of the old-timers let the papertape run through his fingers and wrote the current prices of some of our favorite stocks on a blackboard. Today, I have five computer screens facing me—and four more confronting my two assistants. The screens supply us with price quotes, news, history of customer contacts, charts, and sales and earnings reports—and whole portfolios that are analyzed in a number of different ways. We need two full-time experts writing software and directing the day-to-day functions of our computers. They claim that we have two of everything: if something breaks down, we can continue working.

A few years ago, it was a very bad year for us, I spent over $190,000 to write the beginning of our present customized software. We really couldn't afford it, but looking back, it has paid for itself many times over.

Verbal Reports

What happens when we give a report to a client? His account is in front of us, both in *market value order* and in *purchase date order*. On a third screen we have the list of the reports we've sent him lately.

I'm changing the customer's name—let's call him Terry Remington—but other than that, it's a real portfolio, as it looked on December 16, 1991. (See Figure 10.3)

Hi, Terry, please take a pencil and make notes. By the way, I'm also going to send you a printout of the portfolio, so you can see the numbers. Your unrealized gain is $1,412,000, which equals 53.56%. During the last 12 months, you are up $709,000, which equals 57.98%.

Several of your stocks have already been discovered. HealthCare COMPARE, your biggest position, is up 695% since you started to buy it on May 3, 1990. It was a very big mover this year; your annualized yield on this one is an incredible 434%.

Your third biggest position, Surgical Care Affiliates, which has also been discovered, is up 545%, for an annualized yield of 249%.

Among your newer positions, BMC Software, Fortis Corp., Ross Systems, and Tokos Medical are also getting discovered and starting to move.

Your second smallest position, Home Intensive Care, is down slightly from your weighted cost. It is a new position; we are redoing our research to see whether we should sell or add to it.

Your only other loss is in Insituform Group—and I think we should ease out of it.

There are no other stocks that I would like to sell or new stocks that I would like to buy for you.

I would love to add to some of your relatively smaller positions— if you can get fresh cash. I think it would be good to increase your investment in Ross Systems, Medaphis, and Quantum Health Resources.

Your average position today is $270,000. In the ones I mentioned, I would like to increase the positions to around $300,000.

Figure 10.3
Printout of "Terry Remington's" Account

NOT GUARANTEED - PLEASE CHECK FOR ERRORS

Portfolio Statement   Market Value Order   Monday closing prices   12/16/91

Mr. Terry Remington   A/C #

Current Holdings		Total Return On Investment		+/-	Annual % Rate
Total Cost	$2,637,717.99	Realized G/L		$ 149,432.20	
Market Value	$4,050,600.00	Combined G/L in last 12 months		$ 709,109.58	+57.98%
Unrealized G/L	$1,412,882.01	Combined G/L previous 12 months		$ 544,693.10	+41.32%
Unrealized G/L	53.56 %	Comb GL since acct opd on 10/10/88		$1,562,314.21	+41.24%

#	Shares	Company	Weighted Cost	Price Now $	% off High	Value Now $	$ G/L	% G/L	Annulized Yield	[Purchase Dates] First	Last	% of Total at Market
1	16,000	HEALTH CARE COMPARE	4.40	35.00	5.40	560,000	489,639	695.89	434.83	05/03/90	05/17/90	13.83
2	11,500	OCCUPATIONAL URGENT CA	19.78	31.50	2.32	362,250	134,759	59.24	99.68	02/21/91	09/26/91	8.94
3	8,400	SURGICAL CARE AFFILIAT	6.16	39.75	8.09	333,900	282,194	545.77	249.77	07/25/89	03/23/90	8.24
4	5,500	BMC SOFTWARE	39.36	59.25	20.74	325,875	109,381	50.52	87.28	08/24/89	11/07/91	8.05
5	16,600	ROTECH MEDICAL	13.46	18.75	2.60	311,250	87,732	39.25	266.40	10/21/91	10/28/91	7.68
6	10,000	ORTHOPEDIC SERVICES	24.73	29.50	9.23	295,000	47,706	19.29	53.36	06/04/91	11/01/91	7.28
7	14,000	INSITUFORM OF NORTH AM	13.95	18.38	3.92	257,250	61,972	31.74	103.45	04/22/91	11/07/91	6.35
8	7,000	TOKOS MEDICAL CORP.	26.82	36.75	4.54	257,250	69,506	37.02	91.73	11/05/91	11/01/91	6.35
9	11,200	QUANTUM HEALTH RESOURC	19.32	21.75	9.38	243,600	27,172	12.55	28.20	05/23/91	09/10/91	6.01
10	14,500	MEDAPHIS	15.20	16.00	15.79	232,000	11,612	5.27	31.90	10/11/91	10/28/91	5.73
11	22,000	PHARMCHEM	10.26	10.50	19.23	231,000	5,343	2.37	8.32	08/15/91	09/26/91	5.70
12	11,300	FORTIS CORP	13.96	19.50	17.89	220,350	62,622	39.70	104.19	07/19/91	08/06/91	5.44
13	16,500	ROSS SYSTEMS	10.00	12.25	18.33	202,125	37,202	22.56	59.15	07/12/91	08/06/91	4.99
14	26,000	HOME INTENSIVE CARE	7.74	7.62	15.28	198,250	-2,988	-1.49	-9.68	10/03/91	11/07/91	4.89
15	4,000	INSITUFORM GROUP LTD	7.87	5.12	25.51	20,500	-10,970	-34.86	-26.44	04/19/90	09/11/91	0.51

Average Position Size   270,040

Additional Recommendations

Good Till Cancelled Orders:
B/S Quantity Ticker   LMT

Undiscovered stocks are only for those whose investment decisions are based on KNOWLEDGE, DISCIPLINE and PATIENCE.
We hope that a meaningful percentage will be discovered within three years. Meanwhile, these stocks sometimes
move irrationally.

CONCENTRATE ON QUALITY!

The Lanyi Research of
Landenburg, Thalmann & Co., Inc.
1-800-526-9401
FAX : 212-872-1553, 212-872-1660

The customer tells me if he is liquid, or if he can work on becoming liquid; he may want to sell something in another account at another firm and increase these positions.

If he does not want to go along with the recommendations, at least he made notes. He probably will think about them and I can check back in a few days.

❊

We also reprint another, somewhat smaller account, that of "Bill Stanley." (See Figures 10.4 and 10.5) As you can see, this account was opened on November 12, 1990, so its only about 13 months old.

The conversation will go something like this:

Hi! Your account has a paper (unrealized) gain of $182,000, which equals 37.88%. During the last 12 months, the account's combined, that is realized (taken) and unrealized (paper), gain totals over $112,000, which is a 49.92% return. Your very first two purchases worked out exceptionally well.

Here we would quote from the *purchase date order* report the data regarding SCAF (Surgical Care Affiliates) and HCCC (HealthCare COMPARE). After giving him details on which company is doing well and which company is doing poorly, we would continue:

I like everything you own and do not recommend any sales. On the other hand, there are six companies that you don't own and that I think we should add to your portfolio.

He would get *an explanation* (pitch), *figures*, and *quotations from outsiders* on some of those six companies.

Whether he buys them right away or not, we'll send him detailed reports on the first four. After he reads those, we will probably suggest again that he buy them and send him reports on the last two.

Figure 10.4
Printout of "Bill Stanley's" Account in Market Position Order

NOT GUARANTEED - PLEASE CHECK FOR ERRORS

Portfolio Statement   <u>Market Value Order</u>   Monday closing prices   12/16/91   Page 1

Mr. Bill Stanley

Current Holdings		Total Return On Investment		+/-	Annual % Rate
Total Cost	$ 480,647.78	Realized G/L		$ 14,741.12	
Market Value	$ 662,700.00	Combined G/L in last 12 months		$ 112,854.00	+49.92%
Unrealized G/L	$ 182,052.22	Combined G/L previous 12 months		$ 83,939.34	+ 129.50%
Unrealized G/L	37.88 %	Comb GL since acct opd on 11/12/90		$ 196,793.34	+67.65%

#	Shares	Company	Weighted Cost	Price Now $	% off High	Value Now $	$ G/L	% G/L	Annulized Yield	[Purchase Dates] First	Last	% of Total at Market
1	10,000	PHARMCHEM	10.11	10.50	19.23	105,000	3,886	3.84	12.42	08/15/91	09/03/91	15.84
2	5,000	MEDAPHIS	14.15	16.00	15.79	80,000	9,258	13.09	71.34	10/10/91	10/10/91	12.07
3	2,200	HEALTH CARE COMPARE	12.68	35.00	5.40	77,000	49,095	175.94	272.33	11/12/90	08/12/91	11.62
4	2,000	TOKOS MEDICAL CORP.	21.72	36.75	4.54	73,500	30,051	69.16	97.91	04/02/91	04/02/91	11.09
5	1,800	SURGICAL CARE AFFILIAT	20.55	39.75	8.09	71,550	34,554	93.40	158.54	11/12/90	08/12/91	10.80
6	2,000	ORTHOPEDIC SERVICES	22.25	29.50	9.23	59,000	14,494	32.57	74.98	06/12/91	07/31/91	8.90
7	3,000	FORTIS CORP	12.81	19.50	17.89	58,500	20,077	52.25	127.24	07/19/91	07/19/91	8.83
8	2,500	QUANTUM HEALTH RESOURC	19.68	21.75	9.38	54,375	5,170	10.51	22.39	06/03/91	08/12/91	8.21
9	1,350	OCCUPATIONAL URGENT CA	20.54	31.50	2.32	42,525	14,800	53.38	94.85	05/13/91	08/12/91	6.42
10	5,000	CRITICARE	8.12	8.25	15.38	41,250	668	1.64	7.33	09/25/91	09/25/91	6.22

Average Position Size   66,270

Good Till Cancelled Orders:

Additional Recommendations   B/S   Quantity   Ticker   LMT

1   ROTECH MEDICAL
2   FILENET
3   BMC SOFTWARE
4   INSITUFORM OF NORTH AMERICA
5   ROSS SYSTEMS
6   HOME INTENSIVE CARE

Undiscovered stocks are only for those whose investment decisions are based on KNOWLEDGE, DISCIPLINE and PATIENCE. We hope that a meaningful percentage will be discovered within three years. Meanwhile, these stocks sometimes move irrationally.

CONCENTRATE ON QUALITY!

The Lanyi Research of
Landenburg, Thalmann & Co., Inc.
1-800-526-9401
FAX : 212-872-1553, 212-872-1660

Figure 10.5
Printout of "Bill Stanley's" Account
in Purchase Date Order

NOT GUARANTEED - PLEASE CHECK FOR ERRORS

Portfolio Statement　　Purchase Date Order　　　　Monday closing prices　　12/16/91　　Page 1

Mr. Bill Stanley　　　　　　　　　　　　A/C #

	Current Holdings		Total Return On Investment		+/-	Annual % Rate
	Total Cost	$ 480,647.78	Realized G/L		$ 14,741.12	
	Market Value	$ 662,700.00	Combined G/L in last 12 months		$ 112,854.00	+49.92%
	Unrealized G/L	$ 182,052.22	Combined G/L previous 12 months		$ 83,939.34	+ 129.50%
	Unrealized G/L	37.88 %	Comb GL since acct opd on	11/12/90	$ 196,793.34	+67.65%

#	Shares	Company	Weighted Cost	Price Now $	% off High	Value Now $	$ G/L	% G/L	Annulized Yield	[Purchase Dates] First	Last	% of Total at Market
1	2,200	HEALTH CARE COMPARE	12.68	35.00	5.40	77,000	49,095	175.94	272.33	11/12/90	08/12/91	11.62
2	1,800	SURGICAL CARE AFFILIAT	20.55	39.75	8.09	71,550	34,554	93.40	158.54	11/12/90	08/12/91	10.80
3	2,000	TOKOS MEDICAL CORP.	21.72	36.75	4.54	73,500	30,051	69.16	97.91	04/02/91	04/02/91	11.09
4	1,350	OCCUPATIONAL URGENT CA	20.54	31.50	2.32	42,525	14,800	53.38	94.85	05/13/91	08/12/91	6.42
5	2,500	QUANTUM HEALTH RESOURC	19.68	21.75	9.38	54,375	5,170	10.51	22.39	06/03/91	08/12/91	8.21
6	2,000	ORTHOPEDIC SERVICES	22.25	29.50	9.23	59,000	14,494	32.57	74.98	06/12/91	07/31/91	8.90
7	3,000	FORTIS CORP	12.81	19.50	17.89	58,500	20,077	52.25	127.24	07/19/91	07/19/91	8.83
8	10,000	PHARMCHEM	10.11	10.50	19.23	105,000	3,886	3.84	12.42	08/15/91	09/03/91	15.84
9	5,000	CRITICARE	8.12	8.25	15.38	41,250	668	1.64	7.33	09/25/91	09/25/91	6.22
10	5,000	MEDAPHIS	14.15	16.00	15.79	80,000	9,258	13.09	71.34	10/10/91	10/10/91	12.07

Average Position Size　　　　　　66,270

Good Till Cancelled Orders:

Additional Recommendations　　　　B/S　Quantity　Ticker　LMT
1	ROTECH MEDICAL
2	FILENET
3	BMC SOFTWARE
4	INSITUFORM OF NORTH AMERICA
5	ROSS SYSTEMS
6	HOME INTENSIVE CARE

Undiscovered stocks are only for those whose investment decisions are based on KNOWLEDGE, DISCIPLINE and PATIENCE. We hope that a meaningful percentage will be discovered within three years. Meanwhile, these stocks sometimes move irrationally.

CONCENTRATE ON QUALITY!

The Lanyi Research of
Landenburg, Thalmann & Co., Inc.
1-800-526-9401
FAX : 212-872-1553, 212-872-1660

Old-time customers generally do not wait for the reports, but go ahead and invest based on the verbal summaries. Most newer customers will want to read the reports, but after that, if they have any liquidity, a very high percentage of them will go along with the suggestions.

11

Random Notes

Valery and I divorced 25 years ago. She is still a lively, good-looking woman. She remarried a long time ago and seems quite happy. We speak with each other almost every week. We may get along so well because we are both delighted that we don't have to get along *every day.*

Our first son, George, went to Yale and graduated *summa cum laude,* Phi Beta Kappa, and then got a law degree from Stanford. He was a lawyer for a few years, and then switched to teaching computer science in a San Francisco college.

In early 1990, he died of complications from AIDS.

It was devastating. It still is. It will be forever.

Our other son, Paul, a charmer, is five years younger. He went to Vassar and, he says, "graduated in Hemingway." I suggested that he become a stockbroker. He did—and he didn't like it.

He became a ski bum. Then a waiter. Then he walked into a number of advertising firms, just the way his father had walked into brokerage firms three decades earlier—cold, from the street—and asked for a job. He landed one. He has been an account executive for the last six years. Right now, he's studying for an MBA in Austin, Texas.

He often helps me with my projects, including seminars. Recently he stood in the door during one of my seminars when a gentleman, who couldn't stand my accent any longer, got up and started to leave. At the door he turned to Paul: "I can't understand a word he is saying!"

Paul tried to reassure him: "Don't feel bad about it. I've known him for 29 years and I *still* don't understand a word he's saying."

❈

Of the 250 people in the forced march, we never heard about a single one again. All I can do is hope that we missed each other or that some of them, rather than returning to Budapest, found their way to a foreign country.

My friend, Tom, with whom I escaped from the forced march, moved to South America. When I last visited with him in Rio de Janeiro, he complained that he was having difficulties selling his country home.

"What's the problem? Selling a country house shouldn't be a major challenge."

"Not normally, no. But this one comes with a twelve kilometer private road—and a mountain!"

❈

Beverly, my first secretary, became a successful stockbroker. She is now a vice president of a major firm and is deeply involved in politics and presidential fund raising.

Jim Peppercorn, the successful and wealthy broker who was Beverly's other boss, is retired—a professional investor handling his own very substantial assets.

❈

I come from a country where service used to be very cheap. Consequently, as a boy in Hungary, I had practically never seen the inside of our kitchen.

After my divorce, I decided to learn how to cook. In my hotel room there was only a hot plate. I bought six eggs, some butter, and a frying pan. I would make breakfast.

Unfortunately, I had never in my life seen anyone break an egg. How do you get the egg out of its shell? I recalled that when I was in kindergarten, we painted Easter eggs. We didn't hard boil them. Instead, before decorating them, we took a nail and made a hole in the top and the bottom of the egg—and then blew out the insides.

Try to imagine a man, in his early forties, in a midtown New York City hotel, bending over a frying pan, putting holes in each end of two eggs, and blowing out the contents into the pan!

❃

Can you imagine going home to a wife who, you know, will make you laugh every evening?

All of us deserve a major break in our life. Mine came on June 13, 1989. A friend of mine decided to introduce me to Anika, a German baroness.

We didn't like each other too much. Our friend urged us to "keep an open mind." Why not? We made a dinner date. During that first evening, Anika explained to me that she's perfectly happy alone; the last thing she needs is a man in her life. When I got home, I crossed her name out of my address book.

Next day, Sunday, I planned to work; my backlog was depressing. Noontime Anika called: she's at a street fair, do I want to join her? I told her I couldn't.

"In the afternoon I'm going to a movie," she said. "Do you want to come?"

"Sorry, I have a lot of work. But if I finish at any reasonable hour, I'll call you back."

She gave me her number. I called her at 10. We had a drink. Things changed; they actually turned 180 degrees!

I later discovered that in addition to being bright, beautiful, and incredibly funny, she is a superlative cook.

I had been a bachelor for 24 years, eating out seven to nine times a week, and the pesticides and preservatives in the food were getting to me.

My friend was a healthfood nut. She bought organically grown vegetables, fruits, and meat that wasn't full of hormones. At first I laughed at her, but within a few weeks, my stomach pains disappeared.

One day, I walked into the kitchen. She was standing with her back to me, rinsing the dishes. I asked: "How would you feel about getting married?"

She looked back over her shoulder: "Sure, why not?"

And went back to rinsing the dishes.

Not very romantic. But the follow-up is.

We got married about a year after our first date. It was an unusual wedding. Valery and her husband came, and five of the women I had dated during my long bachelorhood were there, too. Anika has since became close friends with most of them.

When I first met her, Anika's most important qualities were her sense of humor and her exceptional beauty. Now, two and a half years later, the order of her prime qualities has changed somewhat. I love her because she is a good woman, because she spoils Paul and me, because she helps me in my work and personal life, because she is bright and funny—and, yes, very beautiful.

❊

Much of this book is devoted to *making money* on Wall Street. Let me use part of this chapter to give you *the atmosphere* of the place. Let me tell you about a few people I've met on Wall Street over these 33 years. People who are brilliant, exciting—or amusing.

❊

Kenneth was a Bronx teenager, rather introverted and lonely. His world consisted of his mother, father, and a sister; very few others.

One summer, Kenneth decided to try to earn some money. This introvert would sell encyclopedias, door-to-door.

His employer enrolled him in a seven-day course. In the first six days, the instructor drilled the future salesmen in the routine: a script they had to memorize cold. The recruits were supposed to go into blue-collar neighborhoods, deliver their pitch verbatim, without the slightest change, and come back with their orders. During the seventh day of the course, they were told what subjects never to mention. For instance, that there are *other* encyclopedias, *cheaper* encyclopedias, and *higher-quality* encyclopedias.

After graduating from the training sessions, Kenneth rang his first doorbell.

A giant opened the door. Enormous. Rough. Threatening. "Yeah?"

"I'm here to collect data about children's education. Do you have any children?" Kenneth was sticking to the script.

"Yeah," grunted the giant.

"May I please come in?" To his surprise, the door opened wide.

Once in the working-class livingroom, the frightened teenager began to stammer through his script. He was supposed to start with general educational data and slowly work his way to the sales pitch about the value of having children's reference books in the home. He kept talking and talking while the giant and his wife just sat and listened, grimly.

Kenneth had a terrible feeling that he was not delivering the words he had studied in the first six days, but he was repeating the material that was the subject of the *last day* of the course—the things that he was *never* supposed to mention. Finally, he stopped, took out a contract and put it in front of the giant.

An inner voice told him: "He will kill you! This is when he's going to kill you!"

The giant and his wife exchanged a glance and then the man said: "We can use one of those. Do you have a pen?" He actually sounded friendly.

Kenneth was lost forever. He could not consider becoming anything but a salesman.

After finishing college, he joined a brokerage firm—it happened to be the third one I had been associated with—and started to work. And work! And WORK!

I thought *I* kept absurd hours, working from 8:00 in the morning to 9:00 in the evening, and even coming in on Saturdays. Kenneth made me look like a sloth. He was in at 7:00 and went home at midnight and was back the next morning at 7:00 and again went home at midnight—and spent his Saturdays *and Sundays* in the office.

At that time, I was the firm's biggest producer. Within three years, Kenneth was number two, and then he left to take a better offer from one of our finest competitors.

Within a few years, he became one of the highest-paid salesman in the country.

❄

Senator Frank Lautenberg has another "first cold-call" story, from the time when he just became associated with Automatic Data Processing. He was the first salesman they ever had.

I saw a company that seemed to bustle with activity. It was called Merit National Shrinking—and I felt they might need our service.

I walked back and forth across 41st Street, debating with myself whether I should go and knock on the door. I started across the street and I said: "I'm sure they are not interested" and went back to the north side of the street and said: "How the hell do I know?" Back somewhere in the middle of the street again, "Oh, come on, they're not going to be interested"—and finally, after a few excursions halfway across the street, my insurance salesman's training stepped in and it said: "You have to have guts to knock on the

230

*door!" So I went and I knocked. I explained what I was there for
and they said, "We'll let you talk to the bookkeeper."*

*I made a presentation and the bookkeeper said: "That's very
interesting." She called the boss.*

*I repeated the presentation and he said: "Sounds pretty good.
We'll take it."*

I didn't believe it. "You will!?!"

*It was a great experience. I learned that what I'm selling is even
better than I thought. Later it came to the point that if a potential
customer said, "Let me think about it," I couldn't understand it.*

*I am trying to help him run his business better and save money
at the same time. How can he not take it right away?!*

I suppose this is the way every missionary feels!

❋

As I mentioned earlier, people who switch to brokerage from a profession in which you have to explain something with both logic and passion—teachers and
clergymen in particular—usually make terrific salesmen.
So, surprisingly, do many people who compensate for
some problem—and do it with such intensity that they
become a major success.

Mike, whose father owned several Ford Motors deal-
erships, used to sell cars, both new and used, on weekends
and in the summer. He started when he was 14 and
became very good at it.

His life was dominated by one burning desire: to show
Daddy how incredibly good he was. He couldn't do it as a
car salesman; he had to make it on his own. So, at the ripe
old age of 24, he started selling securities.

Mike never *said* anything to prospects. He always
asked questions—carefully leading them to the decision.
In a very rough, abbreviated form, it went something like
this:

"Hi, my name is Mike. You folks interested in a car?"

"If you can find the right car at the right price, are
you willing to buy it *today?*"

"What kind of car do you have in mind?"

231

And then, step by step, question by question he led the prospect further. Finally, "Let me see if I understand you. If you can get this car, in blue, with such and such upholstery, all the special equipment you want, including this radio and all that for no more than"—and here he came up with a figure somewhere between the list price and the minimum price he absolutely had to get—"then you would be ready to buy the car today?"

"That's great! Congratulations! You own the car of your dreams. Let's go to he office and complete the papers."

A few years later, Mike was sitting at a desk, not in a car dealership, but in the most successful retail brokerage office in the country—and he was talking on the phone. The questions were different, but the step-by-step procedure was exactly the same: ask questions that lead to yes answers, and then ask more questions and get more information, and then ask some more questions and get more yes answers, and so on. The customer hardly realized when he *had* agreed to the purchase. But he had agreed!

Mike reinvented the Socratic approach. And he became a master at it!

In his second year in the brokerage business, Mike's take-home pay, before taxes, was $600,000.

❄

Imagine a stunning, elegant, super-bright young woman in her mid-20s.

When Melissa was 18, she met a world-famous European athlete, a descendant of one of his country's oldest families. Great romance. Melissa wasn't yet 20 when she was flying over each weekend to meet her gentleman friend.

There was one problem. Although very much in love, they fought day and night. Maybe if she would *stay* in the

States and he would keep coming to *visit her*, things would improve. It didn't work.

They agreed to the biggest fallacy of all: if the romance did not work because they fought nonstop, maybe they should get married! They did. Disaster. The fights went from bad to unbearable.

After they divorced: "I have to show him that I can stand on my own feet. I'll show him what a terrific girl he lost!"

She became a stockbroker.

One of Melissa's main assets was her incredible beauty—but you don't see that on the phone. All that registered was a charming, laughing young woman's voice.

Melissa was sharp, she was hardworking—and she did something that never stopped making us laugh. When a client was at the knife's edge, hesitating whether to buy what she had recommended or to beg off, she would put on her sweetest, most little-girlish voice and say, with irresistible charm, "C'mon."

Almost without exception, that little "C'mon" pushed the customer into a "Yes."

In her second year, she made about $75,000 net. Within a decade, she crossed the $400,000 mark. Not too bad for a young woman who wasn't brought up for hard work.

Since then, Melissa has remarried. She found a guy who is a real romantic. They have a child. She became a success. In every respect. All on her own.

❄

There are almost as many selling styles as there are successful salespeople. One will get you to buy by making you laugh nonstop, and another by sounding like an undertaker.

I know a salesman who is always cupping his phone with his hand and whispering. He never tells you any secret, but by whispering, he gives the customer the impression that he is divulging such an important piece of information that he doesn't want even his colleagues to hear it.

❊

A few years ago, one of my associates introduced me to Dan Dorfman: he may be interested in interviewing me.

Dorfman had both a terrific and a frightening reputation. He was considered the best, the most knowledgeable—and the most critical—of all business reporters. Before meeting him my associates got from the library everything possible on him: when we met I knew pretty much all available about his professional and even about his family background.

We had a couple sandwiches in his office and he could not have been friendlier or more helpful. I was prepared for a taskmaster—but he behaved like a very sensitive old friend.

At one point I felt that I put my foot in my mouth and asked him: "Mr. Dorfman, would you mind crossing that out? It was really wrong."

He grinned: "It sure would make terrific copy!"

"Yes, but I don't think I should have said that."

He crossed it out.

We met many times since—and he became Anika's witness at our wedding.

❊

Another interviewer who became a personal friend is Gene Marcial, from *Business Week.* After a short conversation I took a real liking to Gene—who wouldn't?—and invited him to my home for a drink. He walked in, looked at my, then, lady friend—this was about five years ago—and said: "Too bad you don't have a sister."

"You are in luck. I not only have a sister, but she is a twin sister—and she is divorced."

Within eight months Gene and the twin sister were married.

234

If you have a sense that, on Wall Street, romance and money, love and money, sex and money, go hand in hand—you've got it right. Monetary rewards give a Wall Streeter the feeling that he is doing something right, something that the world appreciates—and how those rewards are coming in directly influences his emotional and physical condition.

During raging bull markets, the singles bars are full, everyone is dating, everyone is exchanging romantic stories. On the other hand, in a bear market. . .

Karl Berliner, a distant relative of mine, is a psychologist who specializes in marital problems. Karl claims he never has to find out from the news media whether we are in a bull or bear market. During bear markets, his impotency cases multiply, sometimes until they become the overwhelming part of his practice. In a bull market, the number dwindles.

As Bobby Elliot, a salesman friend of mine, says: "*Everyone* is bullish!"

✭

One of my associates is dating an oil trader. She claims: "He gives the word *crude* a new meaning."

✭

In the retail brokerage business, you are only as good as your ability to *open new accounts*. When you stop doing it, you are on your way to turning into a loser.

Henry was the greatest account opener I ever met. His pitch started something like this:

"Our firm has been in the business for way over 100 years. We have 98 partners, and their collective experience on Wall Street adds up to over 2,500 years. These people will never recommend anything that they are not absolutely sure about. Can you imagine that this set of partners, with this immense experience, would ever come up with something that is not exceptional?"

He would go on for almost an hour, spilling out a record of the firm's successes, of the partners' brilliance, of the corporate finance department's and the research department's and the trading department's fantastic capabilities—and all the time dropping hints that there is one stock these departments, these partners, these geniuses, discovered just recently. He implied that it is *the greatest idea* that this wonderful firm has *ever* come up with—but he would never mention the name of the stock!

The poor prospect on the other end of the line was overwhelmed. By the middle of the speech, he was ready to plead for a chance to own this wonder. In his last sentence, Henry would finally name the stock. He'd open the account, say thank you, and start to dial the next prospect.

Henry was so cocky about his talent that he would say to the other brokers: "Name *any* stock and I'll show you that I can sell it to the first qualified prospect I get on the phone." Sometimes they'd name a company, and he'd sell it.

As I said, he was the greatest account opener I've known, but he was not the greatest broker. Very often the stock *declined*, and not long after the purchase. He got tons of new accounts, but his follow-up business was poor.

A broker has to have concern for the customer. He has to increase the client's assets. And by doing so build his own future. Henry, plain and simple, was *overselling!*

❉

At a mixed business and social party, a lady doctor complained to one of our lawyer friends: "Bert, I have a problem. Whenever I go to a social event, people ask me for medical advice. How can I prevent everyone from picking my brains for free?"

"It's very simple. First, you ask them to 'please undress.' And, second, you send them a bill next day."

The doctor thought the advice was terrific. At least she thought so until the next day, when she received a bill from Bert—for legal advice.

❊

My phone rang and the caller—he introduced himself as Doug—announced that he wanted to interview me. He proceeded to ask a number of questions which, I was convinced, were in preparation for organizing a formal, well-arranged interview.

During the conversation we disagreed on a number of subjects, and occasionally our altercation turned quite heated. I was not very comfortable with our first telephone meeting, but I thought, I hoped, I will do much better at the time of the interview. After about 40 or 45 minutes, Doug said, "Thank you and good bye."

I asked when is he going to call back for the actual interview. "This was it." I couldn't believe it: this conversation sounded to me like a disorganized, total mess.

I was wrong. He knew what he was doing.

A few weeks later, I received a tape and a printed summary. The publication contained several interviews, among them mine. He cut and abbreviated the tape; in its final form it made incomparably more sense than what I expected. And the enclosed printed summary was excellent.

My real surprise came a few days later. Our phone began to ring off the hook. Doug's subscribers called and called and called, most to ask information about the stocks we liked—and some to open an account.

First, I didn't understand what was going on, but after some conversations with Doug, my lightbulb went on.

Many years ago, for his own enlightenment, Doug started to call a few famous economic and stock market pros, experts on all kinds of special areas. He wanted to hear their opinion a second time and, so that the conver-

237

sation shouldn't get lost, recorded the answers. After a while, he decided to start to publish the conversations.

Many Americans, especially those who work hard enough to accumulate meaningful assets, find *they have no time to read reports.*

Quite a few of the same people waste a substantial block of time twice a day, when they drive to and from their job. Evidently enough of these traffic-bound commuters decided that, in addition to listening to music and the news, they also want to do something for their education. And it seems many of them decided to get some investment wisdom from Doug's tapes.

❊

One day while we had been prospecting, calling lawyers, I glanced at the card. The name was familiar. "Are you by any chance *Senator* so-and-so?"

He was, and very much interested, too. We started to do business the same day.

He was a customer for many years, and a very pleasant one. We never met in person.

One day the senator called me out of the blue: "Andy, as you may remember, one of my daughters is married in New York. I'm going to come to town and give her a surprise birthday party. Please join us."

I did. The senator was a great conversationalist, sharp dresser—a real man-about-town.

Everyone at the party was very pleasant—except the birthday-girl's husband. I finally asked him: "Is anything wrong?"

"You bet your life! The senator has four daughters, all married, and he claims that I am his favorite son-in-law. I am a sales vice president of one of the biggest brokerage firms in the world, and I can't get a single trade from him. He does all his business with you . . . and he'd never even met you until today!"

A few months later the senator called again. He was coming to New York for two days. "If you're free, Andy, let's have dinner."

"I'd be delighted."

"I'm coming in alone. You know some good-looking young lady, Andy, to keep me company?"

"But, senator, I thought you are married."

"I am—but I'm not fanatic about it!"

We dropped the subject.

❊

One day the prospect on the other end of the line was a Southern gentleman. He was interested. I promised to send a few reports.

The card in my hand said that he was a high-ranking executive of a very large hospital chain, that he previously had been a dentist, and that, for a while, he was the *governor* of the state! Dentist, governor, corporate executive?? We did a little additional research on the man.

It seems that, while he was practicing dentistry, he got so upset about some political problem that he decided to run for office on that issue—and, with no experience, and no major financial backing, he won! Evidently the issue was something that was close to everyone's heart.

By our next conversation, I was well prepared about his life story.

"If it's all right with you, Governor, I'm going to switch you to my right-hand lady, Maureen. You'll like her; she is very bright and quite funny. To open an account she has to ask you a few simple questions, like your social security number and such."

"Okay, Andrew, go right ahead."

"Hi, this is Maureen. Governor, I have to ask you a few questions."

She went through addresses, bank references, telephone numbers, spouse's name—the usual routine.

"Maureen," the new customer interrupted, "I can't believe how much Andy knows about me. He must know everything except the circumference of my navel."

And Maureen said, without missing a beat: "That is the *next* question, Governor."

❊

Surgeons don't like to operate on family members or close friends. They are right.

Every time I have a customer for whom I would like to do a really superb job, he or she ends up among the worst performing accounts in my books. Family members, the Governor (no one can be nicer!), two neighbors—both exceptionally fine men—and some other people for whom I would have liked to do better than for almost anybody else have ended up among my worst performing accounts.

I have learned that if I can't be totally detached, I should beg off!

❊

One day, glancing at the card in my hand, I discovered I was talking to someone in Hawaii. For God's sake, why are we calling Hawaii? We generally saved those calls for late in the evening, when we can't place calls to a nearby time zone. But early in the afternoon?

The man on the other end of the phone was an absolute sweetheart, just about the jolliest person I had ever talked to in my life.

"Andy," he said with a big ho-ho-ho laugh worthy of Santa Claus, "Andy, I've never owned a single share of stock in my life."

We had a five-minute conversation; he totally charmed me.

A week later, I called him again. True, he had told me that he was a very poor prospect, but I found him so delightful, I wanted to keep up the relationship.

240

"Nelson, I know you have never owned a share of stock, but you absolutely have to own this one!"

I told him what and why.

"Okay, Andy," and again came the ho-ho-ho laugh, "you twisted my arm. How much?"

"$56,000."

"All right. You'll have my check."

We started to talk to each other about every second day. Within a few weeks he had more than half a million dollars with me.

"Nelson, I have a great new idea."

"Andy," he was laughing again, "I don't have a penny left. You have all my money."

"Nelson, I don't care how you do it, but..."

"Wait, I have an idea. Sandie!"

"Who is Sandie?"

"My wife."

He turned away from the phone.

"Sandie, do you have some money for Andy in New York?"

Some faint answer in the background, and then Nelson again: "Sandie says she has $263,452—and 14 cents. Can you do something with that?"

I finally woke up. These people are so rich that this is probably the mad money in Sandie's checking account!

We generally do a very good job of investigating a prospect's background. Apparently, this was another case when we'd forgotten to do our homework. I had stumbled, by sheer accident, onto not only one of the nicest men in the world, but one of the richest.

I finally asked him one day, "Nelson, with all your connections, how come you started to buy stock from a man who was just a voice on the phone?"

"Andy, you mentioned the word 'monopoly'; you mentioned the words 'recession resistant.' I've been in dozens of businesses, from dredging to construction, all of them competitive, all of them cyclical. I wanted to know what you meant by 'monopoly or near-monopoly,' what you meant by 'a company that can grow even when the economy smells.'"

He came to visit—and Sandie came along. We had lunch on the day before their 50th wedding anniversary.

I felt life had given me a great opportunity. Nelson had made more money than anyone I'd ever met. Now I would find out how it is done.

I asked him straight out: "Nelson, how did you get your start in life?"

He gave me a big smile and one of his ho-ho-hos: "Well, Andy, Daddy owned a railroad. . ."

12

You and Your Broker

Most brokers start out in some other profession. I was a stage director. Some of my most talented colleagues are former teachers, priests, ministers or rabbis. They are terrific at selling securities because they possess the greatest asset that a broker can have—the ability to express an idea *with logic and conviction*. Even passion!

One of our salesman had for years been an evangelist. One day he rose to his feet—all 6′ 4″ of him—the phone to his ear and his voice rising to a higher and higher pitch. Apparently some customer refused to take his recommendation.

"No? No?! Nooo?!?"

And at the top of his voice: "America wasn't built on a NO! America was built on a YES!!"

He paused, listening. Then, in his normal voice: "Three thousand shares? Thank you."

And he sat down.

We all rose and gave him an ovation.

❊

Another broker was exceptionally bright, nimble, and clever. He came up with more funny lines on his own than Bob Hope with all his scriptwriters. He had so much charm that, when he felt like working, he could open up half a dozen accounts a day.

Unfortunately, he didn't care much about his clients. He just wanted the commissions—and, fulfilling that desire a bit too aggressively, ended up being sued by a number of customers. His story made *The Wall Street Journal* and *The New York Times*.

When one of his clients brought a whopper of a lawsuit against him and the firm, he called the man and volunteered to be a witness on his side. The angle was that if the client won the case, they would split the proceeds 50/50. Unfortunately he repeated the offer later, after the client had gone to the authorities and been wired to record the conversation.

❖

Let's be frank. There is a built-in conflict of interest between broker and client. A broker's income is based on transactions, not results. The more the broker trades an account, the more commissions he earns. The less the client trades, the more money he will make, assuming he owns the right stocks.

How can brokers continue to work with a good conscience?

For one thing, most stocks cannot be held forever. Even if you were lucky enough to be an early buyer of an IBM, a Polaroid, or a Xerox, there comes a time when the right thing to do is to sell them, pay your taxes, and do your absolute best to *find another superstock early in its career.*

❖

Most brokers do care about their clients! They do their best to help the client make money. Many don't sleep nights when situations they recommended go sour.

It's a tough, tough profession. Brokers are always getting sniped at by armchair quarterbacks. "Why didn't you buy before the run-up?" "Why didn't you sell before the drop?" Or, "Why did you sell the stock that subsequently continued to go up?"

If everything works out just right, many clients convince themselves that it was their idea in the first place and it is proof of *their brilliance.* On the other hand, if the stock goes *down. . .*

You'd better face it: for relatively modest commissions you can't get a broker with a direct line to Heaven.

✿

What should you expect from your broker? For starters, you have a right to expect that he will keep you very well informed:

1. He should send you detailed reports on every stock discussed.

2. He should give you objective and factual information, including annual reports, interim reports, charts—all kinds of data—so you should be able to form a reasonably complete picture about what you are investing in.

✿

You've probably heard the old advertising story.

The chairman of a company turns to the head of his advertising agency: "You have been running the same ad for the last ten years. Why do I pay you an additional million every year?"

And the agency head: "You pay me to prevent you from changing the ad."

This translates, aptly, into investments. Not as far as the time frame goes, but the discipline. The broker may do you the greatest service, when *he talks you out of selling.*

Oh, a good broker earns his keep, all right—and if you've been fortunate enough to find one, tell him *thank you,* again and again.

✿

In addition to suggesting what stocks to buy, when to buy them, how many shares, and at what price, your broker owes you several other types of advice—advice that all brokers should give their clients, but, unfortunately, few do. Too frequently you get an excited pitch to buy, then no follow-up, until the broker decides it's time for another commission and calls you to recommend a sale.

Let's look at the way it should be.

You buy 3,000 shares of XYZ at $10. You read the literature, you and your broker discussed the stock and you both believe that in a few years it may be selling at $30.

Assume next that things go well right off the bat. Six months later the stock is selling at $15. A 50 percent profit in such a short time! You are itching to sell.

If you have a good broker and he does his homework, he just may call you and say: "Charlie, I talked today to the chairman of the company, talked to their biggest supplier, talked to their biggest customer—and business is far better than we expected. In fact, the figures are terrific. My suggestion is that you shouldn't take a profit on your 3,000 shares. Instead, you should buy 2,000 more!"

If things go better than originally hoped for, your broker owes you a second service—advising you to *add to your positions.*

Let's assume you get exceptionally lucky. The stock you bought for $10 shoots up in a very short time to $20. This time your broker may call and say: "Charlie, your stock moved up fast all right, maybe *too* fast. It seems to be ahead of itself. Yesterday I talked to the company's sales manager and a couple of its customers. Things are going well, but not quite as spectacularly as the stock's move indicates. My suggestion is that you sell 1,000 shares— and consider it insurance. If it drops back to $11, we may buy back the 1,000. And if the price goes straight to $80, glory be, you'll still own 2,000 shares."

So the third type of advice you should at times expect from your broker is—*sell part and consider it insurance!*

The fourth kind of advice you need, and this is the moment of truth, is *when to sell it all.*

There is only one reason to sell a good stock, and I hope by now you know what it is. While everyone on Wall Street is looking at sales and earnings, you—and, I hope, your broker—are watching *incoming orders and backlogs.*

Let's assume that 23 months after you bought your stock at $10, it is up to $27! You sit there grinning like the cat that ate the canary; you feel in your gut that after two years you will have reached your $30 goal, just as planned.

The broker calls: "Charlie, I want to sell. All of it. I want out!"

"You're nuts! Were almost there."

"Charlie, incoming orders are slowing down, which means that the backlog is turning flat, and six months from now the sales will be flat and the earnings will probably turn down. You, Charlie, and I, have to have more knowledge and more discipline than the rest of the crowd. Lets sell! Everyone is looking at the strong sales and strong earnings of the last four or five quarters. We still have the opportunity *to sell into strength!*"

❋

How about if the stock goes down, rather than up? The answer is obvious. You, your broker—and his trader— have to *reexamine the facts.* Talk to the insiders, the management—and talk to the outsiders, the people they do business with. Only repeated, very thorough research will help you distinguish between a signal of coming bad news and an outstanding buying opportunity. Don't turn one into the other!

Let's face it; a very high percentage of investors act on fear and greed. You have to do the reverse—their fear and greed give you your best chance!

❋

We're now at the final advice your broker owes you. In addition to suggesting what to buy, when, and in what quantity; suggesting when to add to or sell part of your position; and suggesting it is time to get out altogether because inquiries and incoming orders are slowing down—in addition to all that, he should call occasionally and say: "Charlie, *we've found a new company*, one we are excited about and that I think you would enjoy reading about. I'm sending you the report. Read it—and then lets talk."

❈

Of course there are some things you should *not* expect to get from your broker. A crystal ball, for one thing.

Clients are forever asking their broker: "Where is the market going?"

Your broker will have an opinion and he'll spell it out—but he's probably going to be wrong more often than not. Any broker, analyst, professional money manager or stock market guru can be right for a time—but not for long.

Crystal balls and frequent short-term trading ideas are not what you have a broker for. You pay him to put you into stocks of companies you both hope are going to work out in the medium to long term. And to keep checking that the fundamentals are still right.

And then, your broker has to calm you when the stock drops a couple of points, tell you there's no need to panic, perhaps convince you that now's the time to buy more; and make sure that you are not buying more when it's the time to take profits or losses; and supply you with an extra measure of discipline, when it's needed to help you maintain patience.

❈

If you don't have a good broker how do you find one?
I could suggest that you look for brilliance. Unfortunately, your chances of finding it are negligible. Look

248

for what is more realistic: someone who is honest, knowledgeable, disciplined, and extremely hardworking—and mainly, again, someone who is "on your side."

The first consideration, as with everyone else, is his character. You must have confidence in his integrity.

Some of the best clients seem to be the very busiest of lawyers. They have sold themselves on the Puritan work ethic. It is totally legitimate to work sixteen hours a day, seven days a week for their clients' benefit, but it is sinful to spend five minutes a week on their own investments, their retirement funds, or their grandchildren's inheritance.

This kind of investor *really* needs a broker he can trust. Let's call him Michael—and let's assume he is lucky: one of his partners introduces him to Peter, a top quality broker.

At their first conversation Michael listens carefully, makes notes, and then reads the material Peter sends him—but all the time he somehow feels that he is wasting time that belongs to his clients.

Peter is in the habit of talking to his customers at least once every other week. One of the conversations goes something like this: "Mike, ABZ is up 30% from what you paid."

"Great, Pete. Take the profit!"

"Over my dead body. I suggest we sell one-third, no more."

"Pete, come on, I'm offering you a commission, and you can buy anything you want with the proceeds, so I'm actually offering you two commissions!"

"Mike, if you insist, I will execute your order. You are the boss. But I would prefer holding on to ABZ; I think this stock is going higher. I would like to *sell one-third, just as insurance.* As for the rest, I don't want the commission on those shares. I want you to hold them."

Pete is not saintly. It is part of his discipline to take a one-third profit, as insurance, in every company position that ran up very fast.

Michael laughs before they hang up—and that night he tells his wife that his broker is crazy.

When this has happened three times in a row, the lawyer finally decides that he is in the lucky position of having a broker who handles his account as though it were his own brother's. Pete may be crazy, but he is "on my side!"

What it comes down to, and Peter will probably say this to the client straight out: "Mike, we have to decide whether in this game Mike is supposed to make money or his broker is supposed to make money. I suggest it be Mike."

The nice thing is, they both do. When it is time to sell, Peter will get his commission, and if he was right and the stock went higher, he will get a larger commission.

True, if he had gone along with his customer's original suggestion, Peter would have written more tickets. But this way, the client just may send him his wife's account, his cousin's account, and some of *his clients*' accounts.

What's more, he occasionally may pick up the phone and say: "Pete, I just heard about a company that I think would interest you."

And, once in a blue moon, he will be right. A client may give his broker an idea that he—and hundreds of his other clients—end up making money on.

And so may the broker.

❄

After character, the most important consideration in choosing a broker is that you and he be on the same wavelength. His philosophy, his basic strategy, should be the same as yours. If you want high-yielding bonds, you have no use for a broker like me. If you want a guy to help you search for the next Xerox, you are not going to be happy with a broker who believes only in the *Fortune* 100.

It is important that, when you talk with your broker, you feel comfortable. He should be talking your language, inspire in you the kinds of decisions that make you happy. And make you money.

❈

Give him time to prove himself, though. A reasonable time is *four years, or more.*

That may seem long to you, but it is realistic. There will be years, for example, when everyone is interested only in "asset investing" or in blue chips, and your broker's style, of buying small and fast-growing companies, is out of favor.

But, if the idea is right, if the company you have your money in is a good one, other investors will come to agree with your broker and you. It just may take time. To get overly enthused after you've been in the market for a few months and expect all kinds of miracles—or conversely, to be upset because your stocks haven't done as well as the Dow Jones averages for three months—is both naive and destructive. You will switch lanes constantly, losing out every time and making yourself a wreck. That is not investing. That is masochism.

❈

When you choose a broker, ask what he's putting his own money into. Don't be embarrassed, it's a fair question. If you suspect the sincerity of his answer, ask to see a list of his holdings. You may find that he already holds some of the stocks that he is recommending to you now in his own portfolio. Don't be suspicious that he is trying to push up the prices of his securities or that he is going to unload them on you. *These may very well be the companies that he has the most faith in.* He bought them earlier, and he still likes them. He may even plan to add to his own position.

The important thing is not to find out whether he bought a stock at 5—a stock that he now recommends to you at 10. The important question is whether that stock is going to rise to 20, or 50, or 100? Or whether it might

251

go down to 3? Did he do his research carefully enough, has he done his follow-up just as carefully, does he have more than blind faith in that stocks future?

We are back to the triumvirate of *knowledge, discipline, and patience.*

It is a good sign when a broker puts his own money into the same stocks, or at least the same type of stocks, he asks you to invest in.

❄

Indeed, you are facing a real problem when a stockbroker does *not* own the stocks he is asking you to buy. There are too many *brokers who consider stocks something you buy for others*—to make a commission. For them, the customer is a sucker. They wouldn't be foolish enough to risk *their* money in common stocks! They only buy and sell Treasury bills and antiques.

Would you trust a Volkswagen salesman who drives a Toyota? Would you buy from a Gulfstream salesman who refuses to fly?!

If a salesman does not want to show you his portfolio, or if he is willing but his list is in total conflict with his advice to you, you may be talking to a "commission jockey"! He is working for his own benefit and maybe for his firm's, but certainly not for yours!

God save you from him!

❄

Your broker may sometimes act in a way that you find illogical. On the day he recommends that you *sell* part—not all!—of your position in a stock to lock in a profit, he may recommend to a new customer—or to an old one who doesn't own the stock—that he *buy* it.

The reason is simple and quite logical. Selling *part* of a position in a stock that has risen sharply is a good discipline, kind of an insurance policy against totally unexpected events. Your broker still likes the stock, he still thinks that there is a chance for a very substantial

252

appreciation in it, so he wants you to *continue to hold most of it*, and he wants other clients, who have none, to have a stake in it, too. If he decided that he did *not* like the stock anymore, he would have told you to sell out altogether, and he would not have bought it for another customer.

But if you come to believe that he simply trades one customer against the other—then don't do business with him ever again!

I said at the outset that the first thing you have to consider is a broker's character. When you finally come to the conclusion that he's on your side, that *he is more intent on making you a profit than himself a commission*, then don't try to second-guess every recommendation that he makes. If for any reason you have doubts, discuss them with him. If you find that your doubts were well founded—leave.

✤

Another thing you should look at is the staffing and administrative set-up. How is the office structured? How does the broker actually get information from the analysts? How are the administrative details handled?

One of the main problems in major brokerage firms is the breakdown of communications between brokers and analysts. The distance is just too large: physically, time-wise, and in the structure of the organization.

If you have a question about a stock that you bought previously on the broker's advice, if you want to be brought up to date or want a detail clarified, your broker generally has to fill out a form, take it to and have it approved by his manager, and then forward it to the analyst. The analyst will try to squeeze the request into his schedule. The answer might reach you in three days, or three weeks, or an even longer time.

We believe that the broker should be able to get up from his desk, walk over to the analyst, discuss the question with him (if the analyst is involved in something, discuss it with him *within a few hours*), and be able to call you back with a totally up-to-date answer within a short period of time.

It's very important that there should be a high ratio of analysts to brokers. Most major firms have 50 or more brokers to every analyst. In some, the ratio will be worse, in some, somewhat better. In our shop, the ratio is one to one—four analysts for four brokers.

We are in the business of trying to make money for the client and for ourselves. We believe in having enough good analysts covering the small niche and servicing a limited number of salesmen. Let the brokers sit a few feet from research—and also, from administration.

If the client has an administrative problem, his salesman should be able to switch him to someone who is competent, who is near, and who is going to be able to solve the problem—soon.

Making Money and Having Fun

For successful investing, it's not enough to know your broker. It's very important to know a thing or two about yourself first. For example, how do you feel about risk? How much time and energy are you willing to put into your investing program? And why are you doing it in the first place?

❋

Over the years I've come to the conclusion that an overwhelming majority of investors do not go into the stock market to make money. They do it because they want to prove—to themselves, as well as to others—how brilliant they are. They want to have something to brag about during their next golf game.

Some of the worst are those who tried to prove their genius in the market through trading options, buying calls, and puts.* It's how you get rich fast, right? All that leverage, all that action!

I suppose there are people who have made it that way and kept it. But ask any broker and he'll tell you that most option buyers lose money.

Here's a portrait of a typical individual options trader:

It's a roaring bull market. Everything is moving up! So Larry, who's been buying calls with every penny he can get his hands on, is making money hand over fist. From having $500 in his pocket when he started, he now has $500,000 in the market. Larry is more than cocky. He is now convinced he's invincible.

Then the market turns, but nobody puts out a sign that it has turned, and at first Larry doesn't believe it. Nothing but a correction, he says, and he buys more on dips, only to see the dips turn into canyons. Soon he's given back all he's made—and more.

By now he knows that it is a bear market! So he goes out and begs and borrows and puts together a little stake and throws it all into puts.

Before you know it, he's got $500,000 in the market again.

Has he learned his lesson? Not at all. He forgets everything in the glow of the realization that he is indeed the most brilliant investor who ever lived. That he made such a spectacular comeback just proves it.

So he'll give it all back again. He'll go through this routine about twice in every four years, the span of an average market cycle.

❉

Many people get into the market looking for action, the adrenaline of a casino. If that is your bent, you

---

*An "option" is the right to buy or sell a specific amount of a specific security at a specific price within a specific amount of time. A "call" is a contract with the right to buy an underlying instrument at a specific price within a specific time period. A "put" is a contract with the right to sell an underlying instrument at a specific price within a specific time period.

probably should give two-thirds of your money to a charity and take the other third to Las Vegas.

❊

At the opposite extreme is the investor who is paralyzed by concern over risk: "Why should I invest in common stocks at all?"

The answer is simple: if you invest in nothing but fixed income, inflation is going to eat up most, or all, of your return. This is not investing; this is confiscation.

I was born in 1925. Let's assume that my father had $4 to invest for little, newborn Andy.

He put the first dollar into Treasury Bills. By the time I became 65 years old, that investment was worth between $10 and $11. Daddy's next dollar, let's assume, would have gone into long-term government bonds and reached a value somewhere around $18. He invested his third dollar in good quality common stocks, which by now would have been worth well over $500. Quite a bit more than in fixed income! And if he invested the last dollar in relatively smaller stocks—no, not carefully selected small stocks like we suggest, but just run-of-the-mill, average quality small stocks—by the time of my 65th birthday, that would have been worth way over $1,200.

If you invested all your money in fixed income, you didn't even make up for inflation. Not by far.

The standard answer I get is, "But Andy, I can't take the risk."

There is no bigger risk, than taking no risk at all!

❊

Sometimes, experiences that seemed risky turn out to be most pleasant.

Early in this century two sisters lived in New England with their cat, Betty. They didn't go out much, and they certainly didn't let Betty out. "She may meet a tomcat and terrible things could happen!"

256

One day, while marketing, one of the sisters met a very nice middle-aged man—and six months later they decided to get married.

Before they left for the honeymoon, the other sister said: "I don't know anything about these things, and neither does our cat, Betty. We are going to be worried. Please send us a telegram first thing in the morning."

The telegram arrived as requested. It had only three words: "Let Betty out!"

❖

I come from a country where people took some part, say, 10 percent, of their income and invested it in an insurance contract, basically a fixed income instrument, or put it into the bank. After World War I there was runaway inflation, and most Hungarians cashed in a lifetime of savings to buy one loaf of bread.

My countrymen didn't learn much: between the two World Wars, they again invested the biggest part of their savings in some reserve that paid them a fixed return. And guess what? After World War II, they again cashed in their lifetime savings and again received just about enough to buy a loaf of bread.

❖

One of my friends, Barry Ziskin, an extremely bright money manager, published an article in September 1991.[*] Here is his summary of what fixed income investments can do to you.

DOES DIVERSIFICATION BETWEEN STOCKS AND BONDS MAKE SENSE?
Barry Ziskin

Studies show bonds to be one of the worst possible investments for the long term. Only during the very beginning of a recession can a short-term trader do better in bonds than stocks....

---

[*]*Investor Guide*, September 1991, pps. 78-79. Published by Investment Seminars, Inc.

Furthermore, bonds typically reach their peak long before bull markets in stocks are over.

Bond profits in the 1980s were a historical fluke. In the 1960s, 1970s and in just about every other decade of this century, bonds delivered disastrous returns for those foolish enough to lend money—for that's what bond buying is—to companies and governments that are not responsible enough to finance their own growth or survival....

Take, for example, the world's most respected bonds—the "gilts" of London:

In 1990, U.K. bonds ("gilts," as they are called across the Atlantic) performed better than any other bond market in the developed world. But a longer term look at the U.K. stock and bond markets shows the clear advantage of being an owner of U.K. shares, not bonds.

Over the 72 years from December, 1918 to the end of 1990, the U.K. gilt (bond) price index has fallen 52.7%. Adjusted for inflation, U.K. bondholders lost an astonishing 97.7% of their purchasing power. They are left with only 2.3% of what they started with.

Over the same time period, the U.K. equity price index has risen 7,939.2%. Adjusted for inflation, investors in U.K. stocks quadrupled their wealth, while bondholders lost nearly everything....

As undervalued as U.K. blue chips are, none stand out like the smaller company shares traded in London....

Over the long term, the faster rate of growth of smaller companies far outpaces the performance of stodgy blue chips. In periods of superior performance for secondary stocks (such as 1962-68 and 1974-1981, and now, starting in 1991), smaller company shares not only catch up, but go way beyond a catch up in long-term performance.

Studies in the U.K. as well as the U.S. show dramatic long-term results for those investing in secondary shares.

❊

One of my brightest colleagues, Lou Ehrenkrantz, wrote me a note on the same subject:

October 11, 1991

Dear Andrew:

In response to your question regarding bonds as an investment, I referred to my notes regarding a lecture I gave in 1988. The results cover the period of 1926 to 1985, and the experience since 1985 has certainly not changed.

From 1926 to 1985, T-bill returns (the safest known to man) on a compound annual basis were 3.41%. The inflation rate was 2.06%. The real return was less than one-fifth of 1%! *From 1952 to 1985, the T-bill return was 5.27%, the inflation rate 4.26% and the real return less than 1%! No rational person would be satisfied with a return of less than 1%, even in return for safety.*

In any event, the safety involved is illusory. The other day I paid $44.00 for a book that had heretofore cost $7.95 in 1981. I pay more now for one year's tuition at a private high school for my son than my own entire college education cost—and I went to the most expensive college in New York State.

I'll stick to common stocks carefully selected.

❊

If you *absolutely insist* on owning some bonds or other fixed income: I do not believe that more than a minor part, say, 25 to 35 percent of your liquid assets, should be in fixed income. The major part should be in well-selected, high-quality growth stocks, preferably bought well before everyone else falls in love with them.

❊

Another part of knowing yourself is: How much effort are you willing to put into studying and planning? Most people never develop a philosophy, a strategy, a well-thought-out approach to investing. Their portfolios look like a menu in a third-class hotel restaurant: a little bit of this, a little bit of that. If you don't want to devote at least the minimum necessary time and effort to your portfolio, don't get started.

---

*All calculations are adjusted form compounding and inflation.

And don't think you can count on a broker to do it *all* for you. Yes, you might get lucky, you might find that one broker in a dozen—sometimes I think one in a hundred—who has the knowledge, the discipline, and the patience to do a good job for you. The odds are disappointingly low.

If you aren't at least knowledgeable and informed enough to ask the right questions and understand the answers, if you are not willing to make at least that commitment, back off!

❄

You also need a certain amount of money. The minimum is $50,000—but $100,000 would be better.

The reason is simple. Even if you have the best analyst, the best broker, the best information, any one of which would be a miracle in itself, you must own *several* stocks.

Be wary of any broker who tells you otherwise. *You need to diversify!* Putting all your money on one big bet—a favorite move of the man who wants to prove his brilliance—is an ego trip to disaster.

Suppose I currently recommend several companies that, based on our research, probably have a bright future. I may like one, or two, especially well. Still, I will suggest that my new client starts with at least four stocks.

I want to protect him in case one or two do not work out.

Okay, let's suppose a client is very lucky and all four turn out to be winners. Even in that case, you never know *when* the stocks are going to be discovered, or *when* a buying stampede will move them up. One might catch the eye of an analyst in a week and rise sharply, but another one might take several years.

In my experience, if you buy only one instead of all four, you will have bought the one that takes several years.

If you have four stocks, one may catch on in two weeks, two in two months, one in two years. There will always be "something happening." If you are going to get involved with investing, you *need* something to happen. Otherwise, you'll probably lose interest.

After several years in the market, you should own 12 to 15 different stocks. You should have a diversified portfolio to follow, plenty to read about, and companies to be involved with.

Of the portfolio, one stock may turn out to be a disaster, some will do little, a few will go up modestly—but another few may go up substantially, and two may make you the kind of money you have dreamed about.

❈

If you don't have the time, or the desire, to do well in the market through some hard, but interesting work, or if you don't have $100,000 to invest, let someone else invest your money for you.

If it is under $50,000 you should positively consider mutual funds. There are many fine ones. *Barron's, Forbes, Business Week, Money,* and other publications provide plenty of information about them. Put your money in several funds, not just one; the importance of *diversification* again.

If you have more than $50,000 but your heart isn't in handling your investments, maybe you're just too wrapped up in your business or profession, then search for a good money manager. It isn't easy, but there are some very competent "finders," most of them with brokerage firms, who will take a $50,000 account and help the client meet a suitable counselor.

The very best money managers, in my experience, manage private partnerships, so-called *hedge funds.* (Let me warn you, there are some poorly managed hedge funds, too!)

The best brains in the business start to manage their own money, then take in partners so they have more clout with brokerage analysts who supply them with ideas. Since they are so good, these managers ask for up to 30%

of the investors' profits. And if you think they are that good, you will be happy to pay up. After all, 70 percent of big gains is better than 100% of a trickle.

The trouble is that some of the old-time hedge fund managers, who have proven themselves year after year, won't even look at $100,000. They probably want you to give them a million or more. There are younger private partnership managers who will take almost any amount of money to help them get started. But are they any good? The risk is yours.

On Your Own

If there are some good professionals available—mutual fund managers, private counselors, hedge fund managers—why should you bother to invest on your own at all?

One reason is that you have the potential to make more money.

A mutual fund manager owns 30, 50, or several hundred stocks. The better he is, the more money flows into his fund, and the more different stocks he has to buy. In addition, he has to buy bigger and bigger positions, which will keep him out of a lot of small, fast-growing, exceptionally promising companies.

You, on the other hand, can play the field. You are in a position to say: "I will buy only a dozen of the very best ideas. I don't have to buy anything until those ideas come along. And I can buy and sell them when I please, without worrying about pushing the price up or down because I own 100,000 shares of it. I can be patient and wait until a good situation gets discovered, since I don't have to be concerned about my performance being printed in the paper every day!"

In short, you are an individual; he is an institution. You want to find and buy at $5 the stock that he will later buy from you at $50.

❊

Can an individual investor—can you—do the same kind of research I do and find the kinds of stocks I look for? Yes, you can! But it helps to have the assistance of an experienced analyst or broker.

The Wall Street Journal, Forbes, Business Week, Barron's, Fortune, your local newspaper, and the trade magazines—they all carry news of companies, products, and services that can pique your curiosity. *You may get an idea just by looking around you.* As one smart money man said, "All you had to do was see the flower children shed their jeans and become women executives, to know that it was time to sell Levi Strauss and buy Liz Claiborne."

Go to the library and see if you can find more information about the company. And by all means, check with your broker.

The most sensible way to get involved is to find a company in your own city or in an industry that you know well. In such cases you may not even need the library. You may know some people who work for the company, a few executives, maybe some ex-employees—as well as some of its suppliers, customers, its printer, or maybe the builder who put up its offices and plants. All these sources can give you some facts about how the company is doing, what kind of people lead it, and so on. You can do terrific research when you have the personal contacts.

You may find a great company whose stock everyone else will discover months or years later. Call the company you are interested in and ask to be put on its mailing list. Read the reports it sends you, and then call up the chairman or the president.

263

Don't worry, he'll talk to you. You can't phone and chat with the chairman of General Motors, but the management of young companies are eager to hear from individual investors. You have expressed interest in them, you are someone who appreciates them! Many will talk to you as though you were a good friend—some even as though you were their psychiatrist. They will tell you their dreams, they will tell you their worries, they will put their hearts on the table.

A few years later, after their companies have been discovered and 50 Wall Street firms have started calling, it will be different. If you can get through to the president, a lawyer will be sitting on his right side and a public relations expert on his left, and the chief executive will often tell you only what these two people suggest him to tell you.

Of course, you can't just take management's word for everything. Now comes the homework, the checking around. You probably can't do as much as we do, but you can go to stores and ask how a product is moving, and you can ring up one or two of the firms suppliers, and so on. What you want to concentrate on is the *indications of future business*. Is the order picture improving or deteriorating? When you research a local company, or one in your own industry, in many cases you may end up doing a better job than your broker could.

You do what you can—and your broker or his analyst may be able to help you with some contacts of their own. The two—or three—of you are a team; that's what it's all about.

❊

There is another reason for handling your own investment portfolio. *It's exciting!* You learn a lot, and there is always more to learn. The market is fascinating and trying to do well in it is a never-ending challenge.

If you don't find it so, if you don't get caught up in the intellectual and emotional game of ferreting out companies and stocks that may climb higher, then just forget it. On the other hand, if you do, you will have discovered the best reason to be involved—*the sheer fun of it!*

❄

Good old Charlie went to church and prayed: "God, let me win the lottery!"

A week later he was back: "Please, *please,* let me win the lottery!!"

A week later he was back again: "What's wrong? I've been good. Why didn't I win?!?"

From high in the sky, a booming voice: "Meet me halfway, Charlie! Buy a ticket!!"

❄

I am a broker. I am ready to offer customers everything they have a right to expect—and then some. I want to help. That's my business.

But I prefer not to do it *all.* That is *not* my business.

I like to think of myself as *the thinking man's broker.* I cater to customers who like a challenge. I supply them with printed literature about companies we recommend, and when they call, I tell them what's happened to the company since that literature was printed.

But I prefer that the customers make the decisions.

❄

The most rewarding way to invest—and I mean reward and satisfaction even beyond the money you make—is using your own brain and your own talent!

You want to buy a company's stock for $10, watch it split again and again, until your adjusted cost is $2 a share. Then, a few years down the road, you want to hear a friend tell you that his bank's Trust Department just bought him something terrific—and it is your stock! Only he paid $30!

Two dollars to thirty dollars. That's what I call making money!

And that's what I call fun!!

If you put in the effort, especially if you have the help of a good analyst and a good broker who think as you do, you *can* do it. You may end up much more successful than you ever hoped!

If you want to be a winner, you have to do your share. Waiting and hoping are not enough.

As the voice said:

"Buy a ticket!!"

**If you would like more information about
Lanyi Research
and a list of its current recommendations,
please call
1-800-THE-STOCK**

Index